MW00943978

AN
AMERICAN BOYHOOD

growing up in another time

and another place

Charles William Kerber MD

copyright © 2015 Charles William Kerber

All rights reserved. This book, or parts thereof, may not be reproduced in any form without written permission, except for short phrases used for literary criticism.

ISBN-13:
978-1519110275

ISBN-10:
1519110278

For

Grandma, Mom, Judy, Mary Ellen, Janet, Laura, Carolyn,

Claire, Alexandra, Erika and Gracie -

the wonderful women in my life,

and for Charles D,

my best friend

PREFACE

Times change, but people don't, you have likely heard the experts say. In medical school, my professors taught that, when we humans lived in caves even a hundred thousand years ago, we had the same diseases, the same fears, the same neuroses, the same problems to solve as we do today. But hasn't the world today really changed in critical and fundamental ways? I wonder. You may too.

So let me ask: Is it possible to be an average adult, an adult who looks around and wonders, especially one who is an observing parent, and not notice the dramatic change that the appropriately named digital revolution has caused in our children's behavior, their methods of interacting with the world around them, then wonder what this change might portend for their future (and ours)? I thought so.

Perhaps a look at another time might help us understand. And maybe even to predict. Then to answer that fundamental existential question.

So let me take you back to a major juncture point in a boy's life . . .

. . . back to June 1954.

A shy 17-year-old boy had just graduated from the McKees- port Technical High School.

The ceremony and the inane speeches had ended. The new ex-seniors, diplomas clutched firmly in hands, had shuffled back into the school to return their caps and gowns, then move on to parties or reunite with families. The stands had emptied; the stage on the football field was now quiet.

Finally, I am alone, he realizes.

Standing on the highest bleacher seat, he turned back to look at the school. The look back brought a smile – remembering, reliving wonderful memories from the days spent within those walls.

But then, turning to face ahead, his smile faded. Barely visible on the horizon, far beyond the city, the steel mills, the rivers, he could just barely make out the skyscraper the University of Pittsburgh called the Cathedral of Learning. Summer haze and mill smoke clouding his vision of that school seemed a perfect metaphor for his attempts to peer into his future. Try- ing, still trying to see, he felt a vague uneasiness come into his belly. As that feeling intensified, he finally had to admit to himself that what he was feeling was fear…… cold, lead ball in the belly, blood congealing, mind destroying, nightmare generating fear.

World War II had been over for 9 years, but he knew and remembered America's awful experiences of it through the newsreels, from overhearing the adults' worried conversations throughout the war years, but most critically by simply spending time with friends and neighbors, men who had returned broken and in pain. He had watched those shaken but determined men (his heroes, all) try to reconstruct their damaged lives, to try to regain at least some of their lost youth.

We came to call those men *the Greatest Generation*.

To make the future more in doubt, that worldwide war, in spite of destroying uncountable numbers of families, had ended not with a real peace, but with a mushroom cloud, a cloud that still hung over his country, darkening each day.

Then a few years after that awfulness, high school friends only a few years older had gone to a cold and terrible place halfway around the world called Korea. Some returned damaged; some returned in boxes. And even worse yet, that Korean trouble never really quite ended . . .

In 1954, the year of his high school graduation, the overwhelming menace was Russia and Soviet Union/Empire, which at that moment seemed poised to take over the world, just as The Axis had almost done in the 1940s. Practice hiding from nuclear attack was real (the siren went off every Monday morning at 11 AM), and was something the boy took seriously. The movies of the newly invented hydrogen bomb tested two years before made the global fear hundreds of times worse. That fear was the cause of more than one nightmare.

The boy's background, his upbringing, his entire family was poor Appalachian. Knowing and accepting that heritage, then coldly recognizing the obstacles in his path, deep within his mind he had to admit to himself a huge and painful doubt, a doubt that he had the tools to climb out of the poverty cycle that surrounded his family and friends.

The story gets worse yet: neither he nor the people he trusted could even begin to predict what the world itself was going to look like in the coming years – and he heard a small but vocal minority who doubted the world would even exist.

Of course he would try. Of course he would work. Of course he would study. But he was not at all sure that his life to that point had prepared him for what was coming. The future looked cloudy, dark, bleak, unknowable, and in the quiet moments before sleep, even terrifying.

But he had been fortunate, fortunate on many levels. Through his childhood years he had had interesting and uncommon experiences, experiences from which he had learned. And he had even survived errors, dangers and misfortunes that taught painful but powerful lessons. But most importantly and happily, he had come upon kind and generous teachers, teachers who taught with gentleness and understanding, teachers willing to tolerate the wildness and impatience of a little boy. Those teachers were, almost without exception, within his family.

This book is about those experiences that did the teaching.

I write these stories down for my children, but especially for my granddaughters, all of whom I love far beyond my meager abilities to demonstrate that love. And I put my stories down, I suspect, in part for myself, likely as a search for truths I do not wish to forget.

My children, but especially my granddaughters, will see striking differences in their lives and mine, but they will also come to recognize and know critical similarities. And so they too will learn to see further, as I have, by standing on the shoulders of those who came before. And thus their lives will be better than mine, as they should be.

I hope they, and I also hope their friends – this new Greatest Generation – might make use of some new insight gleaned from my stories.

1. THE POND

The two little boys shuffled alongside the macadam, quiet, minds lost in thought, their usual pace slowed by the sultry summer afternoon. Then there, in the distance, a cool dark woods invited, promising relief from the heat.

But first was the swamp. Not that there was anything off-putting about any swamp, especially this one, because just before the woods began, this swamp held a seriously interesting pond.

Sliding and slipping down the embankment, they parted cattails, stirred up legions of sleeping mosquitos and dragonflies, hopped over stands of water, then, finally, came upon the pond. Dense willows guarded most of its periphery, but an open bank faced the woods. And there they stood, cool mud squishing through their toes, absolutely still, looking at - looking into - *the pond*.

"Why is the water so black?" I asked Reed. Reed Gilchrist was my best friend. Reed always knew answers to complicated questions.

"Stagnant," he answered. Actually, neither of us knew exactly what that word meant, other than we had heard the big people use it, and it was certain to be bad.

Some time later I asked, "And what is that green slime over most of the top?"

"Poison." Should have been obvious to me.

More time passed. "Wonder how deep it is?"

"Deep," Reed said with a knowing nod. Of course. We watched . . .

. . . And as we watched, two large bubbles worked their way to the surface, and bursting through the slime made an ugly ominous ploop, ploop sound. We had never heard anything like that. And immediately we smelled rotten eggs. The hair on the back of our necks became erect.

Turning to Reed I asked, "What was *that*? Where did they come from?"

"From the bodies."

Oh yes. I should have known. I could always count on Reed to know the answers to questions of such deep complexity.

We stood there a bit more time, enjoying the delicious tingling feeling of close-by danger. (*Somebody* hid those bodies there, right? And he probably was nearby. Watching us.) But the woods called, and with just a touch of reluctance - but also a little relief, we left our pool, having more worldly knowledge, having laughed danger in the face yet another time.

And so time passed, and we grew, Reed and I, coming of age in a most wondrous time and in a magical place, in an era blessed with fine and patient teachers - learning that freedom was ours, but with that freedom came responsibility, absolute responsibility for the results of our actions. What an American boyhood.

2. TIMES IS BAD

But now back to the present. Let me begin with a certain little girl, the girl who started this word journey.

A deep blue sky, a gentle and moist onshore breeze, creamy oleander roadside bushes in full bloom, and the sharp, sinus clearing smell of eucalyptus – it was a fall afternoon San Diegans often take for granted. Windows down, I was driving slowly through Balboa Park to the Naval Hospital when a pretty little girl caught my eye. The image was so arresting, the picture so sharply and instantly focused that, without conscious thought, I pulled over to watch. For long minutes, I could not move. *Is this for real?* I wondered.

No, it wasn't anything strange or outlandish *she* had done. She was just a four-year-old blonde girl with a charmingly sweet smile, a little girl riding her trike in circles and figure eights. I could tell she was a blonde only because yellow curls peeked out from underneath the safety helmet her mother had clamped on her head - and tightly secured with chin strap. *A hardhat?* And yes, did I mention that mom had also swaddled her in elbow pads and knee pads…. *A 4 year-old? On a tricycle?* Of course mom hovered by – ever so close by. What an apt word. Hovered. What a constricting word. Hovered. What an awful word. Hovered.

Soon mom noticed me, gave me the bad dog eye, and scowling, reached for her cell phone. I knew enough to drive away.

But I could not get that scene out of my thoughts. *This is her life* I realized, *so supervised, so protected, so unfree.* As I drove, that little girl's image brought me back to another afternoon, an afternoon so far away in time and temperament, a moment when I was her age, a time that begins my stories.

* * * * * *

So let's go back to 1940 and allow me to create some background for what follows: A dark winter sky, its low clouds roiling and tumbling over the hill down toward my grandmother's house, chill winds whistling through the eaves sets the mood.

"Times is bad," my grandmother said quietly, almost to herself, washing the lunch dishes.

Huh?

What was it that she was staring at, that something somewhere out beyond her kitchen window? I pulled a chair up and looked too, puzzled, hoping for a better understanding, hoping to find even the smallest clue. But I saw only her chickens. The hens were doing their best to ignore the blustery snow flurries ruffling back feathers as they pecked and scratched for bugs in the garden. Well, there were the winter clouds too. And the leafless apple tree. I believed her, of course, she was after all Grandma, but I was puzzled – plus her words and body language made me worried.

Today, now that I think back to that moment, those cold, desperate chickens were a powerful and singularly appropriate metaphor for the times.

Then even more confirmation: On another chilly afternoon, but soon after: "Times are bad," my mother sighed. I watched her struggling with wet shirts, passing them through the ringer of Grandma's Maytag washer in a dark, damp basement. What little boy would feel a bit insecure?

May I stop at this point to clarify? Obviously the family did make it, otherwise I would not be writing this. But with this beginning you might be wary. I hope you are not thinking *Oh good grief, not another Poor Boy Makes Good/Horatio Alger Jr /Only in America Story. How tedious.* Well, no – it's not. Let me reiterate that what follows are stories from a boy who grew up in another time, a time different from now. And having read the stories, I hope you will analyze, to make comparisons between those years and those experiences to what you see around you today – but, all goes well, only at the end. Only after you have finished reading. And in comparing, to answer that future question asked in the last chapter.

*   *   *   *   *   *

During the dark days of the late 1930s up until the war began in late 1941 and with it, America's economic recovery, everyone knew what those words *times are bad* meant, differences in grammar and accent notwithstanding. And those two simple transactions, both Grandma's and Mom's, which in retrospect I now recognize to be perfect and clear communications, were to define, to limit, and to color my family's and my earliest years.

I should give you a little foundation, first about those two strong women (more about them will come later) and then about the economy.

My grandmother had grown up in Oldham, a small cotton mill town in Northwestern England. She had been taken by her family from school in the fourth grade to work the mills, which explains her poor syntax – and her accent (which she passed onto me). On the other hand, my mother, though she was born in that same cotton mill town, had had the good fortune to have been brought to America – and fortune of fortunes, to have made it through high school.

Mom and Grandma were not alone with those thoughts. However that simple phrase was said, with whatever accent, we heard those three grim words sooner or later during most conversations in our small Greenock community. I heard the phrase even more often in McKeesport, the big city up north, whenever the adults, those who were even able to verbalize their thoughts spoke, much as my grandmother did, staring off into the distance, not quite seeing, quietly contemplative, usually discouraged, and many times near despair. *Times are bad.* And they were.

And now *the* primary cause of those bad times, our economy: By 1935, the Great Depression of 1929 had seemed to be drawing to a close, and the promise of work and better times was in the air. But more ham-fisted and manipulative fiscal legislation by our Federal Government had plunged our country back into another depression. There are so many books about the causes of those sad times that it is easy to be overwhelmed. Worse, the study of cause and effect of the continuing depression seems more influenced by the historian's political leanings than by cold analysis. But for a quick start at understanding, I would suggest you first look to the results of Congress passing the restrictive Smoot-Hawley act, the largest single tax increase on imported products in our history, Mr. Hoover's income tax increase from 24% to 63% in 1932, and, when Mr. Roosevelt was elected in 1936, his raising of the marginal income tax rate to 83%. Parsing the opinions on both sides of the political fence, I believe it was the federal government's misunderstanding of the difference between wealth and money. (Of course trying to understand causes and effects in a large economy is a complex – yet worthwhile quest – but let me warn you, the research will depress you.[1])

---

[1] The most balanced approach I have seen to this history is in Carroll Quigley's book, *Tragedy and Hope*. Make sure you get the first edition if you're going to read it, because I'm told that later editions have been seriously abridged in important areas. It becomes a bit ponderous at times, yet is worthwhile. As for the depressive part, you will almost certainly see parallels in today's Federal governmental activities.

Naturally, the government didn't call its manipulation of our economy and the crash that inevitably happened another *great depression*, but a depression it was, nonetheless. That second depression would continue until we entered that awful world war.

And into these times I was born on a cold November afternoon, in 1936, amazingly, delivered via cesarean section – with Mom under open drip ether, the only anesthesia available during those days. And the story gets more dicey – delivered by Dad's second cousin, a general practitioner. In 1936. And we both survived. Imagine that. In later years, when we learned the awful mortality and morbidity rate of that operation in the 1930s, both Mom and I simply shook our heads in disbelief, looked at each other, and laughed at our mutual good fortune. All these are cold facts, matters of record.

But for the next chapter of this history, we must rely on old photographs, letters, and most unreliable of all, the remembrances of friends and family. (I'm not sure I trust my own memory. Who knows when a child's early memories become based in reality?)

My first 18 months of life were spent in what was then called Lower Greenock– a small community of about 60 families. The settlers were mostly Germans, Scots-Irish and a few English. In fact this little community had been named for the Scottish town Greenoch. We lived on a tongue of land much like a peninsula, bounded by a U-shaped bend of the Youghiogheny River. The immigrants had come here first to farm, then work the steel mills and dig the coal – coal that lay everywhere beneath our beautiful and gently rolling hills.

The poverty during those early years made the awful long, dark winters even more bitter. I was told that my first winter was the coldest in anyone's memory. Coal, though dug locally, was expensive, and the clapboard houses were as difficult to heat as lobster pots. Central gas heating? Insulation? Down jackets? They were in the future. If any family were fortunate enough to survive.

My dad earned $15 per week. He had, by the time I was born, found work in a gas station, yet when he married my mother, he had no job at all. Their Catholic priest, knowing they had been keeping company (I much later learned what that euphemism meant), had urged – even demanded – marriage. No matter what. It turns out that father's family was a Catholic-cursed one, and that rigid mindset pervaded our early experiences. Which is, in itself, an interesting story for later. Do you ever wonder about the power and control of organized religion over us?

My parents set up house in a two-room shack in lower Greenock, at the corner of Greenock -Boston Road and Schweitzer Road. And yes, it really was a clapboard, tarpaper-roofed shack – the rear room was (my mother swore) floored with dirt. This is the only photograph I can find of it – as it was being moved up the hill from its original location near the river (the picture was taken around the beginning of the 20th century). By the time my mom and dad moved in, the storefront windows had been boarded up. Kind of sounds Abraham Lincoln-esque, doesn't it? And, hard to believe, but there you have it.

Mom and Dad told me stories about how they started their marriage – again with that grim, faraway look – in that cold front room. Then almost 2 years later, I came into this world[2].

The only thing I remember about that house is that, once each week, I would be loaded with the dirty clothes on my red handwagon (a gift from Grandfather Kerber), and pulled up Schweitzer hill by my mother to my grandmother's home. Perhaps you can visualize a small woman pulling her new baby and a bushel basket of dirty clothes 2 miles up a serious hill, rain or shine, hot or cold. Well, you see, Grandma had an electric washing machine. (Many of our neighbors were not

---

[2] So maybe they weren't "keeping company" after all. Many years later, I asked Dad if he had been using any kind of birth control. "No, we were good young Catholics." And that was the end of that discussion.

so fortunate, the women needing to rub clothes on a washboard bending over a tub of hot water. And this hand wash practice continued in many homes well into my grammar school years. The women had as tough and gritty a life as the men. One could see it in their red, chapped hands, in their faraway looks. There was scant laughter, those early days.)

Mom would tell me that, once bundled in wool and settled into the wagon, slowly up the hill we went, biting cold winds around us (it wasn't always winter, but that is certainly what I remember). Perhaps I remember the rides because everything changed once we arrived at Grandma's and Grandpap's, because there I became enveloped in warmth, in kindness, held within their loving touches.

By the time I had reached 20 months of age, my parents, at the urging of those same grandparents, had recognized the futility of trying to make it alone, and we moved in with them into their small home. That I had acquired pneumonia that winter might have had something to do with the decision. This momentous move was to change my sister's and my lives – and do so tremendously and forever for the better. But on the other hand, I cannot imagine how depressing and humiliating this must have been for my father.

A few years later, I remember my father coming into the kitchen, laying down three 5 dollar bills on the small kitchen table, his week's wages at the gas station. He looked at my mother, expecting her to run the house for the next week. Today I remember those looks of worry and fear. You can't fool little kids; little kids read body language – until they are later taught not to.

And thinking of my parents today I can see why they were often distant, embittered, and intensely insecure about their future and their ability to feed their growing family. There was no thought of "getting ahead" – their thoughts centered on simple survival. Their Catholicity precluded – at least until after their fourth child came – any form of birth control. There simply was scant money, and precious little opportunity to earn more. And, being the obedient Catholics that they were, our family got larger every two years.

My grandparents' house – in stark contrast to the Lower Greenock shack – was warm in all respects. "Snug as a bug in a rug," Grandma would often say, smiling, hugging us. They, Grandma and Grandpap Mason, were kind, generous, more than willing – even anxious to hold and touch my sisters and me, accepting of our intrusions into their home and their life. But above all, throughout the years of my childhood, they gave my sisters and me unconditional love, and lots of it. Today I am certain that is why we, all four of us kids, grew through those bad times with only trivial scars.

Most mornings I would wander over from our side of the house to theirs, sit on my grandfather's lap, and help him eat his breakfast. Crispy bacon, eggs with lacy brown edges fried in the same bacon fat, yolks still liquid for toast dipping (does anyone in any other part of the country refer to this preparation as "dippy eggs"?) – a steamy kitchen, sweet English breakfast tea. Could life be any better for a little boy? No surprise and invariably, in the middle of all of this wonderfulness, my mother would come over from her side of the house, chastise me that I should let my grandfather have his nourishment, as he would soon "catch the bus" for his day's work at the Christy Park steel mill. "Oh," he would answer, "Leave the boy be . . .," helping me with the next fork full of egg. And I would smile smugly back at her – and snuggle back into his protective arms.

That I would remember his words exactly from age 4 is an important part of my story – my quest to reach maturity. His words represent a little boy's first recognition of a need to understand what adults were really trying to say.

Sunday mornings were even better. First, off to early mass (parents had to be fasting to take communion, and the earlier services were short), then home for a big breakfast, and, afterwards, delight of delights – to sit on my grandfather's lap in his favorite rocking chair for him to read the Sunday comics to me.

But one day, instead of just reading to me, he asked, "What is this letter?" And so he taught me the alphabet. And then, "And what does this letter say; what does it sound like?" "Now slur the sounds together." It took a while, but we kept practicing, then in a flash – an *aha* moment – understanding came, and I recognized that I could sound out not only letters but even a whole word. This concept – I didn't know what to call it then – was simply breathtaking, something making me a little lightheaded. Letters represented sounds; slurred together they made words – real, actual words. Words had meaning. A solid bubble around the words meant that Dick Tracy was speaking. A cloud-like bubble showed what Dagwood was thinking. I still remember that Sunday morning when the sudden flash of insight happened. I sounded out some long word, realized what had happened, and turned to him, awe on my face. He knew; he smiled. And so he continued teaching me. In fact, he continued for the rest of his life.

Grandpap had taught me to read. And had done so before I went to school. Pure phonetics. Words lead to thoughts, thoughts to ideas, ideas to actions and inventions . . . What power. How can you ever adequately thank the person who teaches you to read?

And he encouraged me to draw – again, from the comics. See the form – reproduce the form. Faithfully. Perfectly. And so he also taught me to see.

I'm embarrassed today (well, maybe only a little) that my early drawing interests almost invariably led to my reproduction of Tommy guns, airplanes, and wonderful, voluptuous women's forms from some of the racier comics. *Smiling Jack* comes immediately to mind. Ah, I can still see my drawing of the magnificent, exquisitely beautiful curve of a woman's breast. At age 4? I guess more stuff is hardwired into our brains than we like to admit.

In time, as the war inevitably approached America and the steel industry picked up, my father found a job as a clerk on the Pittsburgh and Lake Erie Railroad. That job eventually was to lead to a white-collar position called Yardmaster. So as times – and prospects – were improving, during the latter part of my fourth year, my parents bought a house about 500 yards down the road from my grandparents. Small, three bedrooms, a white clapboard Pennsylvania farmhouse built before the time of the first world war. The white house was not too far away from Grandma and Grandpap for me to ask for help, not too far away for me to learn fundamental rules of life from them. But once in the white house, my parents had achieved independence, an independence that would slowly grow with the onset of that fearsome and all-encompassing war.

So the first question you might wonder about was whether this continuing reminder of "bad times" imprinted into a little boy's head was the cause of any continuing angst or psychological scarring.

Nah.

And the second question: Was this an auspicious start for any family? Frank poverty, poor economic prospects for the future on one hand; committed parents and loving grandparents on the other. Let us see.

3. IN THE COUNTRY

And from the times, now to the place.

My sisters and I were blessed to have grown up in the country. Perhaps *blessed* is not a strong enough word.

I should explain what was meant by that phrase, *in the country*, during the 1940s – and even into the 1950s …. back in the day.

The cities were easy to define. In cities, people knew about, and more importantly, accepted the idea of boundaries. The houses tended to be close together, fences separated properties, people walked on paved sidewalks, and if you asked someone where they lived, they could say without hesitation, "McKeesport." The size of the city was unimportant to the definition. For example, the small town farther south along the Youghiogheny River, *Buena Vista* (shortened and corrupted to Beuny and pronounced in two syllables, *beu* as in view and *ny* as in knee. Who cares how any Spaniard thinks it should be said?) had only about 50 families living in it, but the lots were small, the houses side-by-side, there were sidewalks, they had their own barbershop and gas station, so Buena Vista is was most definitely not *in the country*.

If city were one end, the other end of the spectrum was easy to define too. Ask, for example, our cousin Katie where she lived, and she would answer, again without hesitation, "We have a dairy farm down on Guffey Hollow Road."

And that left *in the country*, in between. This place, this concept of space was so important to my sisters and me that I feel the phrase *in the country* should be capitalized and made bold. **IN THE COUNTRY**. There. I feel better now.

We lived between the farms and cities. Yes, there were paved roads - but no sidewalks or streetlights - and water usually came from a spring, a well, or a cistern next to each house (though by 1940, there was Township water available – if anybody ever wanted it). At one point, we had, behind our house, cistern (rain) water for washing (rainwater was soft beyond belief – but tasteless). Plus, we had a well in the garage. Yet, for reasons that escape me, the prior owners had hooked the house up to Township water. My grandparents on the other hand refused to connect to Township water – they were quite happy with their well, because for taste, there simply was no comparison, and of course their water was free. By the 40s, most houses in the country had an indoor bathroom. But sewers? Forget about them. We used septic tanks, whose out-flow dumped into local creeks (in which we played).

No surprise, in the country, just about everybody planted a big backyard garden, and also depended upon their fruit trees to put food by. We had two kinds of apples, plus peaches and blackberries. Grandpap grew two kinds of apples, plums, peaches, grapes and currants. When fall came, Dorothy Carloss (she lived up toward McKeesport – in a city named Christy Park) would come to our back yard, and she and mom would put up peaches and apples, and boil tomatoes to bottle ketchup. And naturally, we kids would help. At least they made us believe we were helping. It's nice to grow up around kind adults.

Though our mother's preserves were good, my grandmother's were, quite simply, the best. World-class as a descriptor would be about right. She kept her canning in a chilly part of her basement – a room cool even in the hottest part of summer – a room she called her root cellar. Potatoes, sweet potatoes, and newspaper - wrapped apples were kept above the dirt floor in wooden crates resting on old bricks. Open the door into that space and the wonderful, moist smells of slightly damp earth, acrid green and blue molds, and sweetened fruits enveloped you, smells exploding into your nose, immediately making juices run.

Speaking of explosions, on occasion a jar actually did blow up. It was a rare happening, I should quickly say, because of Grandma's meticulousness. If one jar had somehow become contaminated during the canning process, the bacteria invariably made gas. And the jars being tightly sealed, when the gas pressure reached the tensile limits of the jar . . . we could hear the results upstairs. So we realized there was some risk going into that room. But what kid could not help but feel a delicious thrill of danger as we slowly opened the door, inhaled the complex smells – quickly picking the jar we had been told to bring to the kitchen, then as fast, leaving. We learned to look at and tap the lids before opening. A concave lid meant there was still vacuum – and the contents were thus safe; a convex lid meant that some gas forming bug was at work.

By the way, *canning* was a euphemism – everything was put up in sterilized-by-boiling Mason jars. For the jams and jellies, we poured liquid paraffin on the top. The high sugar content precluded bacterial growth – but strangely, not fungus. Scrape off the gray and green molds, and the jam was good as ever. No, better than good; best ever.

But by living in the country, shopping for essentials – or for food that you could not grow – became a problem. Want to buy groceries? Travel all the way into McKeesport. The bus came by only half a dozen times a day (nobody had two cars, and dads needed the family car to get to and from work). Once a week my grandmother made the trek into Balsamo's, what then passed for McKeesport's first and only supermarket, bringing home paper shopping bags of food[3]. Of course nobody knew about the concept of a supermarket back then, but I believe Balsamo's would qualify today. Well, almost. Balsamo's did have something you don't see on the floors of a modern supermarket: sawdust. Probably never get that sawdust practice past today's health inspectors. Strange though, nobody ever seemed to die of food borne illnesses. To a little boy, going to Balsamos with Grandma was an adventure - until we had to come home, that is, because she would get off the bus at the bottom of Constitution Hill and walk the last two miles to save a dime. And I got to carry the heavier bags. And sweat.

Coming south[4] from McKeesport on the bus, the road home generally followed the Youghiogheny River. Not that we

---

[3] Balsamo paper bags were used and reused by mill workers carrying their dirty work clothes to and from the mill. No prideful man wanted to be seen on the bus wearing dirty clothes. The men irreverently called the bags "hunky suitcases". "Hunky" the word, is one I will explain better in Chapter 7. It had an almost always derogatory connotation and was used to describe immigrants from Eastern and Southeastern Europe. Mostly by those immigrants themselves, much the way blacks today use the n word.

[4] Coming south from McKeesport on the bus……. Wait, I should say something about that word *south*. Kids in Western Pennsylvania had no idea of compass direction growing up. Our landscape was about as different from Kansas or Iowa as can be imagined. The roads followed land contours, the rivers and creeks, and out near our place, old deer or cow paths. It is only now, looking at contour maps or Google Earth, that I can know which way our house faced.

could often see the river – because the steel mills always took the prime land next to the water. But we knew we were getting close to our home grounds when we crossed the Boston bridge. (And no, Boston was not named for that city in the Northeast, but rather for an early inhabitant.)

But to get home, there was no way that the bus could have negotiated that hill ahead even in summer, so we turned left, contouring along the river, through Boston and its brickyard, eventually turning south again to begin a long climb up the hill, still on the Boston-Greenock Road. It was not an easy job for a bus in the 40s, and it was only many years later that I realized that not all buses wheezed. Nearing the top of the hill, we passed by my parent's original home, and farther, near the top, an overgrown cemetery from Civil War times. Years later I found a small marble headstone simply inscribed *Anne Kerber*. Could she have been a relative? Another few miles, and the bus would drop us off at 1514, now on the Greenock Buena Vista Road.

Our home, like a few others in the region, lay in a gentle hollow about 400 yards wide and about 2 miles long.

Walk with me out our home's back door and we'll explore . . (Come to think of it, our back door was in the front of the house, as was the front door. I will leave the analysis of that Pennsylvania naming logic to someone else.) If we walk straight ahead across the road, we will climb up a gentle hill. We pass first through blackberry briars, then softwood sumac bushes and locust trees, finally entering second growth hard-woods. Continuing, a quarter-mile farther, we come to an active coal mine.

When I was five, one of my neighbors from way up the road, Steve, walked down to the house. "Let's go up to the mine. Somebody fell into the tipple. Dead. Want to see a dead man?" Was I not a boy? Of course I went.

Steve is an uncommonly good friend to this little boy. He is a rare adult, a trusted adult, because his communications with everyone – but especially toward us kids – are straightforward. We wonder about this clarity, about his being different from other big people, but being kids, we cannot express our confusion in words.

An aside: Steve is so unlike other adults who so often say one thing and mean another. As we grow, complex, mixed communications from adults continue to confuse us all – in fact to confuse every kid I know. And my quest – my sometimes seemingly hopeless quest – will continue to be to understand what the adults really want. I recognize today I was not alone in my confusion.

As for the trip to the coal mine, my mother, without much thought, gives her permission. Could you do that with a kid now? Back then nobody seemed to think much of a little boy's going off into the woods, riding on a neighbor's shoulders – to see a dead man. I suspect that today, my mother might be arrested. As would Steve.

But too late for our grisly voyeurism, the unfortunate miner had been retrieved from the coal tipple, and taken away. So it goes.

Another half hour's walk beyond the mine, the hill drops precipitously away 400 feet down to the Baltimore and Ohio railroad tracks along the Youghiogheny River bank. From here, Reed and I spy on the hobos cooking chickens they have stolen from someone's yard. Dad warns me, "Stay away from them." I reply ever so cleverly, "Why would I go near chickens?". "Don't crack wise with me," he says sharply, "I mean the hobos, not the chickens." I am at least smart enough to keep my mouth shut from that point.

And a story about that precipitous drop-off. Well, it's a cliff, actually.

In sixth grade, one of the kids from the city asked to come to visit with me. He was curious about us and what it was like to live in the country. After mom fixed us a bit of lunch, I took him exploring in the woods. We walked up the hill toward the river, picking and eating blackberries, then I started climbing down the cliff, holding on to small trees growing out from cracks in the rocks. This climb was something Reed and I did without much thought. After a few yards, I stopped, curious. Sammy was not moving. He was still, hugging his body to the rock, holding on to two tiny trees. And he was crying. I should mention that Sammy was a pretty tough kid, generally respected, even feared at school. I climbed back up, helping him back to the top. We walked back to the road, saying nothing, and waited in embarrassing silence for the next bus so he could go back to the city. He was comfortable in his jungle – he was even respected there. But when in mine, he felt small, inept. And when I thought about it, I was just as uncomfortable in his jungle, down in the slums of McKeesport's First Ward. It was a lesson that stuck with me as I grew up. I would, I must remember to be more careful with others' feelings and not expose their fears.

Walk up the road from the house, and on the right we will first pass a small woods, then find ourselves looking down into a dark swamp, a swamp that you came to know in the first chapter, one that continues to excite a certain delicious twinge of fear in my friends Reed and Jack – and me – throughout our childhood years.

The swamp (you have met the swamp's pond in Chapter 1) lies in a low area between the two hills. The creek running languidly through it gives it its character – making the mud and muck that sucks at our bare feet, and in summer's heat, gags us with disgusting fetid smells of rotting vegetation. Cattails grow in profusion, taller than our heads, showing us where to avoid standing water. Further back toward the swamp edges, low willows entangle us in their branches, and are thick enough to make exploration difficult. That is, when we work up the courage to explore.

Which we regularly do. What little boy could bypass such an excellent place?

Walk further, on the opposite side of the road, and we come to my grandparent Mason's house, then a few hundred yards further, on a dirt road leading left toward the river, a cluster of three substantial brick homes. That road lies adjacent to what we called *the streetcar tracks*. No steel tracks now, just a now unused right-of-way, which is to us a gently graded path allowing us to explore the woods with ease.

The main road, a minimal two-car macadam – too mean even to have a painted yellow line – leads up to the crest of the hill where one incongruously finds a first rate upper class golf course and country club. We used the term "up the road" to the country club, and "down the road" to go to Lower Greenock. You may wonder, but I can tell you, no one has ever figured out why such a superior golf club was located on our hill so far away from the city. But I didn't care about why – that country club will turn out to be the key to my entire future education and life.

Walk from the house to the left along the road, and a little lower than us – as the hollow falls away to the creek behind our house – lies Wilfred and Evelyn Brown's house. The Browns are our closest neighbors. Fortunately for me, the Browns have a son, Jack, about my age and temperament (and I must add, a beautiful younger sister, slim to the point of being petite, who looks at me with shy eyes and innocent smile, a girl all freckles and strawberry blonde hair). About once a week Jack and I prove the adage *one boy, half a man; two boys, trouble*. And when we break a limb off the apple tree while climbing, or manage to injure ourselves falling down the hill, or have one of our recurring fights, Jack's dad actually hits him, something my dad never does to me. We come to fear Jack's dad beyond all reasonableness. And I am particularly afraid, afraid that he will blame me for leading Jack "down the Devil's path."

The Brown house is served not only by a real outhouse but also – a wonder of our Pennsylvania hills – a spring house. The spring house is so seriously excellent that I am, as a kid, embarrassingly jealous, especially when, on innumerable summer afternoons, Jack and I, sweating and flushed from the heat, crash through the wooden door, slap water on our faces and necks, then drink deeply. In this whitewashed stone walled room dug into the side of the hill, a copper pipe has been sunk into the rock. (How did they do that, you may wonder? We wondered.) A constant stream of cold water flows through the pipe into a series of ever lower concrete basins. The first pool is for drinking; in the second, the Brown family keeps their dairy products in stoneware crocks; the third we may use for washing. On a hot August day, there is no cooler place to be than in that half cave/ half springhouse.

I am furious when Dad refuses to build us a spring house.

Beyond Brown's home, a little farther on the right side of the road and beyond the red dog road leading to the mine, we come to an ancient graveyard, its tilted stones commemorating early settlers back at the time of our Civil War, and some even older. One day as we are walking down the road, Grandpap Mason says, with just a hint of a smile on his face,

"You might be surprised how the people in that graveyard keep voting Democrat." "How can that be," I ask? He does not answer, but just smiles and looks at me. It's one more puzzle to file away and, I hope, someday understand.

Behind our house, the land slopes down to a crawfish creek, one that floods regularly during spring rains, and then climbs up again to the old streetcar right-of-way (which I'll tell you more about later), then up further another half mile to the crest of the hill. We called them hills, but they were more – not quite a mountain, understand, but if you stood on the crest, you'd still have to walk a mile or two and start down the other side before you could see Boston and the river. And throughout these early years, I never see another person during my almost ceaseless wanderings and explorations. These hills were mine and mine alone. Or so I felt.

This land, these woods, and the space between houses give each family surprising privacy, a privacy we may not have quite appreciated as small children. Neighbors, by and large, are warm and friendly, and will gather together for just about any excuse. Most importantly for us kids, this is a land that gives us almost absolute freedom. Though there were many factors growing up during those times that formed us, made us what we are, that freedom was near the top of the list. Of course, with freedom came responsibility, and that's another part of the story.

From my tone, you can tell that times are getting better, because work is to be found, though the dark clouds of war are on the horizon, and adults talk through worried frowns about the country's future. It seems that all are united in their determination to keep us out of "another European war".

Until I leave high school for college, and except for going to school in the city, this land is the center of my universe. When I close my eyes in reverie, when I remember these times, I realize I was blessed to have grown up in – to have the freedom of these hills and hollows – *in the country.*

4. THE GIRLS

The girls? Would I ever refer to my three wonderful sisters as *the girls*? How depersonalizing, how objectifying, how abjectly and awfully inappropriate, especially as sensitive as we are today.

Before any feminists get up in arms, let me start with a disclaimer – when we were growing up, I never called my three sisters "the girls". Never. Well, maybe once or twice. It was my mother who started the practice. And my grandmother picked up on . . . well, the convenience of the phrase. And then of course that made it okay for everyone else in the family to use the convention. It was, for example, "...... and yes, next Tuesday, bring Chuckie and the girls......." Both Mom and Grandma would be severely censured today as being su-

premely politically incorrect. Lumping three young ladies together like that? How *lacking in sensitivity* (that word again).
But I digress.

At this point you have every right to wonder where this is
going. Easy answer: I must tell you about the three wonderful,
lovable, frustrating, anger producing girls in my life, sisters
who (only in retrospect) enriched my life - and tried to teach
me how to relate to the opposite sex. *The girls.*

This story began in the spring of my fourth year. I had become
obnoxiously independent, and by my own modest and objective self appraisal, clever, independent, accomplished, savvy,
and remarkably world wise. Then again, maybe not so, because today I'm embarrassed to admit that I hadn't noticed
anything unusual. Particularly in my mother's developing
pear-like shape. Nor did I notice that mom had gone away for
a few days - until she returned on a warm and sunny spring
day in May. Now you may think this strange in view of what
is about to happen, but I don't have enough imagination to
make this stuff up.

On that special afternoon the big fuss on the front porch of my
grandparent's home attracted my attention. Rosie and Ernie,
(English immigrant friends of my grandparents, but Aunt Rosie and uncle Ernie to me), my Mom and Dad, Grandma and
Grandpap were, well, fussing. Even a four-year-old boy could
feel the happiness. Joy was, like the scent of Grandma's
blooming lilac, in the air. It was certainly air palpably
charged, far beyond that brought by the onset of a warm

spring afternoon. I had never seen so many smiles, so much happiness. Investigation was clearly in order.

All the adults had tightly gathered about a small, pink blanket-wrapped, wiggling bundle lying in a wicker basket on the front porch swing. I did my own wiggling, got on the inside of the circle, moved the blankets back, and saw . . . a baby. It turned out to be Judy, my sister. There she lay: all pink herself, a gummy smile, plus constant motion – a squirming head, arms and legs moving – and moving, and moving. And that was to be her personality: smiling, no matter the darkness, and actively exploring, wanting to reach out, to touch and experience the world.

I was awestruck. Wow. And yeah, yeah I know what you're thinking, thinking that was made concrete later – many years later in medical school. I learned what I was supposed to have felt: rage, jealousy, fear that my parents would care for me less – you know the Freudian words.

So much for Sigmund. Maybe it was the four years age difference. Who knows? What I felt was, in fact, awe. I had a sister. MY sister. In a few short weeks, I had become protective, a feeling and behavior that continued when I would, five years later, shepherd her to St Peter's School.

Then about two years after Judy's arrival, another beautiful baby, Mary Ellen. And about two years after that, another beautiful baby, Janet. *How did they do it, I wondered?* Clearly, my parents had figured out something big. I had three sisters. Three. (*What've you got? I got three sisters.*)

No, my sisters were not all sweetness and light. At one moment they could be exquisitely lovable and beautiful, and the next, maddening, infuriating. They intruded. They pushed into everything I wanted to do; my priceless privacy was irretrievably and forever gone. The girls stuck to me like the flies on the cellar flypaper. One sister even weaseled her way along on my first date. On my first date! My sisters. Was I lucky? It would depend upon when you asked me. But in general, yes. Nonetheless, I have to admit that there were times – so many times – when I understood why murder is almost always a family affair.

My sisters were not similar, despite the adults' verbal grouping them as *the girls*. They had a few things in common – two X chromosomes, for example, but each was her own person. Three prime characteristics though they did share: first, their extreme independence, second, to my great and continuing annoyance and frustration, their pervasive curiosity, and third, they could *do things*. Anything. Iron clothes? No problem. Read a novel? No problem. Outrun most boys? No problem. Climb an apple tree faster than those same boys? Oh yes. And they were generally fearless and trusting, especially trusting of an older brother.

Ah, but the intrusiveness: Turn around quickly, and I would bump into one of them. Unlock the door to my bedroom, and I would likely find them inside. *Looking through my stuff.* My most personal private stuff. To this date Janet can press my guilt button by reminding me that I had *more* – after all I had my own room, my own private stash locked away (old medals that my grandfather had won, trinkets from my grandmother, a set of pastels and paints -- I liked to draw -- and other precious things like rocks and used horseshoe nails). And even a cubbyhole/closet where all manners of secret things were kept, including Dad's and my 30-40 Krag rifle and its ammunition. On the other hand, she will not accept any guilt for her frequent rummaging through my stuff. More about that later.

In the cellar one afternoon, I was melting lead to make toy soldiers. (Yes, yes, I know, I know. Kids alone, wood house, open flames, molten metal. Our parents should have been dragged off to jail as we kids were taken to Allegheny County Child Protection Services. But there you have it.) Somehow I had gotten a bit of water into one of the molds. And of course Mary Ellen, being Mary Ellen, infinitely curious, sticking to me like duct tape, was leaning over as I poured. A small explosion – the molten lead falling on the droplet of water turned it immediately to steam, spattering lead over the ceiling – some landing on Mary Ellen. She bears scars to this day. Then again, I am more than moderately guilty that all my sisters bear scars caused by my misadventures. They may forgive me someday. At least I hope they will.

There was, on one single occasion, mild revenge for my loss of privacy. When my parents went out together on a rare evening, I was empowered to watch my sisters. Let me say it again: empowered. (My recurring fantasy was to have *power over the girls* when I think back to those days.) Ordinarily, we played well together – our play inevitably involved excitement - and always some aspect of mutual trust. (And danger - we are reminded by our scars - only some of them mentioned above.) But trust and play were not on my agenda this night - power and control were: "Tonight we will organize the house." Actually, I never used the term organize. In our community the term was *rid up*. It meant simply to put toys away, wash dishes, and generally neaten up the house. They whined to my parents repeatedly that I tortured them. I categorically deny that charge. Who knows when the statute of limitations runs out on these things?

And for another look at intrusiveness (and a brother's revenge), you need some background. The two cellar doors led out to a back yard that sloped gently down to the creek some hundred yards further. Go out those doors, face the creek, and about 30 yards away to the left you would come to our chicken coop. It was my job to feed and water the chickens, and . . . now on to the story: On this certain memorable, fateful Sunday morning my mother said, "Get me a chicken." May I translate? She meant: 1) fill the washtub in the cellar with water and put it on to boil; 2) catch a chicken; 3) cut off its head; 4) dunk it in the boiling water to loosen its feathers, then pluck every single feather off; 5) using the open flame of that same gas burner, singe the hairs on its now bare skin (bet you didn't know that chickens had hair on their skin); 6) cut it open and remove the guts – but save the liver, heart, and gizzard for making stock; and 7) do this all in the next 30 minutes. It was a common command, one I understood well.

You want chicken for dinner? You kill a chicken. Simple. That's what you did when you lived in the country.

Step one: identify a good young bird, then, step two, much more difficult – catch her. No bird would go quietly into that dark night when caught – and none of them ever did. Peck marks on forearms was one price of protein.

Dad had sawn a cherry tree down, leaving the stump flat and about 2 feet high: The chopping block. Holding the bird's legs in my left hand, I would lay the chicken's neck on the stump. The bird would invariably move, usually to look up at me. After all, had I not been feeding her and her sisters every morning for the last six weeks? After some period of time though, she would quiet down, and I would slowly move the hatchet around from behind my leg, then bring the blade down swiftly across her neck just below the head.

You've probably heard the term *like a chicken with its head cut off*. It's perfect description of what happens next. I could either hold the chicken's legs, neck pointing down as it underwent vigorous agonal movements, squirming, flapping its wings violently until completely dead. The result would be to cover myself with chicken blood spurting from the cut carotid arteries in the neck. Or to avoid the bloody mass, I could throw the chicken away a few feet, when, now headless, it would run around randomly, flapping its wings, blood spurting up to the sky - until it collapsed.

Judy saw all such happenings as adventure, and glued herself to me during most of the preamble. This closeness I had come to find inevitable - and this day I remember it as being quite annoying - but when it was time to swing the ax, closeness became dangerous. I had her move well away.

Now close your eyes and try to imagine what comes next. (I am not guilty; the devil makes me do this.) The ax blade moves lightning fast down, the head flies off . . . and I throw the spasming, squirting chicken - directly at her.

In milliseconds – even before the bird hits the ground – Judy has turned, and with a long high-pitched scream that curdles milk throughout the county, begins to run down the hill toward the creek. (Did I mention she is also fast?) She ziggs left, our headless chicken follows, spurting blood, flapping its wings. She zaggs right, the chicken follows, still spurting blood, matching her every move. Her moves are of course as random as are the chicken's – but our headless protagonist matches her moves perfectly, as though *it knows*. They both run all the way down to the creek at which point the hen collapses, stone cold dead at last. But not Judy – continuing her scream, she bounds across the creek more agile than any frightened fawn, finally to hide behind an elm tree.

Long minutes pass. She finally peeks from behind the elm. Some sadism gene deep in my DNA has been switched on; I cannot stop laughing. Not so my mother, who has been attracted to the kitchen window by the scream. Mother's flash of anger undoes me. Again, my only defense: the devil made me do it.

I know she bears deep psychological scars of the experience to this day. I often wonder if she will ever forgive me. I have been afraid to ask.

I have mentioned the woods, and especially that elm.

During the late 1800s, the entire state had been clear-cut, but the trees had grown back and had become mature by the 1940s: wild cherry, beech, walnut, maples of all variety, some oaks, and along the roads, softwood locusts grew. In the deep woods, which meant a short hundred yards from the house, the trees sometimes became tied together by entangling branches of wild grape and Virginia creeper. But above all else, giant elms ruled our woods. Elms with trunks four of us kids, arms together could not encircle, elms with horizontal spreading branches bigger than my chest.

One massive elm though was the star. Its first huge branch, nearly parallel to the ground and half as thick as my dad's chest, was the locus of *our tire swing*. I should probably put *our tire swing* in capital letters, it was that important to us. Over that branch, which at its closest point to the gently sloping hill was 10 feet above us and 15 feet beyond the tree trunk, our dad had secured a stout hemp rope, and had tied its other end to an old tire.

So as soon as the snows left the land, we would burst out the cellar door, run down the hill, jumping stone to stone across the creek, up the hill through blossoming mayapple, catching, then bringing the tire to the upslope. Now if you grew up in Iowa – or any flat land, it would be difficult to visualize how we used that swing. First, no one ever actually sat in the tire; sitting was sissie stuff. And second, no one ever expected another kid to push them back and forth - more sissy stuff. Consider the slope of the hill falling away from the branch. We would pull the tire back as far as we could on to the upslope, then, holding on to the tire's bottom rim, run as fast as possible along the contour, then, when the hill fell away, we would launch ourselves hanging, spinning, swirling, free in space. Seen from above, the path of the tire would be an almost perfect circle. But during three quarters of that circle, we were in the air. It was critical to time the spin in the air just right, or the flier would come back to earth dragging heels and backside on damp black forest floor. That would have been an ignominious end, an obvious-to-others clumsy end to a thrilling, gorgeous, glorious ride in space. We seemed never to tire of our tire swing. What kid would?

The girls and I developed significant upper body strength, an inevitable byproduct of the flight. Nobody died. Nobody fell off. Ever.

Sometimes brothers have responsibilities that outweigh the daily aggravations that happen in any family. Let me say categorically: There have always been bullies. There will always be bullies. And this is about bullies. For a reason that I no longer remember, my mother had sent me to Aunt Rosie's, about a mile and a half away. And I was to take Judy, now aged four, with me. Just after lunch, we started our trek along roads, cutting through backyards (there was no such thing as a fence in the country) and finally through a broad hayfield.

Unnoticed, and as if by magic, the bullies appeared – three bigger boys. They grabbed us, pushed us around a bit, and crammed us into an abandoned dog house, blocking the doorway with an old door and some rocks. They peered in from time to time, then shuffled around laughing. Judy looked at me with wide eyes. "Don't cry," I whispered, "they're just trying to make you cry." She snuggled into the corner, put her arms around her knees, and smiled. I was not nearly as confident as I let on. The bullies became bored and left, since they could not get the reaction they wanted. Try as I might, I could not get us out. Hours passed. Finally, about dusk, fearful that adults would come looking for us, they returned, and let us out.

She looked at the bullies. I didn't know that a four-year-old girl could smirk. How proud I was of her.

I did my best to protect my sisters. Later, shepherding them to and from our awful school (which you get to see in future chapters. You are forewarned.), other bullies appeared from time to time. We survived. But thinking back, I am a bit guilty; I know I could have done a better job.

And another sadness: the 1940s were times when people didn't touch very much, and though we played together, there was in retrospect, not nearly enough touching to reflect and reinforce the tender feelings I had for them.

As they entered adolescence, developing their own individuality, moving further from the family into their own lives, we spent much less time together, save for the picnics, the parties, and the holidays. Each of my sisters developed and expanded those strong personalities I saw during their early years. And each has become remarkably successful in her own career. How proud I continue to be of what they have accomplished.

Here they are in 1949. I am, as appropriate for a big brother, in the background. But even at this age, they are no longer *the girls*. Judith. Mary Ellen. Janet.

Today I do wonder if my sisters know how much I have always adored them.

5. THE WHITE HOUSE

No, not the one in DC. Our *white* house. May I explain?

From my grandparent's home, let us walk down the road toward Lower Greenock. We will likely walk quickly past that swamp I told you about in the prior chapter, then come to some woods, then along a scant quarter acre of timothy grass covered field - and finally, behind massive sugar and gum maples and a small front yard, we come to our house, our home, our white house.

Uninsulated, the white house is cold in winter and hot in summer, but it will become the fountain of growth, of knowledge, and more importantly, will provide security to my sisters and me until we are old enough to venture alone into the world. From a vantage point many years later, I now see we took that security for granted, my sisters and I. Mom and Dad did not.

An American Boyhood

The house is a typical wood frame Pennsylvania two-story farmhouse. It has been built in the early part of the century on a little more than an acre of sloping wooded land. Porches cover the entire front, and bizarrely, both the front door and the "back door" are built into the front of the house, so both face the road. Somehow, everybody coming to visit (everybody who lives *in the country*, that is) knows to go to the back door. Neither door ever was, to my knowledge, locked. It is in this home that we learn to tie our shoes, to prepare food, to study, to share meals, and to learn to get along with each other, not a small accomplishment for four vigorous kids.

A knock on the front door meant STRANGER. If you were that stranger, you would approach our front door, announce yourself, and when the door opens, enter the living room, immediately facing a stairwell leading up to two bedrooms. Step to the right, past a steam radiator and you come into the living room, with a coal-fired fireplace to your right. This is a real *living* room. Look at old grainy and faded photos and home movies, and you will see pretty little girls (my sisters, of course) running, jumping, doing front rolls on the carpet while approving family and guests smile on and encourage their tumbling efforts. You will see Christmas trees, a kid-made creche occupying the fireplace during the holiday. On a Saturday afternoon, you might see Pete Peterson, the milkman, nodding off in the easy chair after one too many highballs he enjoyed during one of the family parties. You would certainly see our grandfather reading the Sunday paper while our grandmother knits, sipping her sweetened English tea.

You would see one of us on the floor, chin on elbows, reading or drawing. No guests-only living room for us; it would be better called a lived-in room.

From the living room, pass through a wide entryway, and you come to the dining room. Dad has removed the old narrow doorway, and enlarging the passage almost to the width of the room, makes living room and dining room a single integrated homey space. Here we share dinner with guests, we play Wagner or Gershwin or Gene Autry recorded on shellac 78 RPM records through a windup Victrola. (Yes, it's strange. *Tristan und Isolde* one moment; *Rudolph the Red Nose Reindeer* another. But there you have it.) Oh, and along one wall Mom's old upright oak veneer piano lives. Since there is no television, we provide our own entertainment. Mom plays *Peg o' My Heart*. Then *Heart and Soul*. Dad's clear tenor leads. We sing. Loudly. Happily. Perhaps not well, but we make each other and the guests laugh. Talent is not a requisite; a best effort is.

Passing through the dining room and through another doorway to the right we enter a hallway, and another 90° right turn brings us to the back door. It is obvious that this part of the house has been added on later. But don't turn right at this moment; instead go straight ahead to enter a large kitchen.

On your left, you come upon our 1940s chrome and vinyl dinner table. At this table we have formal, sit down, take -your - time dinners. Every night. We sit together, we share food, we bitterly complain about the nuns in school (" Stop that. Show some respect", our mother says. Father knows nuns better; he stays quiet). The girls whine about having to eat the peas.

And peas begin another story. It turns out one of my sisters doesn't like peas. Fresh, canned, frozen – no matter. So surreptitiously she (could more than one of them be guilty?) places her peas on a ledge underneath the table. Many years later, when dad and I disassemble this table for the junk pile, we find a mountain, then an avalanche, pounds and pounds of shriveled, black, hard – as - ball bearing peas. Girls are so clever. To this day I have failed to find out who the guilty party is. Or was.

Dinner complete, there is, every evening, dessert. Usually cake, sometimes pie. (Is my mother not English?) On the one hand, being English, she bakes flawlessly well, but on the other, the meat presented is usually a dark, shriveled, brown lump (nonetheless we did get our protein). It would be the greatest kindness to say she was an acceptable, average cook. No matter, her strengths lie elsewhere. But we talk, we discuss, we learn manners, we are disciplined for our transgressions, and we coalesce. At that dinner table, more than any other place or time, we come together as a family.

Had there been, in those days, iPhones, and had we dared open one during dinner, my mother would have, in a voice low but heavy with threat, said "Turn *that thing* off. **Immediately.**" No further discussion would have ensued. My father's reaction to such an action would be different – and might be surprising to an outsider. He would likely say, "How interesting. May I see it? (*This may end well, the outsider might think.*) "It looks strong, well made". (*I'm feeling better about this transaction ending well.*) Let us see if it will withstand a ball peen hammer." (*I should've known better.*) Crash. The situation is ended. And of course we *should* have known better. I do not exaggerate. In fact, I admire his approach – which expects and demands all of us to have common sense – and I have incorporated his approach into my views on handling the world's problems. And do so to this day.

The cellar, which you will soon enter, will turn out to be the heart of our white house, but this kitchen, our kitchen, is our home's soul.

So let's go back to that hallway between the kitchen and dining room. Just inside the back door, open another one, and you will descend dark, steep stairs to the cellar. Almost every adult male who attempts this passage – no matter how many times we warn – opens a small but painful horizontal gash on his forehead by striking said forehead against a low traversing 2 x 12 beam. We gather together to watch each of them in wonderment. "Watch your head on the beam," one of us says. Then we wait. Thunk. A curse word or two, then the men continue down. The girls and I look at each other. We smile, we giggle. One more grown-up male who doesn't listen to kids, one more victim. My sisters and I are certainly easily entertained.

An American Boyhood

The cellar divides into two large spaces. The first, which we have just entered, contains laundry tubs, a Maytag washing machine, gas-fired burners to heat water for the wash (and to scald chickens so I can remove the feathers) and a hot water heater.

On to laundry: Each and every Monday morning, when my father returns from work at about 7 AM, our parents begin the wash. There are hundreds, maybe thousands of (okay, I sometimes exaggerate) kids' dirty white socks to get clean – plus our other clothes. Dad presoaks all in the tubs, then washes, rinses, and rings the water out using our old Maytag wringer washer. We learn mom and dad do things, well, carefully, and the wash is just one example. And our grandparents reinforce: "Do it well, or not at all." The message is clearly: do it right – or else. Our socks are blazingly white. The *do it well or not at all* lesson sticks throughout our adulthood, becoming hardwired into our brains. By the way, the *not at all* part of the aphorism was never a real consideration. Thought I ought to emphasize that.

After washing and wringing, dad puts the clean clothes in a wicker basket, and my mother hangs them outside in the side yard. In the winter, they freeze solid, but dry nonetheless. Freezing and drying? It is a phenomenon that fascinates me. I confess it still does.

Over the years, my father and I rebuild that washer many times. The grease from the Maytag's gearbox will come off my hands. But only eventually.

One day another device shows up "Brought home a mangle this morning," Dad says, proudly surveying this contraption. It is as high as my head, and about six foot wide. "Rescued it from the dump. Needs a little work." And so, over the next weeks, he makes it work. Then, a few days later, installing his machine against a wall, he says to me, with just a touch of annoyance, "No, you can't open up the gas line. You'd help me more just by standing there and watching." (I hate it when he says that.) So he connects the natural gas line to the machine, plugs its power cord in to an electrical outlet, and a few moments later I watch a large roller pressing a bed sheet against the curved heated plate, efficiently, flawlessly removing wrinkles. From this point on, our parents press all bed sheets on this huge drum-like machine. And my sisters and I admit to each other that true luxury is to climb into clean, silky, fresh pressed cool sheets on a sultry summer evening. Way to go Dad.

In late summer, Mom gets out a huge copper pot, we clean it, and we wash two rolls of pennies. All tomatoes are picked from our garden, blanched in scalding water, peeled, and mashed through a strainer. The pulp goes into the pot with salt, vinegar, brown sugar, and other spices. It is my sisters' and my job to stir continually. The pennies, moved by the paddle, scour the bottom, preventing the thickening tomato paste from sticking to the pot. We make enough ketchup to last the whole year. Dad and I cap each bottle with our cast-iron capper. (Yes, we also have a cast-iron cherry pitter for our cherry tree pickings. And a cast iron apple peeler for the apple tree's bounty.) We freeze the apples, cherries and everything else. Even as kids we recognize this food is so much better than any store-bought stuff. And, as we have all gotten into the act, it is *our* food.

Ah, but the other side of the cellar holds the action. The furnace (coal-fired, steam). The coal cellar (filthy, dusty). The workbench (heaven). And in a board covered concrete pit, a water pump.

Why a water pump? The search for good drinking water seems to be a never ending quest that has brought us today to the bottled stuff that costs more than gasoline. The water from the faucets in our homes we take for granted as being safe, but perhaps not so tasty. So it was when I was a kid. Then, people would travel miles to a favored hidden spring to fill their jugs.

When we move into the house, water is supplied by the Township. But in the garage, which is an open shed attached to the side of the house, we have a well, about 3 feet in diameter – but how deep? In my imagination the well casing penetrates almost to the center of the earth (I'm exaggerating again, I know). It is impossible for a kid to get the cap off that well (you may wonder how I know), but my dad satisfies my curiosity one day, removes the concrete cover, and allows me to satisfy my curiosity, to look in. What I see is completely and absolutely terrifying. To look down – so far down – into that hole – to see shimmering black water so, so far below. Way below. I visualize kids falling in and never being found again.

I visualize *me* falling in and never being found again. I shiver a bit, and step back. "Satisfied?" Dad asks, looking hard at me. He knows I won't try to get the lid off ever again. Another one of Dad's powerful nonverbal lessons.

In case you're wondering after that last anecdote, and comparing us to the little girl on the tricycle all padded and protected, it was dangerous in those years being a kid, especially when the kid lived in the country. But danger never stopped my sisters and me. And today, when we get together and talk about those times, my sisters and I recognize with a certain awe, sometimes a chill, how close and how often we came to dying as we grew up in this house. So a question: how do *we*, how do *you* explain the security we felt, the near absolute security we took for granted living in the white house, when we recognize and consider the dangerous positions we placed ourselves in? It's a question I have never been able to answer. It is a question we should, maybe *must* consider in the last chapter.

Let's explore some more: walk out the back door of the cellar and we come to a buried concrete cistern – about 10 feet in diameter. (But again, the little boy wonders, *how deep?*) All roof gutters from the house lead to the cistern, allowing us to collect rainwater. So my father hooks up the cistern to the hot water heater (how does he do this, I wonder?) Thus we have silky soft water in the left faucet, relatively tasty limestone-hardened water in the right, and now we have the best of both worlds. And that explains the need for a water pump in the basement. Dad always seemed to be doing clever and thoughtful things like this. In case you are wondering (and I know you're probably not, but I thought I'd bring it up anyhow) cistern water tastes so bland as to be slightly disgusting.

As for the cistern, there is . . . a wooden lid. A really old wooden lid. A dangerously degenerated, fissured, wobbly, and in spots rotten wooden lid. Hornets live beneath the cracks. Which visiting kids regularly discover when they sit on the lid. Dad and I one day make a concrete lid so no kid can fall in. Again, during the lid's building, I look down into that pit of black water – no light down there – and the hair on the back of my neck stands up. I feel relief when the concrete lid is finished and solidly in place. This fear is atavistic, and is shared by my friends. There is no exit from a well or cistern, and sooner or later, the kid must tire . . .

Enough of that. The thought still brings shivers to my spine.

*   *   *   *   *   *

The furnace tending, during each freezing Greenock winter, is my job.

My dad, after all, works night turn for 20 years on his railroad. Who else would keep us warm? Was I not, in his absence, the man of the house?

You may not believe this, but coal burning furnaces have personalities. Changeable personalities, neurotic personalities, aggravating personalities much like many people we both can bring to mind.

Our furnace has, by the time I am 10, earned my respect, and I have given it a name. *The Brown Beast*, a name which comes from the brown rust on its surface, and the beast part – well, read on. On the one hand, coming into the cellar from the backyard on any dark January night, shedding coats and galoshes, and standing near the radiating heat of *the beast* is as close to heaven as a smile from a loving mother. Well, almost. Because the beast has a dark side.

I learn that I must become attuned to the beast's changeable, even capricious moods. I must learn its ongoing needs. And I become responsible for feeding it, and thus responsible for our family's comfort. By and large though, ours is not a nice relationship. That beast, I come to recognize, at least during the winter, *owns* me, and its appetite for coal is voracious and unending. There are certain few times I love it; in general, I hate it.

Before I go to bed each winter evening, I would *bank the beast*. Banking is a precise and careful job needing correctness of quantity and knowledge of geometry. Maybe throw in a little chemistry, too. Throughout the day, it is necessary to toss in appropriately timed quantities of coal – say a shovelful every two or three hours. But this kind of fire can not last an entire night. So, if I do not conserve the fire correctly, when morning comes, it will take me the better part of an hour to restart a fire and warm the house. The secret, taught to me by Dad: Scrape just the correct amount of glowing embers into a furnace corner, cover the embers with just the right amount of small granular coal, and turn the air vents down. Too much or too fine the coal – the fire will smother and go out. Too little air, the fire will starve. Too little coal – the coal would be burned away by morning. When done correctly, I will still have red coals underneath the ash when my morning alarm goes off.

Of course morning is another story. A banked fire gives off essentially no heat. It is not actually freezing in the house, but cold feet on icy linoleum bedroom floor puts me instantly and painfully awake. Find the slippers, bathrobe on, and down to the cellar. The correct and careful application of coal, a shake of the grate, a wide opening of the air vents, and in 30 minutes the *beast* has steam up, and the house begins to warm.

One evening I decide to do an experiment. My parents are out, and are not expected back before 11. I am, once again, babysitting my sisters[5]. The mercury level in the outside thermometer hovers near zero on that windy, but typical January night. The steam gauge on the furnace is to be my guide. First, I check the water level – okay. Next, check the pressure gauge. Dad has taught me to keep the pressure needle at about 2 pounds per square inch, but, as he continually emphasizes, "Whatever you do, never let that needle get above 4. Never." On the other hand, the gauge is red marked at a never-to-exceed 15. "So that would be where the whole thing will blow

---

[5] Their complaints have no basis in fact, and I absolutely deny their charges that I was a cruel babysitting taskmaster, threatening them on occasion with an actual horse whip. Ridiculous charges, all.

up," I infer. But, I say to myself, Dad is often way too conservative. This brilliant thought causes me to congratulate
myself on my profound insight. And as day follows night,
then the next obvious and logical step is to wonder: What
would happen if I brought the steam pressure up to – say –
13, maybe even 14 psi? It takes me more than an hour caring
for that fire to create exactly perfect combustion. (The girls are
upstairs playing – completely unaware. At first.) Shake the
grate, open the air vents, add the right quantity and correct
size of coal lumps. Watch the fire. Nurse the fire. I finally have
it roaring. Quite literally. That beast is making real noise – and
lots of it. The steam pressure slowly rises. *Yes, a perfect experiment*, I think. Then the needle starts to move faster, to rise really, really fast. I begin to sweat. It is after all, pretty warm
next to that fire. But there is something else, something darkly
ominous happening, and I begin to wonder if my sweat is
caused by more than just the temperature. To add to the problem, my sisters are yelling down the stairs to me – making
remarkably unkind, unsisterly comments. They have opened
every door and every window in the house – in January,
snow on the ground, cold north wind blowing. I investigate
upstairs. The red liquid in the dining room thermostat's thermometer had pegged above the scale. There is a knock at the
back door. Someone, passing by, has noticed that our chimney
is on fire. I become mildly concerned. But after all, the chimney is brick, and it's probably just the soot in the chimney
that's burning. I think about calling the fire department, then
decide that's a really, really bad idea. After some further
thought, I go back down to the cellar, approaching the beast

somewhat reluctantly. It roars, its cast-iron sides glowing red. I see 30 on the gauge – so far above the red mark. Thirty pounds per square inch. Impossible. Obviously, this is now time for real problem solving. Throw water on the fire? Isn't that what firemen do? I find a pan in the other side of the cellar, fill it with cold water, open the furnace door, and am driven back a bit by the heat. But eventually, I manage to throw the water in – creating a cloud of steam that nearly blinds me. Just at that moment – a massive explosion: the overpressure popoff valve opens. Steam screams out, filling the entire basement, blinding me, the noise nearly deafening me. I run, opening both cellar doors, fill my lungs with great gulps of crisp cold night air. An hour later, all is normal.

It is, all in all, a good experiment. I have learned a great deal. The beast works as it should, and importantly, I am in control. Since the beast does not destroy us, we all go to bed.

Neither my sisters nor I think to mention the experience to our mom and dad the next morning.

By the way, have you ever actually seen or held coal in your hand, or lit it on fire? I didn't think so. And yet during those times, it was central to our comfort, and it was central to the region's economy.

*   *   *   *   *   *

But back to the house.

The bedroom above the kitchen is mine – and mine alone. My sisters hate that perquisite, no surprise. Because they three must share a single bedroom. (Hey, life is not fair.) My parents own the third; theirs is above the living room. (Why is there a lock on their bedroom, we all wonder?) My bedroom is, by my own impeccable logic and analysis, sacrosanct and absolutely private territory. Girls may not enter. Which they do, with glee, every time I am not there, despite my lock, my pleadings and their promises. They open every drawer – careful not to disturb. But I can tell. They work their way into the locked wicker basket where I protect my most private possessions. I suspect this violation all along, but one day there is absolute and incontrovertible evidence of their trespass. Plaster bits lie scattered on the linoleum floor; plaster bits completely cover my bed like snow dusting a harvested wheat field. They have discovered that, if they firmly hold a ski pole point up and jump up and down on my bed, they can poke holes in the ceiling plaster. Hundreds of holes, thousands of holes. I am in a fury. A purple rage feels just about right, in fact, totally appropriate, even pleasurable. I revel in how good the anger feels. The ceiling damage is secondary; the violation is the essence. I wait for my father to come home so I can ask him to take his belt off, and beat each of them to the point of needing hospitalization. He arrives. In high dudgeon I pour out my tale – just enough drama tempered with justifiable anger. He looks at me, walks slowly up the stairs, examines the damage, and in contemplation, scratches his chin. And says, " Hmmm." I can't believe it. He – he just walks away. Of course they are not punished. Worse, I think I see a poorly hidden smile on dad's face. I am devastated.

Of course this transaction is important. And critically so, so Reed and I do our best to analyze it in depth, and even go so far as to ask his older brother for advice. We eventually formulate an important lifemanship rule: pretty little girls can get away with anything. It is a rule that we test throughout our early years, and even into our teen years, the rule seems to hold true. And extending the rule beyond our adolescence, we realize that the girls don't even have to be little. Think about it; you may not agree. But if you grew up with sisters, or if there are women in your life, you probably will. Agree, that is.

Every few years, white frame houses in that climate need painting. (By the way, real Pittsburghers say "needs painted". Don't ask me why. I've always wondered myself. Pittsburghers often omit or disregard using the verb *to be*. A particularly smart and insightful physician at the University of Pittsburgh said, "If Hamlet were a Pittsburgher, his soliloquy would simply read '…. Or not……… That is the question.' ")

At age 11, my dad and I both – and once again – take on this tedious, messy, and unpleasant task. So we paint, and we paint, and it takes forever to cover that much clapboard. But generally we do not work together because we have only one ladder. I paint while he is at work; he paints when he gets home. Truth is, he does the vast majority of work.

Now on this particular afternoon it is my turn, and it falls to me to paint the apex of the wall facing up the road. For a boy, even getting an extension ladder to that high point is an accomplishment. And *up there* is so, so high. Today it might not look so high to me, but for a little boy, that apex, that last painting area was terrifying to contemplate.

Let me take a moment to tell you about hornets. Western Pennsylvania hornets. Mud nest building hornets. (They are actually wasps.) I'd like to say hornets could be considered pretty by someone who has not had *the experience* – as they are an iridescent green, and are good flyers. But to us who know them well, they are nothing other than malevolent. We country kids see them as being lethal, unforgiving creatures. Hornets fly with their stinger hanging  down – loaded and ready. And oh so aggressive. Hear a hmmmmmmmzzzzzzz? Time to look out. And unlike bees, which have only a single stinger, hornets can keep injecting till they run out of poisonous painful juice.

And they love building nests in the eaves of our house.

You might want to close your eyes to visualize this. A boy, bucket over one arm, paint brush in the other hand, holding on with dear life to the side of the ladder, climbing up, and up, and up. Now at the very top I hear .... Bzzzzzzz. Too late. Can't move anywhere anyhow. WHACK. Just below the left ear. The sting feels just like a nun bringing the flat side of a 16 inch ruler down on my neck with all her might. The natural reaction would be to let go of everything to get rid of the hornet. But doing so, then to die, by falling down, breaking neck and other important body parts, mashing soft tissues, then slowly fading from existence in this world. So I hold on. Tightly. Where the paint can falls onto the garage roof is still visible to this day. The hornet then crawls down my neck, under my shirt, giving me three more whacks along my back, going down further, now along my right butt, another hit there, and then two more (it was running out of juice, thank God) along my right leg finally to crawl out of my pants leg and fly off. Probably for reinforcements. I break all records climbing down. I have had enough painting for one day. *Mad as a hornet* has new meaning for me.

When I recounted my tale at dinner, mom becomes pale. The girls giggle, thinking it is an amusing adventure. My dad does not find it amusing; he looks grim. He says nothing, but finishes the painting by himself.

Many years after we kids left our homestead, and it was time for my parents to leave for a smaller place to live, they sold the white house to a nice lady who kept it in character. And who, I believe, enjoys the happy ghosts of children past. I like to believe that on quiet winter evenings hearing the faint laughter of four little kids brings warmth to her heart and a smile to her face. I'm rarely back in Greenock these days, but when I drive by the white house, I hear that faint laughter too. The laughter brings a smile. But then a tear, for my sisters and I are children in our white house no more.

6. PLACE, an overview

Let me interrupt the people narrative at this point to give Mister Beatty his due. His well-deserved due.

Mister Beatty, one of my heroes, the man who toiled mightily to teach us English composition in high school, kept pounding into our heads that *place*, the characterization of *where* the action occurs, was an important part of any writing that was worth reading. Thus, without digging too deeply into the nature/nurture debate at this point, you might want to know the character of this complex region of hills and hollows, because our geography and our weather profoundly influenced the behavior and the outlook of the successive waves of migrants, peoples of remarkably diverse backgrounds who settled this land.

You already know about the land that lay close to our home; now let us pretend we are using Google Earth and zoom in from space to look down upon this three rivers area of Western Pennsylvania.

Our geography was that of the western edge of the Appalachian Mountain chain. I remember a professor in college describing our area as a "gray brown podzolic glacial pleneplain." He may have been scientifically correct, but he certainly missed the soul of our land. Dr. Edmonds was obviously not a Western Pennsylvania native.

Navigable rivers are the first key to understanding this interesting part of America. Two rivers approach from the South (the Youghiogheny and the Monongahela), and meet the Allegheny river flowing from the north at Pittsburgh's Point to form the Ohio River.

Our immigrants shared one primary and overriding characteristic - a need to escape the awful poverty, the oppression, the rigid class structure, and the lack of opportunity in the "old country." But once here, to get ahead, they were forced to overcome the harshness of geography and climate, and only then be able to survive the drudgery and dangers of mill and mine work. This is what they faced.

The river valleys that led to the city of Pittsburgh – the Youghiogheny, the Monongahela, the Allegheny, and the upper Ohio (which led away) have become known for the remarkable self-reliance and toughness of their people. It was football and fighting (that would be fighting as in wars) that brought our valleys to national attention rather than the mills and mines.

An American Boyhood

When I was in high school, football was the prime way up and beyond the grind of a steel mill job – for the boys. Sadly, for the girls, there was no clear or easy way out.

High school football in the steel valleys was a serious and often disability producing undertaking. A college football scholarship was the goal. The boys I ultimately came to live with in our Dithridge Street college dorm – those skilled[6] enough to be granted a University of Pittsburgh football scholarship – had earned their place in that college the hard way. They paid for what too often turned out to be a minimal education with continuing pain, multiple weekly rib fractures during the football season, and ultimately, with destroyed knees. Rich, a fullback from a West Virginia coal town told me, as we walked along Forbes Avenue taking our 10 PM study break, "I just pray that the pain will go away before the next Saturday game." At the end of his fourth year of college play, he underwent reconstructive surgery on both knees – but still made it to law school. Jimmy Theodore, one of our Pitt running backs, became a medical colleague, a pulmonologist. He too paid for his scholarship with bad knees and fractures. Many fractures. Though my statistical sampling is small, every one of my athlete friends felt the price of their education was worth it. Though few made the pros (Mike Ditka was one), almost all who successfully completed the four years in rigorous academic courses made it into the professions.

---

[6] Some luck was involved too. Mostly the luck involved not becoming injured.

Sadly, the majority of our athletes were shortchanged in their education, often directed by the athletic department into easy courses to maintain the required grade average. I remember helping one of our linemen pass a music appreciation course. Music appreciation. Generally a guaranteed A. By *helping*, I mean I let him see my final test paper. I actually got up to talk to the professor so he could read my answers. And I have no guilt about that cheating, nor did the professor – who knew.

In the field house, when I jumped up to the horizontal bar during gymnastic practice, I realized that our football players (and also to some extent the basketball players) had paid for our top-of-the-line equipment.

To get to that point – to play college ball on scholarship – and so to get out of the danger and drudgery of millwork cost days of sweat and fatigue on high school practice fields. Perhaps football *practice* was not the most precise or descriptive term as what they did on those fields was done with a deadly seriousness that anyone in the stands could easily observe. Nonetheless, theirs is a good story, a particularly American story.

The pundits have called New York the melting pot – but consider how these valleys had absorbed, integrated, and melded together successive immigrations. The waves came first from the British Isles and France, then northern Germany, then from Ireland and Wales, then Southern and Eastern Europe, and most recently, from Italy[7]. Of course, if you read our early history, we didn't do so well integrating with the French. Nor with the Indians. We called that time in our history the French/Indian wars. The French in Montréal still have not forgiven us. But all told, and admitting my native son's prejudice, I would recommend the river valleys around Pittsburgh as America's truest melting pot. And later, the summer I was working in the mill, watching the ore, the coke, the limestone, scrap, some heavy metals come together in the furnace to make ultimately a beautiful steel rail, that melting pot analogy seemed especially powerful and appropriate.

We in the valleys accepted and even liked this idea of national identities. For example, in the sixth through eighth grades, that time when boys and girls are beginning to recognize and appreciate the opposite sex, we would first ask, "What's your name?" Then, "What are you?" Which meant, *where did your family come from*? And what you were ethnically was defined mostly by pre-World War I political boundaries as they were drawn at the time of your family's immigration. Irish, Croatian, Serbian, German – OK. Yugoslavian? What was Yugoslavia? I remember one young heartthrob smiling at me as I was ineptly trying to strike up conversation, replying, "I'm

---

[7] Two superb books detail the difficulties the immigrants faced (and ultimately overcome). The first, *Out Of This Furnace (A Novel of Immigrant Labor in America)*, by Thomas Bell; the second has recently been reissued by the University of Pittsburgh press: *Homestead: The Households of a Mill Town* by Margaret Byington.

Anna, and I'm pure Hunky[8]." We were, during those innocent days, remarkably politically incorrect; more importantly, remarkably free of prejudice. There were more important things to consider. (Will she let me hold her hand at the movies? Maybe even kiss her?) At least in that accepting respect[9], we lived during better times – and I know that's a value judgment, but it is mine.

As for religion and culture, Greenock was staunchly Protestant – Lutheran primarily, but also Methodist – except for the families in two homes. And those were the homes of my parents and my grandparents. Yet I felt essentially no prejudice directed toward me. When in later years I wondered if I had been simply naïve, I was told that the people were more concerned with survival than with religion, accent, or skin color. Prejudices did not become obvious until much later, after the Second World War, when the first generation children of eastern European peoples began to acquire political power, moving out to our community (to *the country*) displacing the WASPS. Couldn't blame them for moving out and up. McKeesport was still filthy; Greenock idyllic. It was only then that the term "hunky" began to be used and heard as a derogative in our little community.

---

[8] "Hunky" began as a derogatory term, much like Spik, Wop, or Greaser, and may have evolved from the term Bo Hunk, applied to Hungarian immigrants. In time, as here, the word became to be used with pride.

[9] Sad to say, acceptance rarely extended to the black kids — and vice versa. There was still a great deal of prejudice, but more about that in chapter 22 where you get to meet Marjorie.

And that little community had developed in a fertile piece of land bounded by a U shaped bend in the Youghiogheny River. But it was not so much the fertility of the land that attracted later settlers -- it was coal. You might think that since iron ore is heavier than coal and thus more difficult to ship, the mills would have been located close to the ore deposits. But furnaces needed four times as much coal (ultimately in the form of baked coal called *coke*) to make steel. And they needed water, large amounts of it. So steel mills took the prime land, lining our river banks, and were built in our coal country.

The coal mines entered the hills anywhere that a seam presented itself to the surface. Miles and miles of tunnels crisscrossed the land under our house. The mineral rights under the hills had long since been sold, well before our family came on the scene. In the back of my mind was always the thought that, one day, our house would slowly sink out of sight as the tunnel roofs collapsed.

Greenock had become a community of about 80 families by the 1920s. It had been named for the town of Greenoch, Scotland by one of the earliest immigrant settler families, William and Isabella Black, shortly before our Civil War. In 1936, at the time of my birth, Greenock was composed almost entirely of Germans, Scots-Irish, and a few English. Go to the map of Western Pennsylvania, locate Pittsburgh, and draw a line almost due South through the steel making communities of Homestead and McKeesport, and, just shy of the West Virginia border, you will find Greenock.

By the time I was born, most of the smaller mines had closed, but two were still operational. One about 5 miles north in a town called Versailles (pronounced locally as *vur*, as in fur, and *sails*. Who cares how the French say it?) This mine was the source of the many shafts and tunnels under our house. And the other entered the hill just across the road and 400 yards closer to the river from our home at 1514 Greenock Buena Vista Road.

Greenock, as it lies in the northern and western foothills of the Appalachian Mountains made us, like it or not, Rednecks. We were scant miles north of the Mason Dixon line. The sons of our first German and Scots Irish immigrants had fought the French Indian wars that came 40 years before our country's War of Independence. The French had long since left after that disastrous war, but family lore tells of a trace of French in our genes.

As for fighting, the original Scots-Irish who populated the Appalachian chain rightly feel they have fought – and won – the nation's wars – from times even before we were a country, and more so, especially to the present day. Greenock men in their 60s still talk bitterly about the politicians who lost the Vietnam war for them. My opinion is, they have a right to all their convictions – and their continuing anger.

Our settlers had not only fought in French Indian wars, and in our War of Independence, but had once left their hard-scrabble farms and mines to walk across the Alleghenies to a little town in central Pennsylvania called Gettysburg.

So this area, and all of the Appalachians in fact, down through Tennessee and Kentucky -- is even today known for the remarkable self-reliance and independence of its people. Go a few miles further south and east from our home, and you come to the land of the Whiskey Rebellion, the first test of our new federal government's power.

And about that rebellion: By 1789, the farmers, no fools, recognized quickly that it was not so easy to transport their corn either to Philadelphia (Route 30) or to Baltimore (Route 40) across those formidable Appalachian Mountains, and that the job was simpler if they rendered their corn into its more condensed and nonperishable form. Thus the whiskey trade. Our brand-new federal government, in need of tax revenues, passed a law requiring taxes to be paid on all intoxicating liquors. Our people – frontiersmen with rifles – no surprise, took offense. Warning shots were fired. To quell that so-called insurrection (you can tell where my sympathies lie), the federal government sent troops via Routes 30 and 40, roads still in use today, and some of our people were shot. When I was a boy, the people who lived farther out in the hills (and who still drank moonshine) complained even as late as the 1950s about "the revenooers."[10] We rednecks still hate the federal government. Maybe, no probably, even more so today.

Weather certainly played a major role in forming the character of our people. Look at a contour map of the Northern Hemisphere. Arctic winds swirl down through the plains of

---

[10] Local slang for the Revenue Agents of the federal government.

central Canada, sweep across the Great Lakes, pick up awesome quantities of moisture, and then, when those masses of air come up against the first mountains – the Appalachians (we call them the Allegheny Mountains), those air masses rise. And that lifting releases tremendous energy, causing the storms – the almost unpredictable, violent, and frequent storms that made the early airmail pilots refer to our area as the *Graveyard of the Alleghenies*. You can still find airplane parts today on many mountain ridges.

You might think from some of my words and descriptions that it was cold all the time. It was not; it's just that I remember the cold most vividly. We had, just as likely, wild and violent (and interesting to little boys) summer thunderstorms. So given the geography and the general wind flows, what we endured was weather that was changeable. And unpredictably changeable. And violently changeable. That meant that, unless you were willing to ignore the weather (something almost impossible to do), the unpredictability made planning outdoor activities well, difficult. Oh, I should quickly add that a bit of rain, sleet, or snow didn't make the activities impossible, as we continued no matter what. It's just that we could never be sure of what the skies would hand us.

In the summer, we regularly suffered through 90° temperatures with 95% humidity. And the winters – oh my. What was so discouraging about our winters were – again – the frequent and extreme changes. For example, the valleys averaged 40 freeze/thaw cycles a winter. What that meant was that, when the storm passed through the area, we would have freezing temperatures for several days, and as the cold front passed, yes, the temperature would remain bitterly low, but crystalline blue skies holding fast moving, beautiful cumulus clouds would appear. We would get used to the coldness, take a deep breath, clear the roads and driveways, and get on with life. But then warm breezes would appear as though by magic –a 50° swing in a few days. The ice would thaw, the roads would crack, and, I swear, every third person would come down with a cold. This temperature swing became absolutely depressing in May, when, after a long, gray discouraging winter, a soft warm breeze would bring the forsythia and tulips to bloom, our hearts and moods would lift – and then, a week later, another ice storm would crush our hopes of an early spring. As the blossoms died, so did our good humors.

You must not get the idea that the weather is always bad in Greenock. Absolutely not. When spring finally comes, and dogwood, trillium and bluebell fill our hollows, speckled blue eggs appear in Robins' nests, and the breeze becomes soft, our people begin to walk with a livelier step, smiles appear, and even a visitor from Mars will recognize our renewed hope about our future.

Perhaps fall is even better. The lush simmering summer greens give way to intense, almost violent reds and purples in our hardwood forests' leaves. With a luminescent harvest moon rising over the hill adding to a crisp coolness in the air, the pulse, for some atavistic reason (perhaps the thought of harvests and their bounty) will quicken. And fall brings corn roasts, pumpkins and Halloween. And best of all, fall brings

Thanksgiving feasts, plus the most major of all religious holidays in redneck Western Pennsylvania: the opening of deer season[11].

On the other hand, the advent of fall also brought a return to school. And that was a sad, sad story for a little boy, a story for those chapters about Saint Peter's.

But kids rarely care about weather – unless it interferes too much with play. For us, a Greenock childhood was as close to free and idyllic as it's possible to experience on this earth, no matter the season. But, in the late 1930s and early 1940s it was not idyllic for our parents, nor for family friends, nor for our neighbors. Whoever coined the term "grinding and gritty poverty" described perfectly those conditions our parents survived. The sky was usually – except for the one or two days after passage of a cold front – dirty gray from mill smoke, the summers were stifling and sticky, the winters were bitter, the homes either too hot or too cold, but, the one constant, the money meager.

Of course it is difficult for anyone to know whether first memories are real or whether they come from others' descriptions or even from photographs, but at age 4, I remember, more than anything the winter's piercing coldness more than the

---

[11] Are you surprised that I say the opening of deer season is a religious holiday? Had you watched the preparations, the rituals, the solemnity, the celebrations you might conclude this was a religious event. I'll go into this complexity more in the chapters entitled WOODS.

summer's enervating humid heat. And I remember the images in my mind of people during those short dark wintry days, people dressed in many, many layers -- of threadbare, once-white shirts, worn and dark no-color sweaters, baggy, poorly fitting suits of some color I cannot today name, and tan-gray overcoats. They called the overcoat color *covert*. What a perfect name for that color. Those overcoats looked dirty, mean, and old; they usually were, then again they looked the same when they were new. The men wore, almost invariably, dark brown felt hats with snapped down brims, and they always – always – wore neckties. Even automobile mechanics wore neckties. The women – faded house dresses. The image was that of everything and everyone being somewhat *worn out.* As root cause, there was not enough money.

Yet we all felt -- in this condition and during those times -- *in it together*. Never once did I hear talk of class envy. There was no talk, no expectation of the government – any government – taking care of us. Without exception, those adults around me -- those who cared for me and my sisters, fed us, educated us, tried to help us reach our potential-- kept alive their hopes for the future, but especially they kept their dignity and their pride. "Hold your head high," my Grandmother demanded of me one day. She certainly never did. Nor did my mother. Nor did anyone I knew.

In summers, the adults organized picnics. In winter, parties. We shared food and iced tea, sang, played badminton in the side yard and caught fireflies in the evening. The adults around us made us laugh -all together, and instilled in us the knowledge that the future could be better -*if we worked for it.*

The adults in our community stood tall. You can see it in the old photographs. In the face of their poverty – a condition which so demoralized them, even embarrassed them, it seemed most important to maintain their pride. Perhaps pride – pride in work well done, pride in surviving yet another year in a harsh land, pride in children cared for and loved was the driver that got them out of bed to start the next day. Pride may have been all they had. Whatever it was, it was enough.

7. COAL and STEEL (More About Place)

And now the second part of the *place* equation, the equation that leads to understanding us melting pot people: Creating steel was the essence of our region's work, the primary generator of wages, and thus wealth, in our valleys. Every person in Southwest Pennsylvania, everyone who provided services and goods, depended upon the money generated by the hard men who dug coal and made steel. Steel was, after all, the foundation of our American civilization during my early years. Today the Three Rivers economy may be based upon electronics, medical care, and information technology, but in the 1940s and 1950s, America was building – and we were doing it with steel. Making steel was dirty, hot, unhealthy in the long run, and dangerous-every-day work. But it was work that was ultimately and concretely creative. Most of the steel workers I knew were proud of what they could do in the mills, proud that, at the end of their grueling eight hour shift, they could touch what they made that day. If it had cooled enough, that is.

The miners, on the other hand, had touched more than enough. They came out of the shafts completely, absolutely, discouragingly black. Coal dust was everywhere upon them. And in them, especially in their lungs, a sad fact brought home during my medical school autopsies.

These were tough men, men to be admired; men I admired.

Steel and steel products were all around us – in every part of our lives. We could see steel's reality in and on the railroad cars and river barges carrying away the I-beams, railroad rails, pipe and rolled sheet. During the war years, long trains of flatbed gondolas loaded with tanks, jeeps, artillery pieces and armored personnel carriers rolled through McKeesport every day. The might of America was on display for all to see.

On the other hand, the reality of steel's creation also altered for the worse the condition of our rivers, our hills, and sadly, our skies. No fish could live in our rivers, and respiratory illness plagued us all, especially during the winter months.

For most workers' wives, dirty gray skies – strange as it may seem – were a comfort. Bad air, air that even in summer kept plants from growing on the hillsides near the mills, air that made it difficult even to see that hillside across the river meant *the mills were working*. Clear skies meant a strike – and so – no money. The families would then be forced to meatless dinners of, for example, pasta fagioli (pronounced *fazool*, just oil, beans and spaghetti) or fried cornmeal mush. This blue sky anxiety was so pervasive that in the 1950s a communitywide push to clean up the rivers and improve the quality of our air met a strange resistance movement especially from the workers' wives. Some atavistic fear of clear skies expressed itself in their resistance.

My father worked for the railroad, and his (notice the possessive) railroad, the Pittsburgh and Lake Erie Railroad, was originally built to bring iron ore from the Great Lakes to our coal rich valleys. And with our broad and deep rivers, river barge traffic and steel wheels on steel rails were both economical and efficient transport methods.

For the prior hundred years or so, much of the coal came from underneath the hill our home and neighbors' homes was built upon. When my sisters and I realized this, it caused certain anxiety. Walking in the woods behind the house, seeing so many areas of cave-in, I always wondered...... when might I disappear into the depths, to say nothing of whole houses? Our fears were unfounded.

Actually, by the time the Korean War started, most of the mines had closed, but in the 1930s and 40s, there were mines everywhere along the rivers. The biggest surfaced in Versailles (remember, it's pronounced *vur sales*). Three conspicuous parts of the mine told everyone *here we dig coal*. First was the elevator house which brought the coal up and the miners down, a dirty, brick- red or black corrugated-steel covered, 50 foot derrick-like affair that housed a huge motor and the elevator itself. Second was what everyone called (somewhat incorrectly) the tipple[12] – the elevated storage bins for the different grades of coal. Trucks or railroad cars could be driven underneath the tipples, filled with coal, and sent on their way. Here you can see the elevator, the storage bins, and tipple have been combined

into one building. Notice that wheel on the top. Going to school on the bus, we would watch it spinning at dizzying speeds, paying out the single cable, wondering about the fate of the miners plunging into those black depths below. Later, when they returned to the surface, we watched them through our bus windows as they moved away from the mine to bus stop or car, marveling at their black hands, black faces, black clothes, black boots, and carbide lamps on black caps. At the end of their shift, those miners walked with heads down, slowly, with shuffling gait. Today I recognize that walk as one

---

[12] the real tipple was the cart carrying the coal, which, when it came over the storage bin, was tipped sideways to discharge the coal.

diagnostic of depression. The only brightness about them was the unpainted aluminum lunch buckets they carried and the shiny reflector of their headlamp. Flat black those men were – both in appearance and mood. Later, I would dissect lungs that looked exactly the same: black, and hard.

Sixteen tons of coal was the goal for each man, each shift. Sixteen tons.

And the third part of the mine was the nearby gob pile. Yes, *gob* is an ugly word, but a perfectly descriptive one. Shale and low-grade coal got dumped on the gob pile. Sooner or later, gob piles all caught on fire, and smoldered away for years. They reminded this little boy of scenes from Dante's Inferno: a small mountain, black on top, twisting tortuous holes leading into the center showing red fire below, other spouts pouring out smoky blackness, further polluting our air with darkness and sulfur fumes. To walk on the gob pile would be to fall through into red-hot coals. The gob pile was a perfect metaphor for hell.

And I should mention *red dog,* something you have probably never heard of; a material nothing as pleasant as it sounds. Once the gob piles had burned out, the residue was a soft reddish rock that found its use in paving home driveways and little used parking areas. It had no structural strength; it could be used for nothing else.

But the coal was the basis, the foundation, of the steel industry in our three rivers' valleys.

Once dug, washed and graded, its path led to the coke plant. It was this carbonized form of coal that led to iron furnaces' efficiency. Before the turn of the century, Mr. Frick dumped coal into his brick beehive ovens – mostly south of our community, near Brownsville, Connellsville, and the other river towns – then set the coal on fire. Once aflame, the air into the oven was restricted, so that the volatile tars boiled off – yes, into the air. It was the same procedure one would use to make charcoal. Sadly, the smoke further dirtied our air, but when the process was complete, what was left was pure hard carbon.

The ovens looked like hemispheric beehives – firebrick arched about 15 feet across, and about the same height. This broken down remnant is what they looked like when we ran across them during our runs through the woods. The ovens were usually built into the side of a hill, and had an opening in the top – a circular hole about 2 feet around, and a door in front. A small coal fire was built to warm them up, and then, when warm, more coal was poured in the top. Depending upon the weather, the process usually took about a week to make an entire batch. Serious judgment was required by the workers to determine just how much air to let in.

Fortunately, some good basic science, primarily from German chemists, showed that the coal tars had intrinsic value. It turned out that one could make everything from aniline dyes to synthetic rubber from the volatile hydrocarbons, and bee-hive ovens quickly fell out of utility. The downside for kids was, of course, falling *into* them – over the years they became covered with grass and dirt, their roofs decayed from the freeze thaw cycles of our winters, and young boys and girls playing on them were likely to get a terrifying surprise.

The actual iron furnaces were, quite simply, awesome. The furnace itself was a massive vertical tapered tube, wider at the base than the top. A continuum of buckets on an endless chain ran up a track along the side of the furnace, allowing the en-gineers to charge it with coke, iron ore, and crushed lime-stone. To one side, four or five giant vertical tubular air heat-ers stood as tall as the furnaces themselves, and next to them lay half-mile long sheds to handle the processed iron.

This photo shows the National Tube Works, the mill in McKeesport where I worked one summer. The vertical tubu-

lar heaters capped with rounded tops are easy to see – the actual blast furnaces themselves are immediately to the right of
them and are obscured by the hot-air pipes leading to and
from the actual furnace. Iron ore – and rust – colored the furnaces, the air heaters, and everything near them a dirty, dark
reddish brown. It may have been a discouraging color to
many, but brown was the color of our economic success.

It took the better part of a day to charge the furnace. Once the
furnace fire was lit and the raw materials dumped in, the hot
exhaust gases were piped through labyrinthine firebrick in
the air heaters. Once the heater bricks became hot, massive
pumps 20 feet tall pushed superheated air through them into
the base of the furnace, creating the high temperatures to allow the coke to reduce the iron oxides. The exhaust gases

went back and forth through the heaters. As one was heated up, the air was reversed, and the cycle continued.

A batch of completed iron was known as "a heat." It was an appropriate term, as when the ram (or in some cases, one of the workers) punched a hole in the bottom of the furnace's firebrick and liquid iron ran out into troughs, the iron was water thin and a light yellow temperature. On the one hand, tapping a furnace – especially at night – was thought by some of the men to be a scene from hell – dangerous molten yellow-white iron running into and through sand troughs, sparks flying, smoke everywhere – most McKeesporters recognized that this act was the essence of the three rivers economy.

The limestone, once it had absorbed impurities, had its own handling problems.

The iron having run out of the furnace, one had to dispose of the residue – the molten, sulfur-rich limestone. It was known simply as "slag". It was poured into cuplike railroad cars that you see here, and carried to the slag dump.

Watching the slag dumped at night was – I can't make this stuff up – a favorite adolescent Three Rivers date. Narrow gauge railroad tracks ran around the periphery of the dump which, by the time I could drive, had become a semi-mountain filling one of the valleys opposite the Allegheny County Airport. A small switch engine pulled the cars across rivers and up hills, and, when in place, one by one, they were tilted, emptying, disgorging sparkling yellow-heat molten rock down the hillside. Park the car along the road, bring cokes, popcorn – feel the heat on your face. Who could ask for anything more spectacular? And for free. So the making of steel found its way into every part of our Three River existence, even to include adolescent romance. "Wanna go see them dump slag tonight?" No, no one could make this stuff up. At least none of the kids I knew could.

As for the next step, iron isn't good enough - for just about anything beyond making cheap sewer pipes. (Further, I'm not sure that there ever was much of an "Iron Age", but that's just my opinion.) I suspect our ancestors pretty quickly figured out iron's deficiencies, most notably its brittleness, which made it difficult to forge into tools and weapons.

So let us go back to the mill. The blast furnace had given us iron, but now we must remove impurities and carbon to make it into ductile and tough steel.

At the moment the blast furnace is tapped, we have liquid, yellow-heat iron. I say *yellow heat* because color is the way we determine iron and steel's temperature. Now, let us make real, pure, made-to-order steel.

There were, when I was a boy, three potential paths to that goal.

First, to make specialty steels, especially stainless steels containing large amounts of nickel and chromium, the iron and the alloying metals were put in a huge ceramic pot . Electric energy was used to raise this mass of material to high enough temperature to allow the other metals to mix, so forming the specific alloy requested by the customer. Though energy intensive, crucible steels were wonderfully pure.

And second: In 1850 Henry Bessemer brought another technique into commercial use – a quick and easy way to get rid of the impurities in iron while reducing the carbon content. The liquid iron was poured into a large vat, open at the top, with pipe ducted into the base. Compressed air was blown into the pipes, causing oxygen to react with the impurities and carbon. Sparks as big as basketballs, 20 feet of fire, and greasy black smoke poured from each mouth. Three converters working together lit up the entire Monongahela Valley night sky – even as far away as Greenock – and put enough smoke into the air to hide the sun for a day. By the time I went to work in the mill, thankfully, the Bessemers were gone. You can walk around this one today in Station Square in Pittsburgh.

And third: Regular carbon steel was made by dumping the iron (and usually some scrap and other additives) into a huge bathtub-like, firebrick lined furnace. A significant part of the furnace was underground – where natural gas was burned in a honeycomb of firebrick. This heated plasma-like gas was blown over the surface of the steel until adequate mixing of the additives and oxidation of the carbon occurred. Here

you're looking at the inside. Notice all the firebrick. Those brick didn't last forever.

Which brings us to the worst job I ever had in the mill. A team of 12 common laborers was directed into a recently shut down open hearth. We were to remove the worn-out firebrick so that the furnace could be rebuilt. With crowbars, we would pry out a firebrick. It would still be lava red underneath. I know I say this often, but you simply can't make this stuff up. The temperature in there was – oh – 200° F, and it was summer. We had no knowledge of protection from heat stroke, nor was there any protective equipment supplied by management – other than salt tablets. We wore heavy pants, mill boots, shirts, and sweatshirts. That's all. One really smart kid fell down almost immediately, catching his sweatshirt on fire, slightly burning his right arm near the elbow. The burn was not too bad – but bad enough so that he did not have to go back into the furnace. I envied him his cleverness. A few days later, new brick had been laid, and the furnace was in use again.

Unlike the Bessemers, this *open hearth process* allowed the engineers to fine tune the amount of additives and carbon in the heat. Four to six guys would make a daisychain, hand shoveling additives – cobalt or chromium for instance – into the furnace doors. With our McKeesport furnaces, we could make about 100 tons of steel at a time. Yes, a hundred tons.

Think this might be a little dangerous? This guy is dipping a ladle on a 10 foot steel handle into the molten steel. He will then run the sample  to the lab for testing. I thought you might ask: yes, there were leather aprons, which gave some protection, and there were dark goggles, and we were just beginning to get hardhats – but there was not much else in the safety area. On the other hand, is this process not spectacular?

Once the engineers were satisfied and the heat was com-

pleted, the whole furnace rotated, dumping the steel out into carriers to be held for processing in other ways. At National Tube, because of our work making pipe, most of the steel was poured into cylindrical molds – to form billets. Today, we are used to things – mostly electronic things – that are small. Most of what we use we can hold in our hand. It is almost impossible to comprehend how large, how massive these devices and tools were. That ladle above? Almost twice as high as a man is tall. And also today, every one of these photographs scream *danger*, and truth is, many of the men I knew bore the scars of millwork. Uncle Ernie, for example, had lost the thumb of his right hand. But it's surprising how rare actual accidents were by the 1950s.

So, as a common laborer in the McKeesport plant, National Tube Works, United States Steel Corporation (at a 1.545 cents an hour) one summer, until we went on strike, I got to see just about every possible part of making steel.

I've already told you about my open hearth experience. It gets better. The awesome product of our mill was to create seamless steel tubing. How else are you going to drill an oil well a mile or two deep? Making a tube with that kind of strength and reliability may sound easy - when you say it fast.

A billet at medium yellow heat would be picked out of the soaking pit (a gas-fired furnace that held the steel at just the right temperature) and placed on powerful rollers, directed to two huge barrel shaped drums. The drums rotated eccentrically, and were positioned such that they would grab the billet, inducing a rotation, plus a forward vector – all about 30 miles an hour. The forward vector and the rotation pushed the billet against a pointed piece of steel on a long shaft. This rapid action caused the point to perforate the billet, which flowed over it along the shaft. Then the shaft was removed. At this point, we have a piece of seamless steel tubing. The rest is just lengthening, straightening, and enlarging the tube. To me, this process was magnificent. The men were incredible. The engineers godlike.

One expects a certain amount of hazing of any new employee. But when the men found I was going to go to college, it became something else. The term, even today, is *job action*.

The first threat came from a union shop steward who, when I was sweeping the floor, told me not to clean up too much. He was quite explicit – no vague meaning; no chance of my misinterpreting him. It was a transaction of one adult to another: "The man on second shift will need work to do. Leave enough for him." I didn't. When I left, the floor was pristine. My first big mistake. The management – the supervisors – did not dare interfere.

My job rotated each day and depended upon which skilled worker had taken the day off.

The next threat came when my job was inspecting finished lengths of oil well pipe. They were superb pieces of work, each embossed with our mill's name. The threads at each end were square cut and generally flawless – but errors were sometimes deliberately created. But only sometimes; it was rare to find defects, and I was proud of what our mill did on that day. The union shift supervisor came to me, and said that I was to miss four defective pipes, and allow them to be loaded on the barge. Seems that there was a final, final inspection when the pipes were on the barge. "Joe needs to find four bad pipes a day – he gets $20 for finding a bad one." I asked,

"But what if he misses a bad one, and that bad one fails when it is 4000 feet down an oil well? Then what? How will that make us look? " No bad pipes got past me. My second mistake – a massive mistake.

So then my jobs got more dangerous. Pipes – large pipes, 14 inches in diameter, 20 feet long were fed out of the soaking pit to run down a raceway to be further processed. My job was to throw a half shovel mixture of coal dust and salt into the orifice of the pipe as it ran past me. Yes, the pipe was at yellow heat. So I would climb four steps, time the throw just right, then, before the heat of the pipe would burn me, turn and run down the steps. For eight hours. Summer in McKeesport. Heavy pants, gloves, and sweatshirt for protection. Thirty minutes for lunch. But that awful job wasn't enough of a lesson – I let them know I was enjoying myself doing it. Seventeen-year-old kids can be so stupid.

Cranes carried loads of pipe overhead. Before they passed over any worker on the floor below, the crane operator was required to sound his siren, which alerted the worker to look up – and be ready to move should a hitch failure occur. The crane carried at that moment about 2 tons of 14 inch elbows. The operator positioned his load directly over me, sounded the siren, watched for me to look up, and when he knew he had my attention and I was looking up at the load 15 feet above my head, released it. One more time: You just can't make this stuff up. Of course there was plenty of time to get out of the way. If one were a rabbit. Heavy pipe elbows bounced everywhere as I hid behind a support beam. I got the message from the union. Finally.

And then the United Steelworkers of America decided to go on strike. Probably the best thing that ever happened to me, though the lack of money I would have earned during the last few weeks of that summer made that fall at school austere.

*   *   *   *   *   *

In this picture, taken from the McKeesport collection (author unknown), you can see trouble.

The management – in top-coats – in confrontation with the jacket wearing workers. Silent. Sullen. Ominous. No good can ever come of a meeting like this. And, it didn't. The union struck. In the end, the union got the men a raise, which made it easier for the Japanese to compete with us. Now, in the Three Rivers valleys, I see a single functioning steel mill. Just one. Maybe I am missing some.

There are those who are happy that our steel industry is gone. We breathe clean air, trout and bass now swim in our rivers.

An American Boyhood

What could be better? Is Pittsburgh now not one of the more desirable and livable cities in America? But the other towns – McKeesport, Monongahela, Monessen, Homestead (the locus of the great strike of 1892) – along the valleys are, especially today, desperate. I feel that those who applaud the going of the mills are wrong.

Anyone too young to have actually experienced the might we produced in our valleys cannot understand the magnitude of our – more importantly, America's – loss. And it's not just the absence of what could be touched. To stand on a loaded gondola of mainline railroad rails (at a full 110 pounds per foot of rail) looking up the river at workers' houses clinging to the hills was, at least to this boy, infinitely more powerful than standing atop the Giza pyramid. And that power is now a rapidly fading memory.

More importantly, I feel the absence – the profound loss – of those men. Tough men, strong men, men of sinew and determination, men who went daily into our mines and mills, ran our railroads, piloted our riverboats. Men I looked up to and learned from. I fear we will never see their like again. I pray that I am wrong.

I fully know that it is difficult – no, impossible – for anyone too young to have experienced the might produced in those valleys to understand what the loss of our great industry means to our valleys – and to America. By the fifties we were well on our way to cleaning up valley skies and our rivers.

Now we import steel from China and Japan. And we are the poorer for it.

Please tell me, where have the strong American men gone?

In our feminized society today – in this age of the wimp – one must ask difficult questions. Questions about roles, questions about differences. I cannot help but wonder, if the mines and mills were still working, would feminists press for equality? This is an important question, one not given to glib answers or dogma from either side. It is one we will touch on from time to time in these reflections, and do so in depth. There are no easy answers to these critical questions.

.

8. REED

One day Mister Lenhart walked from his orchard across the field over to my grandfather's garden and, nodding a greeting, said to him, "A new boy moved in just up the road. Reed Gilchrist. Send Chuckie over."

A couple of observations about that transaction are pertinent. They are pertinent because you may have noticed that today it is unlikely that anyone – man or woman – would make so direct a transaction.

When you think about Mister Lenhart's words, though they may have seemed like an order, they were just an example of a good, clear adult to adult communication.

And the second observation: Back then, men were more direct. They were unafraid to take charge, unafraid to make decisions. Most especially, men in my circle were energized; they seemed to enjoy the power that comes from making good things happen. And now a new boy had moved nearby, both of us about the same age. Men knew that boys needed other boys for their absolute and ultimate work – which was – *to play*. So it was only natural that the new boys should get to know each other, should become friends. And so the men, once again, did what men did then: and what they did for us was to bring two boys together, so creating a lifetime friendship.

Of course I did as I was told (there was no thought of direct disobedience). I walked a half-mile up the road, from Grandpap's garden, to Reed's house. Right then.

Approaching the house, I timidly knocked on his back door (nobody, I mean *nobody* ever walked up to a neighbor's front door), introduced myself to his mother, and asked if I could come in to play with Reed. She looked at a scrawny little kid she had never seen before (I think it took just seconds to make up her mind), shrugged, smiled, invited me in, and called Reed downstairs. And of course we became best friends.

We were both short for our age, physically adept, not terribly interested in school, and – wonder of wonders, *we lived in the country*.

This magnificent, magical land was ours, ours where we could do (almost) anything we wished.

Having no mechanical means of transportation, we ran up the hills and into the hollows on foot – climbing down the cliff to the railroad tracks, trying our best to get into abandoned but boarded-up coal mines (*attractive nuisances* the adults called them. Figure that wordage out.), coming home only when hunger or thirst or darkness drove us back. We were utterly and truly alone, and we reveled in our privacy, and in our freedom of being able to do, well, *anything*. What heady power for little boys. Even then, we knew what we had. How lucky we were.

I cannot remember ever seeing an adult or another kid – once we had walked a few hundred yards away from the roads and the houses. Of course there's another side to this *freedom* coin – we were responsible for any trouble we caused ourselves. Absolutely and irrevocably responsible. And, from time to time, we paid. We paid with twisted ankles, cuts, black eyes, and burns, and in not a few instances and once our heart rates returned to normal, with the fearful recognition that we had come close to death. We told no-one of the close calls. We knew better; the adults might use that information to restrict us.

In those days the adults would say "we just palled around." There's a lot to that word, *pal*. It implies friendship, of course, but so much more. It implies trust, sharing, and, unlike today's virtual world, touching. Well, maybe *touching* is not exactly the right word. Sometimes it was just an arm over the other guy's shoulder, but more likely than not, it was seriously vigorous – we wrestled together, rolled down hills together, drank from the same cup, shared the same food. And when we could get explosives, one of us would light the fuse, and the other throw the cherry bomb as fast as, and as far away as our scrawny arms would permit. Then again, maybe *touching* is the right word.

May I insert an aside here, a side bar which asks a serious question? Today we have instant Twitter, Facebook, e-mail, and other too numerous to count means of electronic communications. So don't we today have *friended* hundreds of people? Of course they are *virtual* friends? Doesn't that word *virtual* mean, quite simply, not real, not in fact or reality; imitated, simulated? Is this not a significant philosophical question for today's times? And of course virtual friendship does not preclude, does not rule out the possibility of making physically touchable friends. But how likely is that? You get to answer. I'm just curious.

Back to Reed, now to speak of our attempts at creative photography . . .

Reed's older brother Grover was a professional photographer. We were in awe of cameras, his dark room, but most of all his skills, and, so appropriately influenced and wanting to please an older brother, Reed and I – on the sporadic occasions we felt moved to do so – took pictures with our Brownie cameras. But encouraged and taught by that brother, our photographs became over time weak attempts to learn composition rather than simply record an image. Yet there were times Reed and I were moved by some inner drive to create more than just a pleasing composition. There was a day, for example, when we decided to communicate to the world (through our photographs of course. What arrogance.) what cool morning mist on our river felt like. In retrospect, I don't think we were as much arrogant as simply naïve. Ansell Adams was, after all, successful in that very quest.

But we were not Ansell Adams. Our pictures were simply dull. You are likely not surprised by our failures. But Grover counseled that we should not blame the failures on our cheap cameras.

Then there was Grover's darkroom. It was fascinating –more, it was magical – seeing even our failures memorialized, those images becoming a permanent reminder of our quest. To watch a face slowly appear in the darkroom's developer bath caused us to catch our breath. Yes, magic is the right word for that process.

But we didn't take many pictures. The point wasn't to take the picture so much as it was to watch the images appear. And then suffer a critical analysis by Grover. And always wonder why our pictures could never reproduce or recreate (on yet another day's attempt) the crackly charged air of an impending July thunderstorm. God knows, we certainly tried.

Despite our failures, and in part because of the photographs' rarity, those grainy images remain precious today, dredging deep from temporal lobes memories of our close and wonderful experiences.

And today? Can we not take crisp and perfectly colored photos, photos by the hundreds, even the thousands? Are we better with the wonder of digital recording?

So, another sidebar: Let me ask you to make your own observations. Look at some - any - person walking or riding through a new place. Are they not busily snapping digital images as they pass us by? Are they actually becoming part of the world around them? Or trying to make some connection with us? Do you wonder if they feel the warmth of our sun or feel the softness of salt air on the evening onshore breeze? Some writers ask, has *recording* displaced *feeling*? What memories will their images bring back – if they have not experienced the caress of that onshore breeze?

Some, older people generally, ask, criticism implied in their question, if we have become a society of virtual experiences as well as one of virtual friends? It's another interesting question, isn't it? Again, I'm just curious about your take on the thought. For myself, I think not. And more about that later.

But enough digression; back to Reed.

A day came when we were given bikes, surprisingly, within a week of each other (did our parents conspire? I don't think so, but . . .) Suddenly and together, there they were. Balloon tired, heavy, adult sized 26 inch Schwinns, mine red, Reed's silver. Our world changed.

Learn to ride? Well, yes. Training wheels? What were training wheels?

My grandfather put me on the bike, held me erect, balancing me with his right hand on the seat, then ran down the road, pushing. My feet barely reached the pedals. He let me swerve back and forth, saying, "Patience. You'll catch on soon enough." Then a rest for us both 'till Grandpap caught his breath. Then run again. After many miles, and innumerable "When you start to fall to the left, steer to the left", I began to catch on. Next came pedaling. Similar problems, but problems ultimately solved. My biggest difficulty though, was successfully stopping the bike to get off. As I slowed, I wobbled more and more, and a few times Grandpap let me actually fall. Finally, I learned to steer toward the side of the hill, apply the brake, and then when almost stopped, fall off to the right onto the hillside. Thank God for my grandfather's patience. And for a developing brain [13].

Fortunately for Reed, he too had a patient grandfather, and we soon took to the roads together.

So we learned. And being little boys, soon became proficient riders – and no surprise, skilled to the point of disgusting arrogance (two big words my sisters had somehow learned – and used to the point of tediousness to describe us both).

Because of the war and attendant severe gasoline rationing, few people drove along our country road. On our bikes that weighed as much as our own 70 pounds, we pedaled off to explore every road south, deeper into the countryside. We

---

[13] The cerebellum, that rearward part of the brain, controls balance and automatic body movements (like swinging your arms when you walk). It doesn't develop fully until age 5 or 6, which explains why younger kids need tricycles. But the rest of the brain isn't finished by six – development continues into the early 20s, at least a partial explanation for the sometimes bizarre behavior of us as teenagers and young adults.

even went so far to cross the Youghiogheny River at Suters-ville, and pumped up into the hills of Westmoreland County. But more important than going far was exploring the little side roads leading into the dark hollows closer to home. Get even 50 yards off the blacktop road (what were yellow lines back then?) and we found ourselves on gravel and red dog, then ultimately, on dirt. An occasional gray house or tarpaper shack lay tucked into the far hill, usually across the creek running down the hollow. We saw no real yards, no grass. Hard-scrabble kids played together around abandoned cars. The cars themselves rarely held wheels (tires were almost impossible to find during the war), the cars resting on concrete blocks. One unemployed miner told me, "Being rich here means two cars up on blocks in the front yard." That was an insight I have remembered to this day, an insight that holds a painful truth[14].

We rarely stopped to talk to those people. We felt a reticence – perhaps part politeness, certainly more our own shyness – which we found to be reciprocated in those hills. We respected those families' privacy, and in remembering back, that respect of others' privacy was a deeply valued trait in our community. Grandma so often reminded me, "The gentleman minds his own business." But we did smile, we did wave, and were often rewarded with a shy wave back.

---

[14] Years later, I heard it as a joke told by a WASPy colleague; "Bubba didn't realize he was rich till he cut the weeds in his front yard and found two cars up on blocks." I didn't think it funny. Hit too close to home.

When we were 11 or thereabouts, another momentous change came into our lives. Reed's dad bought two horses.

My Dad's family had been into horses since they moved out of that McKeesport Irish ghetto – Uncle Eddie started his career running a riding stable for the rich people. His stable was up near the Country Club, and you'll read more about it in the Country Club chapter. Aunt Mary, whom you will meet later, had won more blue ribbons and riding trophies than I had ever thought possible. No Western saddles for this family – it was all English saddles, all dressage. My cousins and I learned to use four reins; my legs ached from posting. More Aunt Mary: "The trot is the most efficient gait for your horse. You will learn to post".[15] None of that fancy background would help me with the Gilchrist horses.

Reed naturally got the better horse – they were after all his. Beauty, his horse, was a small black mare, and as a definite plus, she wore a comfortable English saddle. I got Tony, who was settled with an old army cavalry bridle and saddle. And that saddle: Iron hard leather, straps and loops placed just right to irritate calves and thighs. After a few hours astride, I could not understand how we ever fielded any effective cavalry.

---

[15] In a post, the rider allows his backside to hit the bouncing saddle only every other bounce as the horse trots, using leg muscles and a touch of forward lean to add a little lift to the torso. It takes practice and is ever so tiring. Go faster, in a canter, or best of all a gallop, and your up and down body bounce exactly matches your horse's gait.

But more important than a saddle, a word about Tony: On Tony's best day, he was a plug, a plug who would even be rejected by the glue factory. Tony defined sway-back, over-the-hill, ugly plugness.

Tony had actually taught himself the skill of ever so slowly, with each plod of his hoof, to hang his head lower and lower and lower, so after some period of time, when I had become tired of holding his head up with the reins, he could work the bit forward with his tongue, then suddenly take the bit in his teeth. At that that point Tony was in control; in power to completely ignore my inputs from the reins. And then, being a plug, he would turn back to the stable. And on the way, stop when he pleased. Tony never met a clump of grass that didn't require a pause and a munch.

I loved to gallop (what boy does not?). Wind in my hair, swerving around trees, under branches, jumping small creeks. On a real horse that is. But on Tony, galloping was not to be. Not even a trot. A slow clumping walk was his one and only gait. When he decided to go home, my only recourse was to stop, get off, grab his head, and bite his ear to get his attention. I know it sounds cruel, but with Tony, after a while, it was not about control; I wanted revenge.

But please don't think I'm complaining too much. With two horses we were now free of roads, and could move as we wished, through the woods, across creeks, exploring around abandoned coal mines, and when the urge hit us, to dismount, letting the horses graze. Then to lie on some hidden meadow, faces upturned to the universe, wordless, to study billowing white clouds flying across summer skies. Or watch the blood cells scurry along the back of our eyes. Moments like these may define inner peace. And at this moment, typing these words, I wonder when the last time was that my mind felt that completely at peace. You might wonder about such mental peace yourself.

And then a fresh breeze, perhaps a pre-rain wind, or hunger, or the coming evening would nudge us back from our reveries.

When I think back to those days, it comes to me that neither of us owned watches. Think – or worry – about time? What was time to little boys?

In the winter, Reed and I went to the movies most Saturdays. Westerns were our fare, by and large.

I would walk up the road, Reed would walk down his road, and we would meet together at the halfway point, where the old streetcar tracks crossed Greenock-Buena Vista Road. Eventually, our wheezing bus would come, and 45 minutes later we would get off at the end of the line, on Walnut Street in McKeesport. That end of the line was a sleazy spot, a corner where unshaven tobacco and whiskey smelling old men sold magazines and candies from dingy small stores. From our get-off point it was a 15 minute wander into an even shadier part of town, finally to put down our quarter on the ticket sill, then go inside. The Victor Theater showed Republic Pictures – praise the Lord. Hopalong Cassidy, Gene Autry, Randolph

Scott – heroes all, all in white hats. Who said B pictures were not wonderful?

The movies taught us that there were bad people in the world (men, by and large), and more importantly, good men too. Those movies taught us about courage, about honor, about honesty. We simply didn't notice six-guns that could shoot forever without reloading.

And of course we watched the Tarzan movies, eyes wide, wondering about jungles. And about Jane, who was really a dish, and who did not wear that mysterious thing called a bra. And so obviously lived with a guy ... but was not married. Now there was food for thought. Johnny Weissmuller (our Tarzan) was a real Olympic hero who could outswim any croc. And swing through the jungle on vines . . . Swing on vines . . . Now there was more than food for thought; there was a real idea.

Back home, we cut a wild grape vine off near the ground. Presto: Monkey Vine! A run along the hill, a launch, and into the air over the creek, slowly turning, flying, then pendulum-like, back to the hillside. If Tarzan could do it, we could too.

Then our arrogance (my sisters' word again) got the better of us, and we had to swing out one handed, beating our chests with the other, pitifully imitating Tarzan's animal calling yo-del/scream. No elephant came to our calls. Sigh.

Tell our parents about the movies? Tell our parents about what we had learned? What we had planned? What we had done? Not a chance.

The critical premise, in every instance in those wonderful movies, was that the good guys sooner or later would overcome adversity and would win. In those guys with white hats we saw our fathers, uncles, and grandfathers. And we saw the men coming home from the war. Yes, heroes all. Their body language was clear; their words straight.

Saturday double features were the rule, so it didn't much matter when we went in. Of course we tried to get in for the first showing, but were invariably late – I had a fault which was always to be a bit early; Reed's was always to be a bit late. And late was the deciding factor. Then again, at that age, who cares about time? It was common for us to sit through three showings, to leave finally, eyes blurry, headachey, to go outside, find ourselves in pitch darkness, and slowly wander our way up to Reed's dad's moving and storage business. Mister Gilchrist would faithfully wait for us, then drive us home. When the stars were right, he would stop to buy us milkshakes.

Any place in that theater – as long as we sat in center first four rows – was fine. And we usually had another dime or fifteen cents to spend on hard candy – root beer barrels lasted longest. (Is there another candy criterion?) By the time we were teenagers, we each had 20 huge cavities. What did we know about dental hygiene?

I will admit that, as we got older (and we believed we had become Oh So Sophisticated) we did develop a certain suspicion about six shooters that never ran out of bullets, and heroes who never aimed but never missed the bad guys. After all, we could shoot too, and knew it was not easy. And worse, heroes who never kissed the girls made us really wonder. After all, those girls were dynamite. So we became more discerning about our B movies. But minor technical details and doubts aside, the concept, our core belief that good guys always won, remained primary and unassailable. I realize that that belief has stayed with me – a certain and absolute triumph of hope over painful and extensive negative experience. My sisters believe this is my curse - or more precisely, one of my curses.

Then in later years John Wayne appeared. The Flying Leathernecks, The Sands of Iwo Jima. Another hero, grittier, more realistic. You might not be surprised that I joined the Marines and went into military aviation. And that's for sure a story for later.

Now I should tell you about the quicksand incident.

Quicksand is not a writer's invention, a literary device found only in Gothic horror stories; it's a real physical phenomenon. Quicksand is a fluidized bed of solid particles. The concept is used extensively in industry. Say, for example you want to make metal casting of a delicate and complex piece of equipment – like the cage for a heart valve. You can make this complex part of a material easy to form, like wax, then cover it with a sand and plaster material, melt out the wax, then pour stainless steel into the mold cavity you've just made. But if you were to try to roll this delicate piece of wax into sand and plaster, you would likely break it. However, put the sand in a liquid, churn the mixture to keep the sand suspended, and you can easily dip the delicate wax in this sand bath – solid particles which agitated then act as a fluid.

Come to a pond with an active spring somewhere beneath it, and where the spring flows upward, it can keep mud and sand in suspension. There you have it: Real quicksand.

Now back to our story. Just to the right and beyond the road to Reed's place, some developers had put in a road, water lines, and fire hydrants that led up the hill deep into the woods. They were trying to sell housing lots along this road, but ran out of money, and, making matters worse for their investors, the war intervened. Bad for them; good for us, because we resented this potential intrusion into our wilderness. But that road to nowhere drew us as inexorably as Tony's need to walk to his barn. We concluded that that road severely needed to be explored. About 200 yards up the road, we came to the second fireplug, and it was peculiar. No black dirt; instead strange yellow mud surrounded it. Obviously a leak, we surmised. Of course we moved to investigate, but as we approached closer, Reed, a pace ahead of me, suddenly sunk in. Stunned, we looked at each other for long moments, completely speechless. He slowly sunk deeper. He tried lifting one leg. We heard a weird slurping sound. Reed said, "Hey, my shoe just sucked off". Then he tried the other leg. Another slurp, and he sunk a little deeper. A sudden burst of sanity – unusual for me – kept me from stepping closer to pull him out. Now he was at mid calf in the mud, and every struggling move make him sink lower. I lay down, stretching my arms forward, but could not reach him. Finally we decided that I would go get Steve.

You have met Steve before – he's the interesting fellow who put me on his shoulders to take me to the mine to look at the dead man. I ran the mile to Steve's house, knocked at the back door. His wife met me with a smile. "Well, hello. I just made oatmeal cookies. Want some cookies?" Was that a serious question? "And maybe a glass of milk?" Little boys' minds have a definite capacity, and are easily overwhelmed with in-formation. Warm oatmeal cookies and milk did the trick for me. Steve eventually came into the kitchen. Steve and I shared cookies and milk, and talked about his work in the mill. Then in a flash I remembered. When I described the problem, he became pale. We moved briskly back to Old Hills Road. When we got there, Reed had settled down into the mud to his arm-pits. He didn't look too good, but he refused to cry. It took a while to get him out – sans shoes.

Steve left (he wanted no further part of this incident). So I walked home with Reed. I wondered if he would ever forgive me for taking so long, but as it turns out, little boys have scant concept of time. And when, in a few minutes, he had calmed down, we both decided that this was just another fantastic ad-venture. And we also decided that, above all, this day's events must be kept quiet. But there was too much evidence – caked yellow clay mud up to his armpits, for example. No shoes, for example. This one was going to be tough to hide from his mom. We walked slower and slower the closer we got to his home, quiet now, dread filling our heads. Boy, was she mad. Not at his close call – she knew nothing of that, but at his dirty clothes – and that he had lost his shoes. She was enough into her anger fit that she didn't ask too many questions. Good for us.

What separated us – at least for nine years – was that Reed went to the public school, while I went to Catholic school. Comparisons were inevitable, and when the facts emerged and the experiences were recounted, our conclusions were unimpeachable: Though going to school was low on our to-do list, his was often interesting, whereas mine was hell on earth.

About the time we started school, the one room schoolhouse in Lower Greenock had been torn down, and a really cool, first rate red brick schoolhouse had been built down near Red Schaefer's general store. Reed could walk to his school, but I had to board the city bus to get to St. Peter's. Neither of us liked that separation (OK, we did not relish actually going to school, for that matter), and the schools could not keep us apart. Example: Some years later, when I was playing ball in Lower Greenock, Bobby Brian told me that Reed had told a story that morning in school that began, "One day, when me and my best friend, Chuck Kerber ...." Yes. My best friend. And then Reed told the kids about another of our great and continuing adventures. Any real boy had to have been jealous.

Near the Lutheran church in Lower Greenock stood the G B Hive. A play on words to be sure – the G B stood for girls and boys.

Near the war's end the adults decided that we kids needed some place to gather. (I will thank and love them forever for this insight.) It turns out that an abandoned shed behind the church was available for the taking, so they reclaimed it, cleaned it up a bit and found some backless benches. And that modest building became our G B Hive. The adults also scrounged an old 16mm movie projector, and mail-order rented 16mm Tom Mix and Roy Rogers black and white serials. As soon as the word got out, it was standing room only. Ten cents to get in, and worth every penny, even when the film broke. And when it broke, as it did with some regularity, we sat there quietly and talked and giggled with each other. (No cell phones then.)

Some Saturday nights after the 15 minute serial, Howard Ransick's dad called us to square dance. I have no idea how he got to be such an awesome caller. (How does one learn these hillbilly skills?) Standing on a box between the fiddler and the bass player (whose names I cannot recall) Mister Ransick called the moves – and we skipped, turned, spun our partners, and laughed until tears came. Like August Ransick (his distant cousin whom you will meet in the next chapter), he was a tall, gaunt man, dressed usually in dark checkered work shirt, faded blue bib overalls, and mill boots. But with his deep voice and mountaineer's clang dialect, his commands were clear, instantly obeyed, and even fun to listen to. Allamand ? Only in my adulthood did I learn that *Allamand left* and *Do si do* were corruptions of the French – *Allemande* (face the girl in the opposite corner, link arms, turn . . .) And *dos à dos* (literally, back-to-back – approach your partner, and turn around each other back-to-back). And the adults were actually encouraging us. . . *to touch a girl.* How unlike the nuns.

And the best was yet to come. Remember, we had no street lights. So of course the girls needed to be chaperoned home. Who else would protect them at all costs and from any harm? Sweet, warm, summer night air, stars twinkling through the clouds, sometimes a racing moon, a maybe not so accidental brush of hands........ *She actually wants me to hold her hand.* And once at her doorstep, a sweet and tender kiss. I do remember that there have been times, those wonderful times, when it was difficult for a little boy to breathe.

And then, girls delivered safely, Reed and I would walk the rest of the way to our own homes, not speaking, not quite understanding our good fortune in this world. And certainly and absolutely not understanding these soft lipped, exquisite creatures called girls. But we did have just enough insight to recognize they were indeed wonderful, and we were so, so lucky.

How do little boys communicate? That's not a simple question, and is best answered on a psychological level. Though I can't speak for every kid during those years, Reed's communications to me and mine to him were straightforward, boy to boy, with no deception, no hidden agenda, and were completely devoid of mind games. Which transaction characteristics have always been and remain the basis of true intimacy.

And back to that time thing. I often wonder what would've happened to us had we thought – even for a second -about what we were going to do that day, or any other day in our boyhood. Another interesting existential question, isn't it?

Except for school, could life be any better for two little boys? What pleases me as I look back today is that, deep in our hearts, we were pretty sure just how good we had it.

Two friends. Each other. Close. Touching. Now that's my definition of being rich.

9. AUGUST RANSICK

Now I should tell you about Mister Ransick. And what he was to us, what he taught us.

Walk toward the river from Reed's house, past his dad's Great Stone Wall, toward the stable, past the riding ring and you come to a large, gently rolling field covered by thick, reddish - tan, knee-high rye grass. By the end of each summer, we've played hard on that field and know every square inch of it. Now look beyond, beyond another field, closer to the cliff that falls away to the river. And there stands Mister Ransick's two-story, unpainted wood frame farmhouse, a house weathered to an unnamable color. Unpainted? In that climate? Oh yes. In fact, it had never been painted. Which is an essential part of his story.

As with most Pennsylvania farmhouses, a wide porch covered the whole first floor front, a porch cluttered by galvanized tin wash tubs, an old Maytag washing machine, and two gray unpainted rocking chairs. And on that front porch, among the detritus, watching us – always watching us – stood a tall, craggy man. Always the same he stood – erect, wearing heavy grayish work pants, dark blue faded almost to no-color work shirt, gray longjohns showing through the shirt's neck, and suspenders – not over his shoulders, but hanging down, down from his belt line along his legs. He watched us. Wordlessly. Intensely.

We knew Mister Ransick could see into our souls.

We, Reed and I, and I expect most other kids in our hills, were terrified of Mister Ransick.

When we asked about him, Reed's mother had warned, firmly but simply, "Leave Mister Ransick alone." She would not explain further, but her frown and head shake was enough to push our imaginations over the edge – the image of him on that porch (our private Eminence Grise), his penetrating eyes, his silence, his stillness on that cluttered porch – all of it excited our childish imaginations. And so we became afraid. Show me any little boys who wouldn't feel so.

We wondered. We pondered. We asked each other: What awful secrets lay hidden in that dark house? Were there bodies in the cellar? (Of course there were.) Why did he stand each day, all alone? Why did he watch us with such penetrating and disturbing interest?

Grandma would know. (She knows everything.) So I asked her. She answered, but in a way that was so little boy unsatisfying, with words that plainly said *you are too immature to know*: "When you are older, I will tell you all about Mister Ransick. Maybe someday you will understand." And she said not another word about him. Until he died. But I'm getting ahead of my story.

It was late July, the summer of our 10th year, and the afternoon had been particularly and unbearably sultry. Fast-moving late afternoon cumulus clouds built higher and higher, promising a lightning and rain storm, but at this moment there was no relief – the temperature was above 90°F, with humidity at least 95%.

We had played the whole day as only boys can – at full throttle – and now we had exhausted ourselves, chests heaving, lying in the grass, dehydrated. Our faces flushed red, our sweat-soaked T-shirts clung to us, and ryegrass seeds prickled and stung our backs. We had become, finally, thirsty enough to overcome even our great fear.

Reed looked at me. I looked at him. We had been friends long enough that we could read each other's minds.

Wordless decision agreed to, we got up and slowly, ever so slowly, eyes darting back from each other to the gray apparition, walked toward his porch. Now, ordinarily, boys of our age don't stand close together – but now we absolutely needed that closeness – for mutual support.

"Uh, Mister Ransick, could we please have a drink of water?"

There, the die was cast.

"COME. WITH. ME," he said.

We looked at each other. Would we ever be heard from again? Would our parents ever know how we had disappeared? But an adult had given us a direct order, and, back in the day, kids followed an adult's order. So we walked up the hill behind him.

I heard sound before I saw anything. Water trickled into a pool.

There, into the side of the hill, Mister Ransick had pick-dug a semi-cave into the shale, the opening an oval about 2 feet around and 3 feet deep, grotto – like. The opening into the cave was oak framed, and an oaken door swung open on well-greased hinges. "Keeps the critters out", he explained, then handed Reed the battered aluminum cup that lived on a nail half driven into the frame.

Springs first revealed themselves as seepage and wet mud on the side of a hill. If the wet spot persisted throughout the seasons, it became developed, formalized by men into real, usable springs. The men dug the dirt away down to bare rock to identify the main seepage point. Then they dug even more with the small picks they had brought home from the mines. An iron pipe was pounded into the area of main seepage, and over time, the water found its way out through the easier passage and into and through the pipe, increasing the flow.

An American Boyhood

Beneath his spring pipe Mister Ransick had dug out and lined a pool with round rocks. Now watercress grew among the cracks and around the pool's periphery. More rocks led the runoff away from the pond, down the hill. No mud around an August Ransick spring.

Reed dipped the cup into the pool, and looking at me, began to drink. Tentatively at first, but then hungrily, water running down the sides of his mouth, off his chin, on to his T-shirt. He poured another half cup over his head. Without a word, eyes wide, he handed me the cup.

Cold, limestone filtered, spring water on a sultry summer afternoon. I looked at Reed. Words were difficult to find. We could say nothing, but *thank you thank you thank you*.

I still remember the damp-earthy smell of the spring's cave, the tinkly sounds of water falling into that pool, and the taste – the wonderful and satisfying purity – of that icy water. Thus an August afternoon became embedded in my memory. As an August Ransick afternoon.

And we saw Mister Ransick differently from that moment. A gate had been opened.

On another day, he showed us his coal mine. Yes, we had become emboldened, and yes, he had his own personal coal mine. He simply dug into the side of the hill behind his house. This man knew self-sufficiency.

"Want to see what blackness really is", he asked. Well, were we not 10-year-old boys?

He opened the locked gate, leading us into the mine, and just inside picked up a miner's lamp hanging on a nail. He spit into the carbide (spit was the way every miner put liquid into the carbide to make acetylene gas[16], then lit his lamp. Now we had that dull yellow light to show us the way. We followed him, walking together, close, deep into the hill, around bends, pillar supports and twists, following the coal seam, hands on each other's shoulders. Then he stopped. "Are you ready?" Hearts in our mouth, we said *yes*. Then he blew out the light.

We could not breathe. We could not move. Because we could not see. Anything. After a few moments, expecting some accommodation to the dark and at least some night vision, we began to move our hands around in front of our faces. Nothing – nothing touched our retinas. It was a profound moment in time, another experience we would remember, probably forever. And for myself, I have.

I expect that few humans have ever experienced such complete absence of light.

"Enough," he asked? We replied in shaky, squeeky voices, but he never laughed at us, just quickly relit his lamp. As our courage returned, we asked to explore deeper. "No, that is

---

[16] Miner lamps created light by burning acetylene gas which was generated when carbide, a granular stonelike material which filled the lamp base was combined with water. The gas escaped from a small hole in the top of the lamp. Miners wore their lamps on their forehead over a billed cap.

enough for one day." Mister Ransick was a man of few words. He let us lead the way out.

When we had found our way back into the afternoon sun, blinking, seeing again – our world had changed. Mister Ransick was no longer the gray eminence. He had become our friend – one of only a few trusted adults. We had come to trust him because he spoke to us as he would to another adult. There was never a game in his words, never a hidden agenda in what he said. And so as a result, Reed and I became less afraid of the world, and more open to adults outside our immediate families. When I got older, finally I came to recognize that Mister Ransick had showed us more than hillsides, fields, and mines. He was one of the few adults who made us begin to see into the complicated adult world, where reality was often not as it first seemed.

Of course we didn't tell our parents any of these insights. And we chose not to tell any of the other big people about our new friend. At this stage of boyhood, we could not put into words why we felt so protective of him. But we did.

Years later, Mister Ransick died.

It turns out he had kept a journal. He earned his living primarily by digging graves, so he detailed each death – and the likely cause. An example:

1906

Jan 20 – death of Alex Gerogia hurt by fall of slate at Yough #2 mine.

Feb 24 – John W Holsing hurt in a streetcar wreck.

March 14 – death of William Loester killed by a fall of roof and rock at Osceola mine.

April 12 – death of John Pinkerton hurt by fall of roof at Yough mine #2 Boston.

April 22 – death of Mrs. Harry Culbert killed by streetcar, Bunker Hill.

May 2 – Josef Wiggins committed suicide at Boston.

Reading his journal, which he began in 1892, I was struck by the unbelievably high incidence of suicide in these small communities, and by the incredible number of deaths and maiming of those who worked in the mines and mills.

And he sprinkled his journal details with bits of his personal observations and philosophy.

His entry for 1912:

April 1 is called All Fools Day because that is the day people try to make other people look foolish. Those who own and run this country however, make fools of us all the year round. It is April the First 365 days in the year for them, and how the people do love to be fooled. Every four years they hire a new set or rehire the old set of political mountebanks to fool them all over again for another four years. If you kick a dog he has sense enough to keep away from the range of your foot. But kick the public dog and rob him of his last dollar and tell him fairytales of a full dinner pail, and he comes back with a smile on his face to listen to the same old fairytale and gets lambasted in the same old place all over again. Strange isn't it that the four-footed canine gets wise to a few things, but the two legged human never does.

And I had thought my views about politicians were original.

Since he had died, and I was older, I went back to my grandmother for the promised explanation. "Why was he always alone? Why didn't he take care of his house? Why was it never painted?"

She had been washing dishes at the kitchen sink, but suddenly stopped. For a moment, she was no longer aware of me. Rather she lifted her eyes up, staring up beyond the garden toward the woods. Without really seeing, she began, "When he was a young man, he courted one of the Heidle girls in Lower Greenock. I don't remember which one. To show her he was a man of substance and property, he built that house himself. The whole house. For her. But she chose another. And she chose not a good man, in my opinion, not as good a man as August Ransick. From that day, he went inside his house. And inside himself. Yes, he had other chances. Other girls were interested. After all, he was a man of property. "

That kitchen stayed quiet for a long time. Neither of us spoke. And finally I understood Mister Ransick's sad and profound loneliness, best expressed in his eloquent insight, his final gift to us, from that journal.

The day brings with it its work and its play. Its gladness and its sorrow, and time moves on. They say the world has dealt kindly with me and given me creature comforts. It's the end of my struggle with sordid things yet in the midst of pleasure I am sad when I hear laughter. I cannot make merry with spirit for mirth is somewhat mockery. There is nothing to look forward and recalls but hard work. My mirror reflects a face young, yet old and tired. There are those who envy me because my life seems filled with ease. I can go my way and do as I desire, but oh me, they know not my sadness else they would not wish to be in my place. And strange to say, I know the reason of my weary way with all its sameness. The little god that rules the world has passed me by. In the heyday of youth I laughed at love and pushed it away – I thought there was time aplenty; that I had but to call. Alas! I have learned a lesson of loneliness and longing because I did not reach out for love when it came my way, and now it seems so hard to find. Let those who scoff and treat lightly the spirit that moves the universe hear this and know that one must run to meet love at its first sign else the demon of sadness forever holds sway. 14 January 1923.

At that moment, he was 53 years old. And then he died.

How could kids know about such black sorrow?

Even today, with what we believe to be our greater knowledge, with our deeper understanding of human psychology, how often do we work to see into others' hearts? Not often enough, as our own behavior showed. Then again we were just little boys.

But as Reed and I grew, and we remembered Mr. Ransick and his lessons, we eventually came to recognize that we should try – to try to see into the hearts of our friends.

Should we not all try?

10. ABANDONED AND BETRAYED

On one fateful September morning in 1941, Mom made sure that I had finished breakfast, checked my clothes for appropriateness and my hands for cleanliness, and walked us across the road to wait for the city bus. Getting off at the Post Office in downtown McKeesport, we walked through an unpleasant and slummy part of town, crossed the Baltimore & Ohio Railroad tracks, then 50 yards further found ourselves in front of three massive, soot covered, reddish black brick buildings. Standing before those buildings (which Mom did for the longest time), we saw on the far left, the imposing church of St. Peter's Parish. In the middle, the convent of the Sisters of Mercy. And on our right, St. Peter's grade and high school, a three-story dark, forbidding building which, as years passed, I would come to recognize as some author's construction of the center of evil in her Gothic horror novel.

We opened a creaky steel gate then stepped onto the brick paved schoolyard. Mom paused for an even longer moment. I turned to her, puzzled at the hesitation. She was looking up at the portico. The look on her face caused a sudden bad feeling in my stomach. Then, with a deep breath, chin down and grim determination, she dragged me up the steps. We passed through heavy tall oak double doors to enter a dark building smelling of lye, industrial disinfectant, sweaty bodies, mildew, and a more unpleasantly pervasive odor that I recognize (only in retrospect) to be the essence of little kids' fear.

WOW, I thought, ignoring the weird feeling in my belly. This was a quite a place – a place – and a moment rich with potential. This could be another great adventure.

Face full of wonder, looking up at the high ceilings, then at walls covered with pictures of long dead Mothers Superior, I was half dragged to the first grade school room. What an amazing place, I thought.

How naive I was. Mom had delivered me into the cold hands of the nuns. I had been betrayed.

Thus began my nine years of crushing, mind numbing interactions with women who, in general, hated men, but in particular, loathed and despised little boys. My judgment is too harsh you say? Let us see. And then you decide.

But before we begin our journey, first, a question: Have you noticed that when some large organization (more often than not, the federal government) names something, say, for example, their Anti-Poverty Program – exactly the opposite is the result?[17] and now Mom had placed me into the hands of the Sisters of Mercy. Mercy? Sigh. As the years passed, I wondered again and again how she could have done this to me. In the early years, I wondered as little boys tend to do, *Was I that bad? Does Mom hate me?* Kids do tend to internalize these things.

At this point, let us set the scene. I have told you of the pervasive institutional smell. The first grade classroom itself was large (actually huge to us kids). Blackboards we could barely reach covered three walls (except for space for the single huge oak door). High, dirty, multipaned windows faced the railroad tracks on the fourth. From my detail, you can tell how this place's ambience is burned into my memory. Burned into it. And I have found that I am not the only grown up kid from that school with this sharp a picture in his mind.

In spite of the room size, we were crowded, there were not enough desks, and chaos ruled the morning. First, we became registered into a big black book (as names written onto the rolls of those condemned and damned). And that task accomplished, the parents, almost exclusively moms, were ordered

---

[17] Then again, you may believe otherwise, but your conclusion would be a tough sell to most Americans. Or, to further my thesis, you might look at the House of Representatives Budget Committee report, *The War on Poverty: 50 Years Later*. Then again, you may not wish to Google it, because it is a profoundly discouraging summary of the cost of programs – trillions of dollars – wasted – with no scientifically demonstrable effect.

(yes, ordered) to leave, which they did with pitiful and disgustingly submissive smiles at the nuns. Then a few shy and tentative waves to us, and they obediently left [18] . . . at which point the ambience changed. It seemed the very air in that room changed immediately, irrevocably – and painfully. Sister Mary Joseph's first order of business was to teach us . . . who was the absolute and unquestionable boss. And she did so with the back of her left hand across kids' faces, or with a 12 inch wooden ruler in her right hand, a ruler she applied generously to arms, shoulders, and especially to knuckles. In thinking back, I remember with painful clarity that this application was almost entirely to us boys. Even in this beginning of our journey, the girls were immediately, clearly, and obviously smarter than we were. Too bad we did not have the insight to learn from them.

And I was not yet five years old. Could there be any other little boy's conclusion but that his mom and dad hated him? Why else would any mom and dad send their boy to this brick prison guarded by cruel women dressed in stark, black medieval robes? *This is really bad*, I thought. *Abandoned*, I thought, over and over again.

It would get worse. And day by day, it did. Then year by year, it did.

We learned by rote. The whole class repeated the exercises. First the alphabet, again by rote. Immediately some kids

---

[18] Almost all of them were Irish and German Catholic girls who had gone to that same school. And who had not escaped the Pavlovian conditioning.

started to fall behind. But my grandfather had already taught me letters, and more importantly, their sounds. What a relief. After upper and lower case printing, the A. N. Palmer method of cursive writing was introduced. I liked that whole concept, and practiced the technique, filling pages and pages with smooth up-and-down lines and circles. I began to read more, always to myself, ignoring the classes – which caused the nuns significant distress, and even anger. So it likely would not surprise you to learn that I was punished for my frequent mental absences.

In our favor, kids who did survive Catholic school could write cursive script really well. I am searching my memory for other positive outcomes of that education. Give me time, and I'm sure I'll think of something. Anything.

Corporal punishment was not new to kids of our generation. Most of us expected (and frequently felt) a wooden spoon to our behinds when we *crossed the line*. Punishment by adults in my circle was – how can I best describe this – clinical, dispassionate, and appropriate to the transgression. With that kind of punishment, we did not ever feel abused. But the nuns were different. Emotion was involved. Angry violence was visited on us, often, it seemed, for reasons we could not figure out. Punishment was the one subject the nuns, the *Sisters of Mercy* never seemed to tire of teaching.

We were puzzled – we boys especially – most of the time, at least in the early grades about why they continued to hit us.

We were puzzled because what was said was not always congruent with what their body language was telling us – with what they really meant. Understanding the real meaning behind and beyond those nuns' words was a continuing problem for many of us. Later, as we caught on, most of us solved our confusion problem by mentally withdrawing. As a coping mechanism, withdrawal was simply awful. But what else were powerless little boys to do?

A sidebar: Of course this was not the first experience we kids had had with the difficulty in figuring out - in interpreting – what the big people really meant, what they really wanted. Early on, even before language has developed, before a child learns to speak[19], a child can figure out what the adult – almost always mother – really wants, through facial expressions, tone of voice and other nonverbal body language. In this environment, the nuns were talking down to us – as a stern, disapproving Parent to our terrified, naïve, and hoping-to-understand Child.

 The nuns' message was immediately clear: We Sisters of Mercy are the goodness in your world. You are damned-to-burn-forever, evil little children unless – unless we can save your immortal souls. Well, at least that was the message to us little boys. They really did believe in this Catholic idea of Original Sin.

---

[19] May I bring this critical subject up again and expand it in detail in the next-to-last chapter?

This is going to be awful, I thought. Kids hate confusion. Kids hate mixed messages. Kids don't really want to learn Parent to Child communication, with all its complexities, feelings felt profoundly but words impossible to say.

But on the other hand, and beyond the nuns . . . there were girls. Wonderful, dainty, pretty, girly girls. Girls with red hair, girls with black hair, girls with golden hair. Girls with freckles. Girls with dimples. And their smiles. Did their smiles not prove there was truly a spot of heaven in this hell called St Peter's? I found it difficult to breathe when standing next to certain of them. Actually, when standing next to many of them.

In first grade I promptly fell in love with Joan Fullard, deep dimples, blue eyes and short curly red hair. Pink pinafore, white ankle socks, Mary Janes on dainty feet, and a smile that put the beauty of sunsets to shame: What was not to love? We held hands, walked together, went into the back of the church next door, and in the darkness, gently and sweetly kissed. But the nuns soon found out – they *knew,* they said, *everything.* And said that they *could see everything* we did. By and large, for the first few grades, we thought they did see everything. And read into our minds, which often caused a cold sweat when a cold eye was directed toward us. We were naïvely obvious, Joanie and I, and one afternoon they backed us against the blackboard, enclosing us in a semicircle of powerful disapproval. Close your eyes and picture this: three black-clad huge women (in the convent, gluttony was not a sin), arms crossed, glaring down at two little innocent kids. Punishment was swift and severe. Joanie cried, and was sent in disgrace to the principal's desk. An open palm across my face, while telling me how shameful – how sinful – my behavior was. "You are going to burn in hell forever".[20] Forever? I didn't even know what forever meant at that point; in fact, I couldn't even think ahead six weeks to when we would get our report cards. But I simply could not believe the nuns saying that Joanie and my tenderness could be evil. No.

Though Joanie and I were separated – and punished – we learned. We learn to conceal actions, and especially our thoughts and emotions from the nuns. And as time went on, we learned to lie to them, really, really well. But to try to unlearn a child's spontaneity and ability to understand human to human nonverbal transactions, well, that was going to be more difficult.

By third grade, as I was apparently going to survive, Mom decided that I would learn to play the piano. One of the nuns

---

[20] Thinking back, these were the commonest words we kids heard from them. One day - probably about 5th grade - the concept of infinity, of foreverness, came into my consciousness, and that, given how evil a kid I was (I must have been having a bad day), I would likely burn in hell *forever. Forever and ever.* As I had by then experienced a few real burns and knew how much they hurt, this recognition of my foretold and inevitable fate caused a few sleepless nights. Until I and the other boys came to recognize that this was yet another nun baloney sandwich.

gave piano lessons as a method of earning a little extra income for the convent.

Ah yes, the convent. The building where the nuns worked, prepared meals, ate, did their laundry, prayed, and slept. This too was a dirty, red brick building, of architecture similar to both school and church, sited between the two, and only a dozen steps away from the school.

At a certain time, a messenger, the prior piano pupil, would be sent from the convent to the classroom to summon the next learner. The messenger did not go to the kid, but rather to the nun, that all-powerful being, who then excused the kid from class. Even in third grade I found this puzzling. If class were so important, as we were told every day, how could I leave it for the better part of an hour and not miss something significant? But I dared not ask anyone – especially a nun.

But then it was down the steps, and along the walk, that oh so ominous walkway to the convent. A respectful knock on the door, and I was allowed, permitted, but only barely, to enter the sanctum sanctorum. The rooms and hallways were stark, dark, and terrifying. I hated it. The place smelled bad. Not that a seven-year-old boy could describe and characterize the smell any better, but it was just bad. Bad bad bad.

Music theory was fairly straightforward, and anybody with reasonable eye hand skills could learn to pound out a simple tune, but the pounding out was tentative and a bit tricky, as errors were rewarded with a 12 inch ruler crack across the knuckles. What a wonderful teaching system (please excuse my sarcasm). Each evening Mom would ask when I was going to practice, and was as encouraging as a mom could be, but I would not approach our old upright. After some months, with a sigh, she gave up. And I never had to go into that awful place, that convent again. Passive resistance is not a good coping mechanism, but it's the only one a little boy had available.

By fourth grade I thought I had the system figured out. The nuns taught reading by calling on an individual kid to stand, then read aloud a paragraph from our so-called Reader. So 45 other kids sat, painfully bored with nothing to occupy their minds while, for example, poor Richard Rollins – who had already been held back a year – stumbled through the words in a single paragraph for an embarrassing and painful 15 minutes. Today the diagnosis would be easy –Richard was dyslexic. Then, the nuns considered him stupid, and continued to humiliate him daily in class – in front of everyone. Richard, being an older and bigger kid, made us littler kids pay for his embarrassments at recess. Who could blame him?

Hovering parents today believe that if their child is an earlier reader she is likely a genius. What early reading usually means is that, number one, the kid is not dyslexic[21], number two, she may be nearsighted and so finds enjoyment in things

---

[21] Given the power and ubiquity of computers, I have often wondered whether it would not be better to have an app change the text to read backwards so that dyslexic kids could enjoy reading. After all, it worked for da Vinci. Could the problem be similar to the way that teachers used to require left-handed kids learn to write with the right hand?

closer up to her eyes rather than in outside activities[22], but mostly and simply, that she just enjoys reading. And with that in mind . . .

. . . and as it turned out, by the third week of that fourth school year, I had read the entire Reader, a book they had planned to take the whole year for us to get through. ("Get through" is an unfortunate turn of phrase, isn't it? But those are the words the nuns used.) Now please don't think this completion – my completion of reading the text – was important. Reading for pleasure was simply something that I enjoyed doing, something my grandfather had taught me to do before I entered that dour prison. So I asked Sister Mary what's-her-name if I could have another book. "I finished the Reader last night. Can I have another?" Her reply was instantaneous. A flash of dark eyes, an immediate smack – her forehand across my face. "Don't you be so smart," she said, a blush of anger rising up her face [23]. God, did that hurt. The other kids saw the redness on my face – caused more by my humiliation than from the swelling. And of course I would never give her the satisfaction of showing pain. Naturally, the other kids had no idea why I had been slapped, but knew it must have been something really bad. My anger at that humiliation lasted through

---

[22] All kids should have their eyes tested well before they go to school. There's more than one kind of amblyopia, and vision is almost always correctable – if the problem is diagnosed early enough.

[23] You think kids don't notice nonverbal communications like this? Reading nonverbal cues is what kids are really good at doing. And yes, that dichotomy is a fundamental part of these stories.

the rest of the morning, and, come to think of it, has lasted until today. I'm not making this up.

If we analyze that transaction (something I'm still not quite able to do with any degree of dispassionate thought), you will likely understand the root of the then Catholic school problem[24]. First was the nun's immediate and powerful reaction: a slap to a little boy's face. She felt no surprise. No curiosity. No desire to reward. Did she feel a powerful drive to control and humiliate? What do you think? And how about interpreting the literal statement *do not be smart*? In a nutshell, don't be *too* smart was the agenda of those nuns. Get some skills, get out, so you can get married (before you get pregnant, or get a girl pregnant), so you can get a job.

In later years, I wondered about that baseline philosophy, that philosophy that did not emphasize excellence. It has been difficult for me to cut through the myths and the need of elder Catholics to justify and rationalize the Church's abuses. But I offer this synthesis as unprovable hypothesis: the great Irish immigration wave that followed the potato famine and English takeover of the Irish farms created legions of uneducated immigrant Irish farm girls, girls who had no employable skills. No surprise, they sold what they could, and prostitution flourished. I am not sure who gets the actual credit, but church elders, likely led by Boston bishops, decided to do

---

[24] I have been told that times have changed, and that the schools are now "different." Maybe. But people don't change, in my experience. In fact, as we grow older, we seem to become even more like ourselves, with less social overlay modifying our behaviors.

something about it, and invented the parochial school system, the primary goal being to give girls workplace skills. They were taught to be secretaries. More than once I heard from the nuns, "Everybody wants our girls to work for them." More important is what I didn't hear: " He or she will become a great scientist/editor/engineer/you fill in the blank." It's a fascinating history, but a history clouded by hidden agendas and the need to cover up. Who knows where the truth lies? You get to decide.

But now let us speak more of covering up. In the fifth grade, the nuns decreed that I would be an altar boy. *No No NO. Never Never NEVER. Bad. Really, really bad,* I thought. But nuns had spoken. My mother, who had graduated from that same school and who had been unable to throw off the shackles crafted by the nuns (she was the one, after all, who delivered me into the hands of the nuns), was resigned to my fate. After all, *They* had said *it would be.* My father, on the other hand, a man similarly conditioned as a Pavlov's dog from his time in that school, one who generally acquiesced to anything the clergy pronounced, said simply and absolutely, "NO." Mom and I looked at each other, mouths slightly open, surprised. I wondered about this single instance of defiance. It was the only time in his entire life – at least the only time I knew of – that he stood his ground where a priest or nun was concerned. When he was older, quite sick and near death, he admitted to me that his religiously fanatic mother had required him to be an altar boy, and a certain priest had chased him around the altar with lust in his eye. I never asked him to tell me whether the priest had caught him or not. Some things sons do not want to know. Thankfully, for his single defiance, I was spared. But other boys were not.

On to better, brighter things.

$$* \quad * \quad * \quad * \quad * \quad *$$

Thank God for lunchtime and for recess. Twenty minutes in the morning, the same in the afternoon, and 45 minutes for lunch.

Ah, yes, lunches. First, you must understand that only sissies carried lunchboxes. I should say that the men, the real men, those tough men who worked in mines (miners carried un-painted aluminum lunch pails) and mills (steelworkers carried steel black lunch boxes[25]) – those men stood far above our pettiness and concern for group standing. But this was school, and to be considered a sissy was a fate far worse than burning in hell forever, a fate far worse than death.

Lunch consisted almost invariably of a sandwich of peanut butter and jelly, or of chipped ham[26], some cookies, and an

---

[25] They called them "buckets". A wife would say, "I've put a bit of that veal pie in your bucket today." I've never figured out why the usage was so universal.
[26] Unless you grew up in the Three Rivers area, you will have no idea what Chipped Ham is. Sold, and I think invented by a local Dairy/Deli named Isaly's, it is some mystery meat ground and pressed and cooked into a loaf, then sliced paper thin, jumbled on a sandwich (Wonder Bread, of course), and often covered with a sweet mild barbecue sauce.

apple or banana. As the lunch was packed tightly into a flattened rectangular package covered with yesterday's McKeesport Daily News and tied with butcher's string, the fruit mashed itself into the sandwich imprinting it to a hemispheric paper thinness. In the first seconds after opening lunches, trading became furious.

It took maybe 2 minutes to trade, to grab a half pint bottle of Diffendall's milk[27] and to gobble down our food, then explode from the doors, out into the brick-paved yard – the girls to their segregated area, we boys to ours.

The frost-heaved bricks covering the yard were anything but smooth, and the corners sticking up provided plenty of opportunity for stumbles and falls while at a full run. But skinned noses and knees brought a laugh and a "stupid clumsy kid" from everyone watching. And maybe a little tincture of iodine if a nun noticed. But never a lawsuit.

Let's get back to reality. Any time boys get together there is a quest for dominance. No well-meaning but dippy sociologist/educator will ever change that. And older, and especially bigger, always wins. Combine bigger with a little bit of anger – or child abuse in the home, or in our case, abuse in the classroom – and you create a bully in the schoolyard. Our Catholic school was a breeding ground for bullies. As for generalized global anger, what boy, other than the inevitable and disgust-

---

[27] Yep. Milk in bottles - and from a German family (but of course Catholic) dairy.

144

ing teacher's pet, could not be angry at having spent a morning under the thumb (or ruler) of the nuns. To make matters worse, any boy who had been held back a grade, or who had been thrown out of the public school for antisocial behavior, was sent to the Catholic school for disciplining. By the time I was in fifth grade, we had fully mature 14-year-old boys in our class. And rarely could they read well, rarely do the math. Though terrifying to us at recess, they were casualties in a system where nobody knew or cared what dyslexia, a learning disability, or an abusive stepfather was.

The bully rarely varied in his approach. Begin with an angry, semi-sociopathic big kid. Add two to four sycophantic side-kicks, kids who sought protection as subservient allies. The group would roam the schoolyard looking for victims, looking to dominate. There have always been bullies. There always will be. We were appropriately terrified. They could do real damage. And they did, creating fear at times enough to loosen our bowels, and at other times, to cause blood to flow. By the way, it always amazed me how easy it was to make a boy's nose bleed.

Men passing by would often stop to watch us playing in the schoolyard. One particularly vigorous and courageous kid might get a smile, and a "Now that's a real boy," one man to another. Today that kid would likely be medicated.

And then back in our world, we would, at the tolling of a bell swung by an unsmiling nun, change from sweaty, flushed, breathlessly exuberant boys back into glaze-eyed students, and shuffle inside to our prison, to sit at our scarred oak desks.

Not all of us survived this harsh environment. From time to time, we would come to school one day and find an empty desk where someone, always a boy, had sat among us. We would ask, but the nuns would not talk about that person, and eventually we gave up trying to find out. One more boy, usually a troubled boy, had just ceased to exist. It was worrisome, even frightening, that the nuns could make someone simply disappear. Forever. Now that was power.

School days were filled with our attempts to learn. We were, after all kids, curious kids. And every day we tried to discern truth from falseness, a continuing problem throughout those years.

In that school, I learned that true evil lives in the world. I had been naïve when I first went there, but by fourth grade, I knew. The nuns spoke of being good, of doing good, of loving one's neighbor. We were forced to memorize the Ten Commandments. We learned the Seven Deadly Sins. We were marched to the church to confess our evil ways. Again and again, they thundered at us that we were sinful creatures with uncontrollable lusts, and that we had been born in sin.

Lusts? We didn't know what lusts were. Born in sin? And then, hearing this concept, the picture of each of my sisters as smiling babies in their bassinets, pretty little girls, came into my mind. Those beautiful girls were born with the stain of sin in their souls? Now that was a really, really hard sell. And that realization caused the first crack in the priests' and nuns' stone-like and unyielding philosophy. From that moment on, no matter how hard the nuns enforced and reinforced their Pavlovian conditioning, my first reaction was one of doubt. And I was not alone. I could not talk about these doubts to the girls. But we boys wondered, and whispered quietly in the hallways, at the water fountains. The seeds had been planted.

As we progressed through the grades, our worldly experience and knowledge grew, and we boys learned that there were other places even more awful than St Peter's. One older kid in our class had been required to spend two weeks, for some infraction or other, in a place that was called Juvenile Hall – a jail for kids. When he returned, we tried get him to tell us .... *What's it like?* Mute, he shook his head, staring a thousand yards away, tears beginning to form. The terror in his eyes was enough. We never asked him again.

Then the nuns tried to convince us, once we asked for more information, that, as bad as Juvenile Hall was, eternal damnation in hell was infinitely worse, as it didn't just last two weeks, and we would burn forever. Yet another baloney sandwich from the Sisters of Mercy. By seventh grade, we boys had begun to affect a jaded demeanor.

Some of us learned sooner than others that, to avoid the ruler, we would have to be other than ourselves; we would have to lie. Lying is a really bad thing for a kid to learn. What happens to him later if the essential need for truth has not been taught in the home?

The negative Pavlovian conditioning the nuns used would come back to haunt some of my classmates in later years. The good news is that most of the kids in my class were able to achieve a certain balance, a balance needed to survive and be happy in the real world outside that school.

So slowly my fellow sufferers and I learned the ways of the nuns. We gradually learned to negate their pernicious influences. To lie to avoid an open palm across the face never became comfortable, but it's what we did. As I grew older, the priests' and the nuns' behaviors, as opposed to what they told us, opened profound philosophical questions, the essential one becoming *if this organization, this church, is really about truth and goodness and love, how can their hatred, their sadism, and their sexual perversions exist at its very core?*

Good questions, aren't they?

11. GRANDPAP MASON

There was escape from the nuns.

Escape consisted not only in withdrawing deeply into the recesses of our minds during class times, but ultimately, by leaving that awful building and all that it contained and represented.

Actually, when the final bell rang, we didn't simply leave the building. We exploded out, freed yet again, relief and joy returning once more to little kids' faces.

Best of all, on some of those afternoons, I would burst out, running through the iron gate – and surprised beyond belief – find myself gathered into my grandfather's strong arms. How did he know? How did he find me in the crowd? How did he get here from the mill? Who was going to see to getting my sisters home safely? No matter; he had organized the situation, and I knew at that moment a new adventure would begin.

Sometimes we simply walked around town for a bit, found a cheap diner, and enjoyed a hot dog for dinner. By far the classiest diner was down across from the B&O railroad station. It looked like a stainless steel, all-chrome Pullman railroad car – without the wheels – anchored in place forever on cinderblocks. Steamy inside, and smelling of hot coffee and cigarettes, it was a most wonderful refuge from the cold winter winds. The waitresses wore uniforms – black dresses, dainty white aprons across their front, and tiny white caps on their heads. Theirs were eyes that had seen and endured every manner of man, but still showed kindness –when they sometimes handed an extra large piece of pie – along with a furtive smile and a wink to a little boy.

All the men of my childhood smoked – unfiltered Luckies, Chesterfields, and Camels. (And they smoked a lot[28]) and of course drank alcohol. The inevitable mill valley drink was a shot of whiskey and a glass of beer (*"Gimme shot 'na beer."* Just two words[29]). The whiskey was the cheapest Rye, usually Canadian Club, and was drunk down straight, followed by a gulp of beer, almost invariably Iron City[30]. The rest of the beer

---

[28] So did the kids. My dad started smoking at age 8. Hard to believe, but there you have it.

[29] Or "Gimme 'n Imp 'na Iron", Imp standing for Imperial whiskey. Iron was pronounced arn as in barn. The term boilermaker hadn't been invented yet.

[30] It is possible to buy Iron City beer today, as it has been popularized by advertisements during the Pittsburgh Steelers games. And today it is quite good. Today's Iron City is not the beer of the 50s; that beer was made with truly awful

was then savored, cigarette in one hand, beer glass in the other, before going home. "Cuts the mill dust", one man answered, when I asked about downing the shot first. Since there was essentially no drinking at home, how would I have known in such detail these awful, sordid practices? (Which was how my Aunt Mary described them.) My grandfather – horrors! – took me into smoky, and to a little boy, somewhat scary dark McKeesport bars. That's where the good sandwiches – which we shared – were made. The bars were organized not by place in town but by nationality. There were Italian bars, Slovak bars, Irish bars, Polish bars – bars reflecting the diversity of our immigrant steelworkers. And I was welcome in all.

Oh, and a lesson I learned in the bars: steelworkers to a man carried themselves with pride. "I built the Empire State building," one man on the next barstool said to me. And another: "I make tanks." As in Sherman tanks, whole train loads of them for our military. Sadly, that pride left the valleys when the steel mills closed.

Watching bar behavior with wide eyes, I began to notice that my grandfather rarely drank and when he did, drank sparingly. On our forays into the bars he would order a small glass of beer – six or seven ounces for a dime – but never more. I asked him about that. "The only time I took beer was when

---

water from our then polluted rivers. Even worse was Tube City beer, made from water drawn from the acid polluted Youghiogheny River.

prohibition was on. I'd stop in a speakeasy. Have a glass. None of the bloody government's bloody business." No profanity (unless you consider the English word "bloody" a curse word.) I heard only determination and firmness in his voice. And so I learned about constitutional freedoms and individual liberties. And more importantly, that a man had not just a right but even more, a duty to stand up to the government to defend his own freedoms.

Walking along the railroad tracks usually brought us to the steel mills. We would walk, then stop while he looked hard at the rails leading into the mill. Then toward the gondolas on rail sidings, gondolas filled with seamless steel pipe waiting to be picked up, waiting to be taken to Texas oil fields. He would stand for a few moments lost in thought. Then he would look at me, say nothing, smile, then look back. I finally got the point, looked, but it took me until years later to completely recognize his insight. This coming together of rail and mill was the fundamental source of all wealth in our valley. Many of Grandpap's best lessons were nonverbal – powerful, but nonverbal, this one among them.

The Baltimore and Ohio (pronounced BeenOh, one word) Railroad's mainline rails curved through McKeesport. Wherever streets crossed the rails, a barrier had to be lowered to prevent cars from crossing the tracks as a train was coming. No automation then – small towers located at intervals allowed the tower man inside to determine when to lower and raise the barrier.

You can see one such tower in the center of the photo taken a few blocks from the school.

My dad had pointed out one particular watchman to me. This watchman had no legs, having lost them in an accident. (Brakemen falling under  moving trains and losing legs was, he said, not an altogether uncommon happening.) The watchman asked for no help from the man he was relieving, or from anyone else. He would, overhand, pull himself up into his watch station for his eight hour shift. I pointed out this awesome feat to my grandfather. He knew all about the man. When we talked about this man's daily problem in getting to his work, I came to recognize great and profound respect on Grandpap's face. But never pity. I then looked at Grandpap's mangled thumb (some mill accident), thought of Uncle Ernie's absent thumb (another mill accident), and realized suddenly that *these men do not ever whine*. I wondered, *Could I ever fill their shoes?*

An American Boyhood

When there was a movie he thought we would both enjoy, we would amble into the center part of town to one of the theaters. Unlike Reed and me on Saturdays (we entered when we got there, and stayed the whole day of course), he always knew when the movie was scheduled to start, and timed our walk so that we could get in, get the best seats, and be there in time for the Warner-Pathé newsreel and the cartoon.

I remember more from his reactions to the movies as from the movies themselves.

One particular movie sticks in my mind to this day: *Tom Brown's School Days*. The movie was a study of the English upper class school system (I was confused, as they called them Public Schools, but Grandpap explained all to me). I also remember, in the middle of that stark black and white movie, saying to him, "Wow, that place is as bad as St. Peters." He just shook his head no. He explained after the movie that he believed the English schools were far worse, far more damaging to little boys. As much as I was immersed in the movie, I noticed him leaning forward, totally absorbed. When the movie was over, and we were walking back to the bus stop, I asked him about his intense interest. "Shows you why I left that land, laddie. At least one of the reasons." "Yes, but why was that school so bad," I asked. "Brutality, bullying, and buggery," he answered, never one to waste words. Well, I certainly understood the brutality part. The nuns stood in well for the headmasters whacking thin whips on little boys' bare bottoms. And Eddie Sampson (my personal nemesis during grades four through eight) was the perfect bullying replica of the older boys in the movie. But I couldn't figure out the last part, and said, "but what's buggery?" Then he gave me that adult's answer that I truly hated: "I'll explain when you get older." And he did, when I was older, in a bit more detail than I really wanted to hear.

We talked again and again about England – he always called it *The Old Country*. He explained why had no respect for the English upper class – nor he added, for the lower classes either. "At least the nobles have some self-respect." As we walked to the bus stop, he explained why he had brought his family to America. "What could you have made of yourself if I had stayed in England? Here, in America, you can do anything, be anything. *If you work for it.*" And with that last sentence, he would look directly into my eyes. Just those few words, that eye contact, and I was made to understand. And that understanding has shaped my life, and my willingness to go to school, to serve in uniform, in fact, everything. Grandpap was a good communicator - just what a little boy needs.

After each movie, he talked to me about the bigness of the world out beyond McKeesport, about the need for travel to educate, and what each movie actually said, what it was about. Those were heady philosophical discussions for a little boy, all tempered and interpreted by the world experience, the native intelligence, and common sense of the man I adored.

In our ambles, we finally reached the bus stop – the start point of the Sutersville line. There were no seats; everyone just stood around on the sidewalk waiting, the people mostly withdrawn into themselves, alone with their thoughts. What a perfect place to observe humanity. Even now I wish I had been a more careful observer.

One evening we heard, then saw a nasty man be disrespectful to his girlfriend.

As Grandpap intently watched that painfully public transaction, he shook his head with disapproval, and said: "*Always be the gentleman.*" It was not a matter of *acting* a gentleman or even *behaving* as a gentleman. But that powerful verb *to be* made his words an imperative to incorporate the concept into a personality trait, a way of being, not just of doing. And he was insistent that it was not enough to be *a* gentleman but to be *the* gentleman – in other words, that it was my responsibility to be the leader in the group, the one who would set an example, the one whose responsibility it was to show the way. I wonder if he knew – I hope he knew – how often in later years I had listened to that advice and tried to act on it.

We watched a slovenly and dirty drunk stagger past:
He observed to me *The man keeps his shoes shined, his collars white, and his nails clean.* The man may need to work in a sewer (or perhaps even worse, as he believed, in a mine or steel mill), but when the occasion demands it, the man will dress and comport himself appropriately. Of course the clean hands

and nails problem was not easily solved, especially when one had calloused hands and ingrained grease from the mill. But hot water, lye soap, a brush, and his term, some *elbow grease* eventually solved the problem.

Then I suddenly realized that all the men in my family had hard, calloused hands. Calloused hands were an invariable male property in our family. And then I felt even more proud of those men.

As for the dress code, you might ask if I am remembering correctly? Oh yes. Look at early pictures of men working in the mill – even the men working the gas stations. For church, or other important events like weddings, even the poorest man wore his "good" suit, a starched white shirt, often with darned collar, tie and black hightop polished calfskin shoes. At work, men wore buttoned up shirts – and many of them even wore ties. And this mode of dress was not just for a photo op. It was about the affirmation of their own dignity.

And other nuggets of wisdom:
Put more elbow grease into it, laddie. The same to Mary Ellen one day: "Put more elbow grease into it, lass", as she was about to give up on her attempts to remove blackness from the bottom of a skillet. Easy translation: keep at it; work harder. It is surprising how *a bit more elbow grease* solved so many problems in my life, both physical and mental.

Educate yourself. Note how important the form was to him. We had just left another movie – I don't remember the name, but it was an English period piece – Basil Rathbone had perfectly played the dastardly villain – and were walking to catch the bus. Grandpap was more pensive than usual, and we spoke little. Thinking about that movie, about his home, his England, I wanted to understand why he had felt the need - and had had the courage - to leave. "So you would have opportunity. So you could do what you want. Nothing for you there. You saw what they were like," commenting on the movie. Then immediately, looking directly into my eyes, " But now it's all up to you." To become educated was possible here he knew, but he made me understand that the responsibility was mine. Suddenly, a heavy weight came to sit uncomfortably on all too narrow shoulders.

The craftsman don't blame his tools. Again, more on responsibility. I was whining about having broken a hacksaw blade while cutting some pipe, and had cursed "that lousy blade". (As an aside, I still have that hacksaw. It is more than 100 years old.) Don't blame the tools – look into the mirror instead. This homily served me in good stead when I was learning surgical skills. It was up to me to ensure the patient's well-being. Something about a buck stopping with me.

As we walked to the bus – and I asked why he didn't get a car:
Shank's mare will get you there. Shank's mare is an old English term for a leg. We walked everywhere. Grandpap never learned to drive, and never seemed to suffer for lack of a car,

though we lived well out into the country. A five mile walk to meet with his friend – just for a few minutes to talk over some problem – saved bus fare and was "good for the constitution".

I was complaining about getting only 50 cents an hour to cut grass for Mr. Peters:
If the man is paying you, give him an honest day's work. Notice the emphasis – the lack of victimhood, the lack of entitlement, the emphasis on personal responsibility.

And the words that inevitably followed that last rule:
Always do your best. No explanation or justification needed for that one.

As I complained about Eddie Sampson:
Give the bully a quick bloody nose – then run. Practical advice. React quickly, aggressively, then exit the danger zone.

The man is his word. Perhaps the most profound of them all. Again, form counts: there is no "should" or "ought to", or "try". Over the years this has morphed into much more – being careful with words, recognizing words can hurt, and enough hurts can kill. More, much more about this in the last chapter.

Grandpap – and Grandma too – kind of expected my sisters and me to know about the Ten Commandments[31] as the foundation for behavior, but his and Grandma's homilies refined

---

[31] But in retrospect, that commandment proscribing "coveting thy neighbor's

and sharpened the way we interacted with our world, and did so in essential ways that codified then enriched our lives.

In looking back over these rules, especially the imperatives "educate yourself" and "be the gentleman", every homily placed the responsibility for decisions, for behavior, for actions, squarely where it belonged – on our heads. We had incredible freedoms, but with our freedoms came corresponding responsibility. And considering these imperatives, at least for my sisters and me, it was clear that Mom and Dad, but especially our grandparents, were standing above us in judgment, and were far more immediate, more insightful, and more powerful even than God.

In reading these words, you might get the impression that I had uncommon insight as a little boy. I did not – in fact most adults regarded me as clueless. The ability to verbalize what I learned came ever so slowly, and came actually after I had finished medical school. I suspect that it was that the verbal, but even more, the nonverbal lessons were so profound, and became so indelibly etched upon my developing psyche that I could recall them, and much more importantly, use them throughout my developing years.

Grandpap Mason and I did a great deal of walking together.

---

wife" remained fuzzy to me, no matter how I tried to get any adult to explain it. That understanding would have to wait until later, until high school.

And some talking together. And then we shared the quiet bus rides in the darkness back to Greenock. During those rides, I remember, though words were few and far between, being absolutely protected. And feeling profound closeness to him, feelings always missing in that cold Catholic school.

Where did a man such as this come from? Grandpap Mason began life as a spirited boy growing up in a small cotton mill town in Northwestern England. The town was Oldham, near Manchester. The people in this region were not quite sure whether they were Scots or English; moreover they tended not to care one way or another. When some central authority north of Hadrian's Wall, or far away to the south in London attempted any kind of control, these people simply ignored them. Watch a soccer game on TV today, and my family's people will be the ones in the bleachers with their faces blue-colored with woald, the traditional body paint of their Celtic ancestors, eating pork pies, wearing only T-shirts as driving sleet whites out the playing field. The men too.

Grandpap Mason had been taken out of school in seventh grade to work the cotton mills, but survived, fingers intact[32]. He was unsure what to do with his young adulthood (he told me many years later) and was going to join the Army to fight

---

[32] Loss of children's fingers was the commonest injury in the cotton mills. It usually occurred near the end of the 12 hour work day when the kids were so fatigued they could not pay attention. Noise induced deafness was the other longer-term affliction. The cotton mill machinery was so noisy that the women communicated with lipreading.

in the Boer war – or something – anything. As it was not far to the Liverpool docks, he wandered there, on an impulse signed onto a freighter, then shoveled coal across the Atlantic to America. And after exploring New York, shortly came back to Oldham.

At that point, the story gets muddied by the mists of time and the family's psychological need to clean up our history, but he again left England, this time, it was said, in somewhat of a hurry, pursued either by (story A) the police, or (story B) enraged brothers of an impregnated young lady. Take your pick. I would never judge him; I had made more than my own life mistakes along the way.

Back to the docks with great dispatch, find the first freighter, and shovel coal across the Atlantic one more time.

Now an interesting turn: seven years later, having worked in the coal mines of Western Pennsylvania in the meanwhile, he shovels his way across the Atlantic – now back to England, quickly marries a young lady, quickly adopts a little illegitimate girl, age 7, a daughter of a woman in the same family, (the daughter eventually becoming my mother). And also quickly books passage across the Atlantic to return to America. Let's see, chased out of the country, returns seven years later, picks up a pretty little seven-year-old girl . . . Probably all just coincidence, right?

No matter; who am I to judge? Who doesn't have secrets in his life?

My grandfather works the next 35 years as a millwright in the Christie Park works, United States Steel Corporation. In that mill, he is not quite so lucky with his fingers, and ends up with some severe damage. Loss of fingers and hands in those days was not uncommon (Uncle Ernie, for example, had lost the thumb of his dominant hand. They, and the other steel-workers, take the accidents in stride; I never hear any bitter-ness expressed.)

But he too, like Grandpap Kerber, can do anything around the house, and in all the years of my childhood I never see a plumber, carpenter, electrician, or any of the building trades in our homes. Raise chickens, reroof the house, prune the fruit trees, grow tomatoes – we do it all, all by ourselves. And this is what men in my family do.

By now you may think Grandpap Mason is a giant – in every possible way.

Grandpap Mason is a quiet man, short in stature (something I didn't recognize until a growth spurt during my teen years), light complected, blonde, almost white hair on arms and chest, in later years balding into male pattern baldness, com-

pactly muscular, sure of himself, and uncommonly handsome. He smells of freshly soaped skin. When meeting him, you will likely first notice his eyes. They are as blue as the color of tempered steel. In old photographs, he looks directly at the camera, his broad face open to the world, crinkles at the corners of his eyes, those eyes and his slight smile implying he knows something we do not (as he usually did). And that image is how I remember him best. He is as comfortable in his fine black suit, starched white shirt, silk tie with diamond stick pin, polished hightop black calf shoes as he is in blue shirt, dark millwright overalls and mill boots. Around his yard, he walks with a quiet assurance, with a kind of grace, in complete command of his surroundings. There were times during my childhood when I distinctly remember a kind of halo around him. Then again, kids have wild imaginations, don't they?

Even now when I come to think of it, he was a giant, certainly a man in full – all throughout my childhood.

A story as good as it gets: At one of our many parties, my dad and his friends begin boasting of their own strength, as men are wont to do after a highball or two, then each in turn drops down to the living room floor to see who can do the most push-ups. My grandfather, about 65 at the time, says nothing, continuing to read his paper. When they have finished, are congratulating each other, and are about to leave, he says nothing, gets up from the chair, carefully folds his paper, drops down, does 10 more push-ups than the winner, and then rolls to his weak side, puts his right arm behind his back, and does three more one-arm push-ups, and then rolls to the other side, and does six. With one arm. He says nothing, gets up, and continues to read his paper. The men look at each other. No words are spoken. They leave, deflated. What an awesome statement. Men in groups, more completely and carefully said, the *behavior* of men in groups, is certainly inter-esting, isn't it?

Though I give him more than adequate reason on so many occasions to punish me, he never spanks me, never strikes me. His words are always enough, for I will do anything to win his approval.

Since we go to live with my grandparents when I'm a baby, and stay in their home until I'm about five, I am with him con-stantly during my early years, except for the times he is at the mill working or I am at school. More than anything, this little boy wants to be just like his grandfather. This is a man who has taught himself everything – about how the world works, about how to be self-sufficient, to be in control, to manage money well. He has what we would call today street smarts. One more time we get to question the Freudians about whether boy to mother is the primary relationship.

I have described how he taught me to read before I went to school. More than the simple learning of that skill, he impressed upon me the *why* of reading. "What does it really say?" he would always ask when I had finished reading one thing or another. Did I understand?

And then, almost in the same breath: "Come on boy, there's work to do." He always called me *boy* – like Johnny Weissmuller called the boy in the Tarzan movies. Or *Laddie*. And soon I would be sawing, or painting, even cutting threads on a replacement water pipe. And with his guidance, and maybe a few false starts, things usually worked out pretty well, and the job got done. For a 10 or 11-year-old boy to take a piece of galvanized pipe, measure it to length, cut threads on each end with a die, and then insert and seal that pipe into our water system, turning it carefully – just tight enough – with Grandpap's pipe wrenches (which I still proudly own), then having water flow to the kitchen tap is an accomplishment, an accomplishment big enough to develop pride in anyone – especially in a little boy. About the only thing Grandpap didn't know cold was electrical theory – so Dad took care of most wiring problems.

It was Grandpap Mason who controlled my 22 caliber rifle. He kept it in his bedroom, behind the door. I would first ask permission, have it be granted, then he would tell me to take two rounds, and I could walk in the woods to my heart's content, rifle strap over my shoulder, the rifle's weight confirming my responsibility. On return, the rifle was wiped down and oiled. I was responsible for its good care, completely and absolutely.

So it becomes obvious that Grandpap Mason and I shared, and shared, and shared. We shared time together – more when I was really little, sitting on his lap in a warm and steamy kitchen, dipping toast into the yolks of his fried eggs, sipping his sweet English tea. As I got older, we walked together in the woods, usually saying little, comfortable in our own long silences. We worked together, and during that work, I discovered his philosophies. Later, when I was in school, I shared my experiences, what I had learned from them – and even sometimes told him my fears. And during these later years, despite his firmness, I learned he was flexible, adaptable. Example: throughout his life, Grandpap Mason had not liked doctors. Didn't trust them. Said so repeatedly throughout my boyhood. Then a day came when I told him I was going to medical school. Suddenly, everything changed. "Good for you, boy." A different world had opened up for him at that moment. He changed his mind. Just like that. Another good lesson.

During baseball season, it was his habit to sit in the kitchen, smoking his pipe, right ear next to the small RCA radio, listening to the Pittsburgh Pirates play. And usually to lose. By the seventh inning, he would shake his head in disgust, and turn the radio off. "Wait, it's not over. They could still win," I said. "Bunch of bums," he would say. By the time I was an adolescent, and an insufferable know it all, I goaded him, "If the Pirates are so bad why have you kept listening all these years?" He gave me a long dark look that said *I hope you grow through this phase quickly.* I did not, sad to say.

He retired from the mill, but never stopped working. Every single day he got up early, as also was his habit, worked to keep his house, trees and garden in order, and enjoyed himself and his quiet independence. He would walk up toward the woods, past the chicken coop, look over his fruit trees, his garden, his paid-for house, his grandkids playing in the yard, and recognize (I could tell by the look on his face) *this is good, I am a successful man.*

When I came home from time to time during my medical school years, I looked at his pipe habit with dread; I knew what was sucked into a person's body through that pipe stem. My fear would be ultimately fulfilled in awful fashion.

But that lethal malignancy was in the future.

How can any boy be so lucky as I was? Throughout those years of my childhood, his willingness and ability to teach – not only his many mechanical techniques, but to expose me to his vision of the world, to his philosophies, his ways of thought and action learned through hard experience, showing sometimes with words but more often by example the importance of character and the absoluteness of a man's word. And those life rules made it possible for me to get through school, and to begin to educate myself, a process and a goal I'm still working on, one I'm certain I will one day achieve. I know he would approve of that goal, and that I'm even today going about it.

I smile when I think about him now and how he would appear, as though by magic, outside the school yard gates. How did he know that I couldn't stand another moment in there and was about to commit nunicide? How did he know when to come to save me? How did he know? How did he know so much – about everything?

Some answers are not knowable. But I'm sure glad he did. Know, that is.

12. OUTSIDE THOSE STEEL GATES

But now back to St. Peter's: Beyond the confines of that black steel gated schoolyard lay a whole new world to explore, a world beyond my experience, so far beyond my little boy's imagining.

So, when *they* allowed us out, I began to explore. And as I explored, I found that walking in each and every direction away from that schoolyard showed the depths of our poverty. The homes were little better than slums. It was only if I were to walk more than a mile up to the top of the hill overlooking the McKeesport valley would I come to the upper middle class and even better neighborhoods.

Walk straight out from the school, cross the street, and we come to Paul Klasnic's neighborhood – the ghetto where the German/Irish side of our family had settled before the turn of the century.

I asked Paul about that part of town. "Don't go there. You don't belong. The big kids will kill you," he warned. Nonetheless I walked, but with tentative and careful steps toward the Youghiogheny River through that promised valley of death. A small smile at the kids playing in alleys showed I was no threat, and I made it all the way down to the river. Standing on the river bank I suddenly realized that I stood where Johnny Appleseed[33] had rented land for one of his Apple tree nurseries.

Talk to Tom Kushner, who lived on the other side of the tracks directly behind the school, and he solemnly advised me that I

must never go there. "Bad people. Lots of drunks. They'll kill you." This is a view behind the school taken from the rear gate. Tom lived in

---

[33] John Chapman was a folk hero who became known as Johnny Appleseed. He traveled the river valleys, selected likely plots, planted his apple seeds (which he got free following cider pressings), nurtured his plantings, and then traded his trees to local settlers. Apples were staple crop for those early people in the Ohio, Allegheny and Monongahela Valleys, as apples were used to make the common intoxicating beverage – hard apple cider. Mister Chapman was in fact an astute businessman.

that house just across the tracks, the house barely shown on the right side of the picture.

When I explored that area, walking down those tracks all the way to Walnut Street and Shaw Avenue, I found, yes, poor, unpainted houses but also friendly Italians, men with magnificent mustaches, plump bosomy mothers, and the coolest Italian grocery.

Speaking of which: As part of his display, each morning Mr. Luigi brought out gold-colored rockhard salted fish as tall as me, placing them in a bushel basket on the sidewalk. He then set up his fresh greens and tomatoes in boxes – all in artistic assemblies. And inside his shop he had hung pleated garlic, dried spices, and peppers from the rafters. His store was small, triangular, and lay between a street and the railroad tracks. I was at first a little reluctant to enter – these were after all Italians, not my people, but the smells wafting out to the street from the family's living area in the back told of garlic cooking in olive oil and pungent marinara sauce. Could any combination of aromas be more exotic to a kid from an English household? I could not help myself – I was drawn into the depths of this strange and foreign store.

Mrs. Luigi welcomed me with a warm smile, a pat on the head, and words that were more sung than said. She never did help me figure out how anyone could make those fish edible though.

JoAnne O'Toole lived down in the First Ward – some 10 blocks of tenements at the junction of the Youghiogheny with the Monongahela River. Confluences of any sort seem to be attractions to little boys.

I asked her about her neighborhood. Could anyone actually get to the point of land where the two rivers came together, I asked? She looked troubled. With her head down, she said, "Rough people down there. You don't want to go there. Probably never get back." She shook her head and walked away from me. *So how did she get to school, if it was so awful*, I wondered. During my explorations, I was never able actually to get to the point of land where the two rivers met – there was some industrial place keeping me out, a junk yard as I remember. But I do remember that the big people in McKeesport's First Ward went about their business, heads down, thinking of things other than a little boy wandering on his own. The boys though were another matter. They stared at this outsider with long, suspicious looks, but made no move to attack.

I found myself somewhat reluctant to go to the left of the school however, because that's where the blacks lived. That area was then known as *the Negro section* of town. We had no black kids in our school, something I find curious to this day, but in retrospect, I believe that the nuns were even more prejudiced than most big people in that city.

I wandered into their community nonetheless, at first only with short quick explorations, each subsequent exploration penetrating the area more deeply. And even as a naïve little boy, I was appalled. The other parts of town in which our school was centered were certainly depressed and depressing

173

areas, but the black section of the city was simply awful. Blacks lived in falling down houses, shacks even, and later, after the war, in *The Projects*, brick high-rises that were soulless monstrosities, buildings soon defaced. I didn't get to know any black kids until high school, a story for later. But when I was in grade school, there was certainly no black militancy directed against me. I found only reluctance to engage – even in a shared smile with a little kid (one who certainly had no appearance of affluence) as he explored their neighborhood. Was it humanly possible to be any more naïve than I was?

Once a month my mother gave me money to buy tokens from a certain nun, a thin and wrinkled ascetic, the Keeper of the Tokens, a woman whom no one ever saw smile. Somebody in the parish had made a deal with the bus company to provide Catholic kids with cheap transportation to and from school. I think one token, which would take us into town, cost Mom about eight cents. Oh, but a full roll of tokens in my hand was a hot piece of steel in my pocket. And on a day when the urge hit me, after school was out, I would grab my sister Judy by the hand, help her onto the first bus that came by, and explore The Hill. The bus drivers, knowing that these tokens were used only to go to and from school, smiled indulgently, and never questioned a little kid dragging his sister along as we rode whichever bus came to the end of its line, then to return to our starting point. Mom never questioned us when we got home at dark, but she was certainly disturbed when she found that half the tokens were gone.

When you look at the crime statistics, you find that there were more kidnappings and murders of little kids then than today, so some risk was involved, but we knew enough to avoid the weirdos while talking to the interesting people. In retrospect, Judy and I had two quests. The first, to explore for exploration's own sake, and second, though we didn't recognize it at the time, to search out and talk to adults who would give us straight communications. The latter we found to be almost impossible. When I think about it, both quests, especially the second one, continue to this day.

For example, about that communication problem with adults: once every six weeks I would, 75 cents in hand, walk from the school to the Italian part of town, walk halfway up Walnut Street to the barbershop, passing Mister Luigi's wonderful grocery store and his stacked fish (still wondering how anyone could eat something that's almost solid salt), wave my greeting to him, and enter the barbershop. You could get any kind of haircut you wanted, as long as it was exactly the way the barber's union prescribed. One day I asked Mister Angelone why he stropped the razor before shaving my neck. He paused a few seconds. Nobody had ever asked him this. Then, looking me in the eye said, "Makes the razor hot, Chuck. Hot steel cuts better." I wrote him off my trust list immediately. Never asked him another question after that. Don't adults recognize that kids know when they're being fed a plate of BS?

He made me angry, because it took me a long time to learn what the strop actually does to the razor's edge.

An American Boyhood

My three city cousins lived on the Hill, and when the mood hit, I would bring Judy with me to go to visit them, tokens clinking into the bus's coin counter. Maryann, a lovely and petite strawberry blonde was about my age. Billy and Johnny were each younger, about 18 months apart. Those boys, though young and small, were fierce, and they absolutely controlled their neighborhood. While Aunt Agnes gave Judy cookies and milk, we boys patrolled the neighborhood. "That one's okay for hitting," Billy said, as we rounded a corner, "but don't touch his little brother". Theirs was a harsh code, but one always protecting the little kids.

I admired my cousins; I recognized their life of conflict on city streets as being so fundamentally different from mine in the country.

Their dad, Uncle Bill, saw to it that his kids went to a public school. He wanted them to have an education, he said pointedly and repeatedly to my dad, trying to convince Dad that Catholic school education was sadly inadequate. I wish Dad would've asked me my opinion.

But no matter how far I wandered, the ultimate and depressing fact of life sooner or later hit me: I had to go back inside the gates to that dark place, St. Peter's School.

Nonetheless, outside those gates, I had found a complicated, amazing, and most interesting world. It was a world that begged for further exploration.

13. THE SCHOOLYARD

When we were let out of our classrooms for short times at morning and afternoon recess, and for almost 45 minutes during lunch time, what became obvious even to the most casual observer was the universal boys' quest for dominance. Of course we played semi-cooperative games (but the dominant boys made and interpreted the rules). When we ran, running till we got that sharp pain in our right side, we looked to see *who has beat me*? When we secretly watched and admired the girls, the dominant boys pushed to the front. Did I mention that every boy's quest was for dominance? To determine his rank in the social structure of the playground? Every day.

And the question of rank was never quite absolutely settled. The review by peers was an ongoing phenomenon, and status depended upon a boy's willingness to give his all. Fail during some test of skill or courage, and the boy moved down the social hierarchy a few notches, toward the bottom of the heap.

Though more difficult and often painful, one could also move up. More on that below.

Not so with the girls. They played, well, together.

I marveled at the older girls' ability to jump rope. Two girls would face each other, about 8 feet apart, swinging two lengths of clothesline so the lines twirled in opposite directions – one clockwise, one counterclockwise, perfectly 180 degrees out of phase. A third girl would watch for an opening, time her move perfectly, then jump in, beginning to skip. A moment later, a fourth would join - two girls lightly up-and-down facing each other together in the swirl, now both in, then one backing out, taking turns. When my sisters were jumping, I could do nothing but watch the self confidence, the elegance, and the coordination of their moves.

Girls' play, you see, was almost always a cooperative play. (So unlike us boys.) The girls, my sisters especially, were magnificent. God, I was proud of them.

Boys' play absolutely, fiercely, was and will forever be competitive. Teachers, administrators, helicopter parents: get used to it.

There was no team sport where I lived in the country. The boys were too widely separated. The school introduced me to team sports, though I rarely bought fully into team effort. There were three exceptions.

First, and least important, was our modification of baseball. It was rare that some one of us would actually own a rubber ball, but if one appeared, we would crowd together. The two biggest kids decided a) that the game would be baseball, and b) were the opposing team leaders, and c) got to pick who was on each side. The picking of each team was a drawnout, carefully thought out process. And it was absolutely hierarchical. The fear we had was not getting picked it all. Tom Hickey and I were the youngest and littlest kids in the room. We almost always got to sit out the game. Still depressing to think about that.

There was no stick for a bat. Only the closed fist could hit the ball. (Of course it hurt. It was supposed to.) The bigger kids could hit the ball hard enough that it sailed over the high chain link fence onto the railroad tracks. A home run. No, we weren't allowed to leave the yard to retrieve the ball. Yes, we obviously and immediately disobeyed. Any dolt could hear the train coming. Anyhow, who would know? There was no supervision.

Second, touch football. Almost never did anyone have a real ball, so one of us kids would make one. First, wrap newspaper (from our lunches. No mother would waste money to buy bags) tightly into a cylinder a bit smaller than today's beer cans, tie it together with string, and finally dampen it to add weight. With that pseudo-football, the game would change. As in every competition since the beginning of the human race, the big kids dominated. If Tom Hickey and I were picked for a team at all, we were picked last. Being the smallest kids caused us a great deal of angst. Almost certainly scarring us for life.

But the third was the best, a game where bigness counted for little. What counted was stoic tenacity in the face of pain. Where the name came from, I do not know, but we called it *buckety buck*. One kid would stand with his back against the school's stone foundation. So no matter what force of boy or nature presented itself to his front, that kid wasn't going anywhere. Boy number 2 would bend over at the hip, back parallel to the ground, and hold on to number 1, his arms tightly around 1's hips, head to the side. Number 3 would do likewise behind 2, repeating for a many kids as were on a team, usually six or eight. The defending team would look like a caterpillar with the head pointing the wrong way – away from the wall, all backs parallel to the schoolyard. Then the opposing team would, one by one, sprint full speed across the school yard, then vault as far forward on the caterpillar as he could, belly flopping as hard as possible on to the defending kids' backs, hoping to crush the line, but if it held, then to hold on with all his might. The idea was to make the defenders line buckle - and if it did, they became defenders again. But if the caterpillar did not crumble - with those six or eight kids piled on top of the defenders - the sides could change. And if the piled up aggressors fell off, the common result, the defenders won, and sides changed. Boys' games are rigidly rule-specific though, so there is more to come: If the pile held, after about 4 seconds, the lead defender, the boy whose back was against the bricks would hold up some number of fingers on one hand and call, "Buckety buck, how many fingers up?" The opposing team leader, looking down at the bricks, would try to guess, and if he guessed correctly, his team got to be the aggressors again. We didn't know a lot about probability theory, did we?

I never saw anyone cheat - to try to look at the upraised fingers, or to try to topple the pile by deliberately swaying. Interesting, isn't it?

Buckety buck was the very essence of egalitarian boys play: vicious at times, pain producing often, team oriented, and rigidly rule limited.

I now read that recesses in most schools are no longer permitted. There is too much chance for injury, I hear. There's too much chance for competition. And we mustn't have anyone feeling that he is a loser, feeling anything other than that he is *special*. I read recently of a little boy bringing a blue ribbon to his dad. His dad innocently asked, "Congratulations. What did you win?" His son replied, "We all won." "How is that possible," the dad asked? The little boy simply held up the blue ribbon as proof. Think how that kid is going to be surprised when he tries to get into a good college. Or worse, get a job in the world.

The do-gooders continue to strive to change human nature. Perhaps they may. After all, recesses are all but gone, as is most playground equipment. Too much liability. And we have to keep things fair, don't we? Further, the absence of recess is supposed to cut down on bullying. Good luck there. The adults may as well try to keep little boys from sweating. But I wonder: After a morning in cooped in class, how does today's little boy let off steam?

An American Boyhood

You might observe that as a result, today little boys have become almost completely feminized. Wait: You don't think boys have been feminized? Google *decreased sperm motility*. Or check Christine Hoff Sommers book[34], or the writings of Camille Paglia[35].

Of course there were fights. What would you expect? Were we not boys? Competitive, short tempered boys, boys frustrated by sitting in those classrooms?

Fights in grade school rarely do real damage beyond a bloody nose. And unlike fights later on, for example in high school or on the street, after the kids have done fighting, they usually become close friends (another reason for parents and educators to butt out).

Why grade school fights start is difficult to determine, but in my experience, the fight has to do with no real problem, but rather some fundamental chemistry incompatibility between two boys. And the mutual dislike – even a flash of hatred – can develop and become manifest with surprising rapidity. A quick glance, a glare across the classroom, a prolonged eye contact, and you both know. Sooner or later there will be conflict. The fight usually starts out with some posturing -- ineffective pushing, almost certainly some name-calling and then a few wild swings that often miss the mark. Then the fight degenerates into wrestling on the ground. Skinned knuckles

---

[34] The War Against Boys: how misguided feminism is harming our young men.

[35] Are Men Obsolete? and other essays in the Wall Street Journal

(from abrasions on the bricks rather than the opponent's face), bruises, skinned elbows and knees, and copious blood make it all worthwhile. And then, again for unexplained reasons, the two usually become friends. One more time: adults should butt out. Always. But that is not today's way, is it?

Not counting the bullies, who rarely ever consummated their threats on us littler kids, there were plenty of fights in the schoolyard, none of us was ever psychically damaged, and we learned critically important life rules, especially the one that says *don't get into a fight unless you are willing to get your butt kicked. And be terminally embarrassed in front of the girls.* And the girls always seemed to be closely watching.

We were repeatedly and continually amazed at how exhausting an actual fight was. We were winded, gasping for air in less than a minute. Watching professional fighters, we could not understand how they fought through a three-minute round let alone 15 rounds. On the unusual occasion when a bigger kid actually was willing to fight a littler kid (we had an ethic, after all) it was not important who won, because size preordained the outcome, but that the smaller kid actually engaged. In fifth grade, Richie Corcoran refused to be threatened by our biggest bully, Eddie Sampson (an appropriate name for a tough guy. He even had long hair). Rather than backing down and walking away, Richie took him on, and actually landed a blow, ineffective as it was. When it was over, he was seriously bloodied. But no bully bothered him after that.

An American Boyhood

There was no greater status for the little kid than to have stood up to somebody bigger and older. Bloody, teary but unwilling to cry, sore – so what; it was all worth it. Do-gooder adults, butt out. That's the best advice – priceless advice – that I can give you.

But there was, almost always, more to the fight. No surprise, when it was over, there was nunly punishment. Usually, the flat side of the hair brush or a 16 inch ruler across each butt. Also no surprise, they didn't care who started the fight. (Counterintuitively, at least to the nuns, the same punishment to each boy bonded the fighters even closer together.) Later, there was always the parental response. Mother was expected to be compassionate, caring, and say stupid adult motherly words like, "You shouldn't fight, you know." A good dad would smile, never ask who won (he knew that wasn't important), and offer silent and nonverbal but powerful approval that his son had engaged.

In high school, as we became stronger and more like adults, the fights became no fun. Guys actually got hurt, and knives were a constant possibility. And it was not uncommon for a street smart adult to take on and really hurt an arrogant adolescent male who thought he was a man. It was a mistake not often made twice.

A schoolyard sidebar: Something I have observed about us, we who live and work in the middle part of this nation: our country appears to be run politically by elites – intellectuals, mostly on the coasts, those who believe in their hearts they are smarter than everybody else, especially smarter than us workers. Who are these intellectuals? Where did they come from?

Going back to grade school, and not to put too much of a simplistic spin on it, I have followed up what became of most of us kids. (And I'd ask you to do the same exercise with your own school group.) Though certainly not a statistical sampling, I found that the aggressive kids in the schoolyard, girls and boys but mostly boys, were the ones who later worked in the mill, started and ran businesses, went into the professions, and into the military. In other words, were productive. The teacher's pets, the ones who ran the school rooms, ran the student council, kids unable to compete outside in the schoolyard, became the intellectuals, the politicians, the professors. I expect a fair amount of resistance, even anger, from that observation, especially if you are one of the elites. And I freely admit – even stress – that I don't have a statistical sampling. But statistics aside, we don't always need mathematical rigor to discern trends or make judgments. Just an observation.

The English were fond of saying that their wars were won first on the playing fields of Eton (and their other private schools). They believed that lessons learned there, lessons taught in their sports, provided the ethic for their Officer Corps. Probably true, at least in part. Certainly we learned critical life rules on our playing field, our brick schoolyard at St. Peter's School.

14. GRANDMA MASON

Enough of those darknesses; now for some light.

There has not been a single day in my life – especially when I have time to reflect on my growing up years – that I have not thanked God for my grandmother. I will begin these musings by granting you that it is simply impossible to be human and not have feet of clay. And I'm certain she did – have feet of clay, that is. But this little boy never saw his grandmother's imperfections – nor did I admit to any even as we both aged. So be warned: God help anyone who criticizes her. (Okay, that's a bit more aggressive than I intended, but it's how I feel.)

Grandma was even smaller than what we would call a small woman today. I know she was less than five feet in height, and even as she aged, she never weighed more than 90 pounds, a consequence of scant protein in the lower class English diet when she was a girl. But she was more than big in other ways.

Grandma was a prim lady, a proper lady, a Victorian lady, but in essence and ultimately . . . a lady, always a lady. Even in her 90s, I never saw her walk with a stoop. She carried her-

self with an almost haughty pride, head always erect, unwilling to bow down before anyone. But there was a balance – no arrogance in her feeling of high self-worth. Though she would not kowtow to anyone, she did not feel that she was better either. In her world, one was judged solely by what one could do, and especially by one's ability to keep her word.

She was blessed with the light complexion common to people of the northern British Isles. "A peaches and cream complexion," my mother called Grandma's skin, referring to the highlight of blush on her cheeks, that blush just the color of the peach next to the stone.

So I remember her as standing always tall (not easy when you're less than five feet) whether she was alone ironing clothes or walking into church with others watching. "Don't slouch", she would whisper to us, my sisters and me, especially when anyone were about, and then show us how to walk by her example: head up, eye contact with others, shoulders back. Early photographs show a proper lady, large bosomed, narrow waisted. "Pap (the name she had for Grandpap) can circle my waist with his fingers." And indeed he could – put his hands around her waist, from behind, and his fingers would touch in the front, his thumbs behind. Of course the whalebone corset helped[36].

Coming into my life on a daily basis as she did when we moved in with her and Grandpap, she had even more of the wonderful grandparently influence adults hope that their own moms and dads bring to the family. The smells from a steamy winter kitchen, eggs frying in bacon grease (eggs with

---

[36] Whalebone corsets, tightly laced, were a constant part of the well-dressed Victorian or Edwardian lady's undergarments. If you wonder why fainting was such a common occurrence in the literature of the day, it was because these corsets significantly blocked venous return to the heart, and the poor girls passed out from lack of blood flow to the brain. Passed out with great regularity, as it turned out.

lacy brown edges, no less), butter melting on toast –could any little boy resist pushing through the back door to share? No words were ever needed. She would just smile, look into my eyes, and with a nod and turn of her head, indicate that I was to go sit on Grandpap's lap. "Help Grandpap with his breakfast," she would say. Help? You bet.

Though we moved to the white house I described in chapter 4, I continued to make the trek to her home. Winter Saturday mornings in that steamy warm kitchen were the best – a piece of pork pie (meat pies being an essential part of the Northwest England culture), strong sweet English tea whitened with canned milk, and the Buster Brown Shoe radio show tuned in on the kitchen radio ("Here's my dog Tag. He's in your shoe. Look for me in there too." And I would take my shoe off to look, and the picture of him and his dog smiled back at me.) Let the winter wind storms batter the countryside; her kitchen defined absolute kindness, absolute security, absolute contentedness.

As I got older, she taught me to play card games. I never got good at any of them – she always won (and in winning, showed me no mercy. "You lost. Play harder."). Still, I was willing to play just to learn about life from her. And like my grandfather, though she had scant formal education, she did have what we call today street smarts, handling the small amount of money Grandpap earned so that there was always enough for the basics – plus more for treats, for vacations, and, when needed, money to help my parents.

She taught us old English nursery rhymes from our earliest days. Only much later did I realize that most, if not all of those nursery rhymes carried a political, almost always satirical secret message, as open dissent in Elizabethan England was often punishable by death[37]. *Mary Mary quite contrary, how does your garden grow? With silver bells and cockle shells, and pretty girls all in a row.* And that was about Mary, Queen of Scots. Elizabeth, her competitor for the throne, would ultimately cut off Mary's head. And another: *Ring around the Rosie, pocket full of Posey. Ashes. Ashes. We all fall down.* And that was about the plague they called the Black Death, caused by the bacterium Pasteurella pestis. *Posey* was a bouquet of herbs carried to ward off the plague. *Ashes* – cremating bodies. *We all fall down* – we are going to die anyway. So the English danced, they looked death directly in its face- and laughed. My goodness. Nursery rhymes for children? Indeed.

A day came when she tried to explain English money to me. Pounds I could get. Crowns? Shillings? Farthings? Guineas? It wasn't base 10 money; it wasn't even base 12, as far as I could tell, and then when I heard a word like thripneybit[38], I simply gave up, my eyes glassed over, and she laughed. "American money is better, isn't it?" And she meant that on several levels.

The English can't cook. Bake, yes, but cook – a hopeless endeavor. Nonetheless, I watched her carefully in the kitchen.

---

[37] You might want to check out http://www.rhymes.org.uk/
[38] a copper coin worth three pennies. Actually a three-penny-bit

She certainly did not inspire me to want to prepare food (pork pies, veal pies, rhubarb pies, strawberry pies, apple pies – you get the picture), but as I watched, I saw something else. I saw the root of her prosperity, even the root of her life's philosophy: for example, when she cracked an egg, dumping the liquid contents into a bowl for baking, she would scrape out the rest of the protein still attached to each end of the shell with her index finger. When I questioned her whether that extra bit of egg white was worth the energy, she simply replied, "Waste not; want not." When she peeled an onion, no edible part – not a gram – of that onion went into the garbage. *Waste not; want not* has become an essential part of my sisters' lives and my life.

And this was why Grandma smoked Raleigh cigarettes (a lot of them too. My grandfather disapproved of her smoking, so she never did smoke in public as long as he was alive). She smoked Raleighs not because they were good (they were awful), but because you got a coupon on the back of the pack (four extras if you bought a carton!). Which, when you had accumulated enough, you could send in for a free gift – 229 possibilities, according to the ads[39]. "If you will to buy the cigarettes anyway, why not get something back?" Hard to disagree with that philosophy.

I came to realize in my late 20s, that that with the exception of

---

[39] You might like to see a sample of a 1950s Raleigh cigarette advertisement. *www.youtube.com/watch?v=BOuWGjW7RUM. "Look for the pack with a coupon on the back!"*

two additional lifemanship rules I learned in medical school (I'll try to get back to these later, if you grant me a bit more patience), I had been pretty much formed by these forces I have described by the time I was seven. Well maybe eight. I guess the Jesuits were correct after all. And those forces are summarized in Grandma's and Grandpap's rules.

Always be the gentleman. Not *a gentleman, the gentleman,* the exact same words as Grandpap's, over and over again. It was to be understood that "You might be the only one in the room full of ruffians. But you will be *the* gentleman." As a result, yes, I still open car doors for ladies, and I allow others to get ahead of me going through a doorway. I've never found this practice to be a weakness or lessening of masculinity. And, as I learned in the Marines, one must set standards, but those standards begin within one's own self. (I may not set anyone else's standard, and after all that's not the goal, but being the gentleman does shine a little light into transactions and relationships. Light and air helpful? You bet.)

Good fences make good neighbors. So much in so few words . . . This speaks to a respect for others' boundaries, mostly, actually especially, personal boundaries. Because there were no fences in Greenock. Grandma always listened to a neighbor's troubles. Always. But she never interfered. It was many years later that I recognized this *good fences* aphorism to be a line from a Robert Frost poem. Frost had spent some years in England, and I wondered if this was something he had learned from my grandmother. Nah . . . Probably not.

An American Boyhood

Always put a little by. In my grandfather's best year, 1945, the year of his retirement from the mill, he made about $2700. Translated into today's dollars, that's about 35,000 bucks. Not a great deal. Grandma always insisted on saving a little first before any money went out of the house. And so she was able to help, when times became difficult, my parents, my sisters and even me.

And more repetition: *Educate yourself.* Neither Grandma or Grandpap ever seemed to tire of giving this order. Notice the form: active voice, imperative mode. It was *we* who must seek the learning – kind of the opposite of "getting an education". She knew the value of education, having gained the little she had so painfully. Active voice, imperative mode. An order.

You are known by the company you keep. The form always surprised me as much as the content. She didn't say, for example, "you better not hang around with Wayne W. He's a thief and people will think you're a thief too." The responsibility was always ours to take action – one way or another. The ultimate responsibility was always placed upon our heads.

A penny saved is a penny earned. This one is about efficiency, and efficiency not just in money transactions, but in the human as well.

Don't be penny wise and pound foolish. It took me years to figure this one out. I should have paid more attention during the lecture on English money units. Again, this is about balance, and judgment too.

Neither a borrower nor a lender be. Honored more in the abstract than in the absolute – as she did lend my parents money when they were in need. But, come to think of it, never a penny to anyone outside the family.

Faint heart ne'er won fair maiden. Self-confidence. See below.

Don't be the richest man in the cemetery. One of her best. About bringing balance into one's life.

That thing don't eat hay. For my adolescent sisters, when they were keeping company with males whom my grandmother thought to be less than desirable. The obvious sexual analogy with the elephant's trunk seem to make my sisters angry for some reason. I have always wondered why.

My Dad was about as apolitical as anyone you will ever meet. Well, with a major exception: he was somewhat of a socialist, believing that Roosevelt, with his many governmental programs, had gotten us out of the Great Depression. ("The government will never let *that* happen again.") The reason I make this politics comment is that Dad believed in communal property. If he needed a certain bolt, some paint, or a tool, and Grandpap Mason had it, he would simply walk up the road, and take it. But with Dad that idea worked both ways. If someone – even a neighbor -- needed something of ours, and we had it, they were welcome to it. The house, after all, was not locked. Grandma, though, was not of this mindset. "Charlie's a thief," she would say with a certain grimness. *Well, I* thought, *that's a way to see Dad's behavior that had not occurred to me.* So my sisters and I came to recognize that the edges of her world were sharp and unmoving. Grandma's world was about integrity. And she combined that absoluteness of integrity with a long, long memory.

Though I ultimately came to admire (and use) grandma's aphorisms, when I was a little boy, they quite simply drove me crazy. They were, well, for one thing, unscientific. What was worse, what was profoundly frustrating, was that *she always seemed to be right.* How could any little kid stand that?

Upon entering the absolute and unredeemable jerk phase of my growth and development, well before I had developed the recognition of the value of her sayings, in my near infinite arrogance I determined that I was going to negate every one of her aphorisms with some countering logical, scientific, and irrefutable argument. (You may wonder why any kid could be so unbelievably unkind and stupid. But there you have it.) The first time I countered, she was simply silent. The second episode produced a frown – a deep wrinkling of her forehead, lowered brows, and tightly pursed lips. The third (one of my most brilliant repartees, I thought) brought an instant anger, and "Don't you be so contrary". She pronounced the word with her accent in four syllables – con ta rar ee. She turned quickly, and walked away from me. It came upon me suddenly and sadly: I had crossed a line.

How easy it is to hurt the feelings of someone so loving. With love comes vulnerability.

She forgave me. Showing another one of her strengths.

Then a day came when I realized that she was always right. What she called "her sayings" were founded in a broad life experience, a deep understanding of the human condition, plus a distillation of lessons learned throughout time. And that gave her her insight, which she had distilled into short, almost poetic aphorisms.

This day, this epiphany happened on a spring Saturday morning. I had come into her kitchen, completely brokenhearted. I had fallen desperately, passionately, and profoundly in love with a sweet young thing (I was 10, I think). It was no use; life was not worth living – because I felt I could not even approach this Beautiful Eminence. "I can't talk to her. She is so much above me," I said in the saddest, most pitiful voice I could muster. (How disgusting to enjoy such self-pity). Grandma came over to me, laid a flour covered hand (she was baking bread) on my cheek and said, "She is *above you? Above you? Nobody is above you.*" Then, head close, looking into my eyes, " *FAINT HEART NE'ER WON FAIR MAIDEN.*" (How can some people speak in capital letters?) Then she nodded her head toward the door. I was dismissed, told what to do – or my manhood would forever have been in doubt. What a lesson. Yep, Grandma was always right.

I hope that at least one time during my maturity I told her how right she had been all those years. But I continue to wonder – and fear I had not been adequate in my thanks.

Another insight: Almost every immigrant I spoke to – but especially the Italian men – talked of saving up enough money to go back one day to the "old country," to finish their last days there. But I never heard those words from my grandmother (or my grandfather, for that matter). She knew the grinding poverty and lack of hope she had left "in the old country" and she reveled in what she enjoyed here in America: her freedom, her ability to control her own life, her ability to rise above the class consciousness of Oldham. Here, no one was better than her (nor worse either, she continued to remind me). Here Grandma had power, and she knew it. She never went back to England. "Nothing back there. For anyone." Grandma wasn't one to waste anything (remember *waste not want not?*), especially words.

Now a final aphorism – possibly her favorite, one so superficially simple yet so profound: *an hour of sleep before midnight is worth two after.* It took me a long time to figure out it was not at all about sleep. Of course we kids wanted to stay up late (after all, that's what the big people did, and wanting to be adult . . .) But when we were allowed to or had the opportunity to stay up late, it was oh so difficult to get up early. Actually, almost impossible.

And then I decided to try an experiment. Went to bed early. Not much happened the first night or the next morning. Second night, the same. On the third night, went to bed early again – and then quite abruptly wakened before the dawn. The awakening actually surprised me. The world outside still colored itself in shades and dark hues of blue and purple. No lights on, my night vision still intact, I felt my way down the stairs, through a pitch black cellar, then wandered through the back yard, slippery, dewy cool grass between my toes, the hill behind the house only a darker silhouette cutting across a violet sky. Sitting on the cistern, not a breath of moist night air stirred my hair, and I waited, just allowing the presence of the moment to come into my head, all alone with my thoughts. And as time passed (who could tell how much time?), the sky became discernibly lighter. Then I heard the first rooster crow. And slowly, ever so slowly, colors returned to the world. Trees and leaves that were only dark violet shapes moments before took form and became breathtakingly orange, then sun fully up, their primary green. What a magical, wonderful time. What a magical, wonderful experience. So quiet. So perfect. *An hour's sleep before midnight.* Oh, yes.

From time to time I have wondered (and you might be a bit skeptical too) . . . Am I perhaps hearing more in Grandma's words than those words actually say?

Nah.

That process contained in the "an hours sleep before midnight . . ." aphorism has become ingrained into my daily reality . If

An American Boyhood

I am sleep deprived – usually from being on call – it might take me a few nights of catching up to waken spontaneously before the dawn. But when that morning comes, when I waken in the dark, I leave the confines of the house, the confining bedroom walls, and, moments later, let the cool night air clear the cobwebs from my mind.

As I have grown, learned, and been tempered by my experiences in surgery, I've come to recognize that she distilled her philosophy into two simple commands: First, be true to your word; and second, don't trespass. How can you improve upon that?

Thank you, Grandma. Thank you thank you thank you.

15. ELEVEN YEARS OLD

The present practice of American child raising, which is focused in my mind by anecdotes and experiences I hear from young parents, plus the reading of the current crop of child rearing books, makes me think, to remember, to relive, but especially to appreciate the childhood my sisters and I enjoyed growing up in Greenock. We think we were truly and finely blessed. But you may think differently[40].

Please allow me to muse about some profound differences.

The first story that comes to mind is what it took simply to get to school in the city.

World War II was just about to start. St. Peter's School was in McKeesport. To get there, I waited by the side of the road -- Greenock- Buena Vista Road (what were bus stops?) for the public bus, got on, paid the fare – eight or ten cents for us school kids, and got off in downtown McKeesport near the

---

[40] And we will revisit this observation, which is actually a question in some depth in the last chapter.

post office, then walked three or four blocks past businesses, slums, and across the busy Baltimore and Ohio railroad tracks, to that dirty, ugly, red brick building infested with nuns. But then surviving in that school with those Sisters of Mercy -- who were anything but -- was another story I have already told.

For the first four days of the first week, my mother accompanied me on that bus trip. For four days. Then I was on my own.

At the time I began my solo journeys to school I was four years, ten months old.

And then four years later, I assumed responsibility to take my sisters to school. Then collect them afterwards, and bring them home. Remembering back to those times, I have the distinct impression that my sisters neither needed nor particularly wanted my help. And nobody thought anything of that significant responsibility, least of all me.

Along the way, given the location of the school on the edge of the slums, I ran into, spoke with, and befriended derelicts, drunks, disturbed people of all sorts, plus the majority of adults who were good and hard-working people who lived literally on the wrong side of the tracks. Times were, as I said, grim. But more than the detritus of our culture, men and women who would've made my mom cringe had she known,

I remember most of all those kind adults, people who on occasion stepped forward to protect little boys and little girls from harm. Tell your kids not to talk to strangers? Ridiculous. They won't listen. Tell them not to *go away* with strangers, not to *get in some stranger's car*: reasonable, and they do listen. And yes, we knew the difference.

What remarkable independence.

In Greenock we had no streetlights, and given the continuing depression and later the beginnings of war, there were few cars on the Greenock-Buena Vista Road. When school was out during summer and other breaks, I could leave my home in the morning, then come home only when I was hungry -- or not.

When night fell, the country became truly dark, so we became comfortable wandering along the roads and in the woods at night. Our parents had no idea where we were. Our parents would likely be put in prison today for those permissions, for that *laissez-faire* attitude.

For the next story I was, at that point, 11 years old. I had money in my pocket from cutting neighbors' grass (fifty cents an hour - not bad), and from my grandmother's generosity. School was out. The money was, as Grandpap said, "burning a hole in my pocket"; and the languor of the late summer lay heavy on my head and shoulders. Could there be any more dangerous combination for any boy? So I went up to Pittsburgh — "the Burgh," the Big City.

I waited for the city bus in front of our house, climbed on, paid the money - I think fare was 2 silver dimes when one was not paying the school rate, then got off at the end of the line - Walnut Street, in McKeesport. I walked down the hill to the Balti-

more and Ohio train station (it was right in the middle of town), bought a ticket to Pittsburgh, the fare I think, about 77 cents in coach, and, ticket in hand, waited for the train. (No, the ticket teller thought nothing of a solo young boy's request.) A magnificent locomotive with driving wheels taller than my head enveloped me in steam exhaust as it pulled in. Well, yes, I was standing too close, but all boys did that. This picture is of one of the steam trains coming into downtown McKeesport.

I climbed the coach steps, and settled onto the scratchy horsehair covered seat. Minutes later, the engineer smoothly moved his train out of the center of town, so professionally I could not feel us start to move – the diner across the tracks actually seemed to start moving backwards.

The tracks twisted north, following the contours of the Monongahela River, passing steel mill after steel mill, all the while a little boy's nose pressed to the grimy window. We finally backed into the terminal on Grant Street, I got out, completely ignored by the hurrying people who had business to conduct, then simply wandered around.

I should explain that the big city was old hat to me -- my Grandfather Mason had brought me three times up to Pittsburgh by this very path when I was a little boy. We came each Christmas to wander the streets, watching the puppet shows that Kaufmann's and the lesser department stores put on in their display windows, then finally chilled, to sip a steamy hot chocolate in one of the coffee shops. When he had taken me to Pittsburgh, I was little; now, at 11, I was big.

I explored the downtown area, finding a wonderful and huge Farmer's market in the center of this big city. Best yet, the food tastes of our nationalities were well represented – I found salt dried cod stacked in a bushel basket, barrels of brined olives, hanging sugar cured hams and legs of lamb, pirogies, halopkies, fifty different cheeses, deviled eggs, and pies beyond my imagination. And flowers. The aromas of the flowers, mixing with the penetrating smells of the fresh cut and cured meats, the cooking cabbage, made the juices run, so I bought a hot dog there for lunch (twenty cents), and drank water from one of the fountains.

I wanted to see *The Point* – the spit of land where the two rivers, the Allegheny and Monongahela joined to form the mighty Ohio, but was completely unsuccessful. That whole area was depressingly industrial - mostly covered with fenced junkyards. Even at age eleven I wondered when somebody would clean up the area. (I'm happy to say that finally the cultural and historical significance of this original site of Fort Duquesne was recognized, and is today reclaimed as a park.)

At about three o'clock, the streetlights came on. Streetlights in the afternoon? Yes, the air was that filthy in the 1940s.

With more wandering, I finally figured out Pittsburgh's triangular street pattern and how to get from one part of the downtown area to another. The Wood Street pawnshops were especially fascinating. There, none of the men behind the counters seemed to mind a boy wandering around inside their pawn shop. As I remember it, the adults were kind, smiling, indulgent - even encouraging. But they wouldn't let me handle the guns. Darn adults.

When it started to get really dark, I made my way back to the train station, got the train back to McKeesport, and then caught the last bus at 10:40 on my final leg toward home. I walked into the (unlocked) back door well after 11:30, brushed my teeth, and went to bed. My father had gone to work; my mother and sisters were in bed, and I was careful not to disturb their sleep.

It never occurred to me to ask permission - or to tell anybody about the trip. Until now that is. And when I think back on it - when I think of that adventure - it brings a smile.

There were other adventures of course. Many involved my walking through the woods with my rifle. Alone. Looking at the contour map I have today, I would estimate that I had about 6 square miles to wander through, woods I came to know as well as my own back yard.

But, now I wonder . . .

As I wonder about my boyhood – I have always wondered – and worried whether I had been able to balance freedom and responsibility with appropriate protection as I was raising my own children.

My daughter Carolyn recently told me that when she was 16, to find peace and solitude, she would drive to La Jolla Shores beach just north of San Diego, walk into the surf alone, swim toward Hawaii as far she could, until she could swim no more, then rest on her back, floating gently in the swells. She said her confidence in this power to create aloneness and solitude - this ability to conquer ocean, time and tide - had changed her life. Telling the story, she remembered her adventures with a smile. I thought I saw even a touch of smug satisfaction. I thought of the dangers. She had not asked my permission any more than I had of my parents. What I felt when I heard her story was a great pride and an even more profound respect. I say that now. But had I known then . . .

I would really like to extract some great principle from these adventures and these freedoms my sisters and I (and now I know my daughters) enjoyed. I should do this exercise to help the terrified parents of today's children. Could it be more dangerous today than it was back then? Nah. The FBI's crime statistics just don't support that premise, and in fact child abduction – all parents' primal fear – has been significantly decreasing over the last 15 years.

If there is one word that sums up my sisters and my wonderful childhoods, it is *freedom*. Well, actually there must be a second word. We also felt *responsibility*, a responsibility to pay for our own actions and occasional stupidities. With pain and with blood. Do something really stupid, and my grandmother would smile, look at me and say, "You made your own bed, now lie in it." Only then would the bandages and a loving smile come to take away the hurt and dry the tears.

Maybe this essay should be called not ELEVEN, but FREE-DOM AND RESPONSIBILITY. Or FREEDOM WITH RE-SPONSIBILITY. Or something else. You get to decide.

16. THE FARM

Hardscrabble. It's not a word you hear much anymore. But that word better describes the family farm than any other.

Hardscrabble is an old Appalacian term. It speaks of long hours in relentless sun scratching out a living from reluctant, worn out soil. It speaks of dark, bitter cold winter mornings washing cow udders before milking, of thunderstorms knocking wheat stalks down just before harvest. It speaks of hard work, of uncertainty, of scant financial reward for that work.

This farm caused me some confusion – not so much about the idea of growing crops. That uncertainty I got. But that the farm was said to be a family enterprise.

It was clearly not. Uncle Eddie, being the oldest brother, had in his head this idea called primogeniture; that everybody in the family should work to make his venture, his farm, a success. Especially so his kids, but also his brothers and sister.

For many years, I had no idea of the conflicts this feeling of entitlement caused. I was just a boy wanting to play with my cousins, and the price paid was chores done before play was allowed.

*   *   *   *   *

More on that hardscrabble descriptor: One summer day two men, serious men, humorless men, men dressed in dark rumpled cheap suits and dark ties showed up at the farmhouse – said they were from the Pennsylvania Department of Agriculture. *Why had they come*, I wondered? No one bothered to answer me. "Here to sample the soil," they said to Dad and Uncle Eddie. I must give them credit for being thorough – they took small jars of dirt from most every part of the 240 acres, from every field, even the woods, and, when the report came back, they had pronounced our land *severely depleted*. So we had to work hard – and work smart – to get that land to produce. Hardscrabble: from the dictionary, land that is barely arable.

So hard work was what we kids had come to expect – what we had been taught as the price of food on the table. And the men in our lives, dads and uncles, taught by example, with their own hard work. Hardscrabble, you bet we were. And proud of it.

On the other hand, if you will permit me to be a bit critical, I was never sure our family had the smart part figured out. Cousin Annie said one day, "Any Kerber can work the next two people into the ground." True, but not necessarily desirable under all circumstances. And, as she said those words her wry smile made them a family curse.

Two remembrances poke to the surface through my memories, the first when I was really small, about five, standing amid the ruins of a shed that had fallen down. All my cousins, Dad, and Uncle Eddie were prying boards apart, trying to salvage lumber – all during bitter biting winter wind and crossways sleet. *I hate this. Hate it.* And shivering, I could not stop myself, and finally, so cold I could not stand it, I began to cry, embarrassing myself in front of my dad. *Why is Dad doing this to me*, I wondered?

And the next, when I was older, another bitter winter during my 11th year, tugging bales of hay and ensilage to the cows, air so far below zero I felt I was drawing fire into my lungs, it came to me *there has got to be an easier way to make a living.*

Nonetheless I went to the farm with Dad as often as I could. Playing with my cousins was worth the price of the drudgery. How close we all became.

And danger? Of course we knew the farm could be dangerous. Did we not all have cuts and bruises the majority of the time? Did we not push ourselves to the edge of barely tolerable fear jumping off high beams into hay piles? Of course. But we never could conceive that our farm would be actually lethal. It ultimately came to be so, but those stories come later.

I was always puzzled by the organizational procedures of the farm. There just didn't seem to be any, organization that is, and each day's jobs were given out, seemingly haphazardly, at breakfast.

Yet during harvest times, on a given morning, I was surprised to see a dozen hard men gathering at the barn before dawn with their wives, smoking cigarettes, quietly talking among themselves, waiting for the sunrise. (Uncle Eddie never included us kids in his plans, an omission we found disconcerting, frustrating, often even anger producing. We wanted to know everything. How would we know how to run the farm one day when he was gone, I wondered to my cousin Eddie? His dad's indifference to us, worse, his sneering condescension was yet another adult disregard of kids wanting to learn, to grow.)

With the dawn, harvesting oats and wheat was to begin. A threshing machine had come the prior evening (from where I wondered), and, once hooked up to the rusty red Farmall F 30 tractor, the tractor pulled it slowly through the fields, cutting great wide swaths through the golden grain shafts, arranging those shafts on to a conveyor, the machine tying the shafts into bundles, then dropping those bundles on the ground. The men followed, stacking seven or eight bundles together into what was called *a shock*. By 11 o'clock, everyone was exhausted, and ice cold buttermilk was passed around. As the men worked through the morning, the women had been just as busy, and had created a massive dinner feast. Under the shade of a walnut tree they had built long tables of boards placed on sawhorses, covered them with cloths, and presented a magnificent meal to the men walking in from the fields. The women had roasted three kinds of meats, prepared a half-dozen vegetable dishes (but no bother with salads), mounds of potatoes, had baked huge loaves of fresh bread, thick cut, to be spread with jars of homemade jams and butter. And at the end of the table, so invitingly, lay more pies than a little boy could count.

After the dinner, the men rested in the shade, smoking, talking little, then, an hour later continued their work until sundown. At day's end Uncle Eddie wrote checks in his careful script, and everyone went home to sleep and recover for the next days' labors.

And then on another day, maybe a week later, when the shocks of grain had dried, these same men piled the shocks on to wagons, and brought them to the barn where another machine had appeared. The men fed the shocks into the maw of this huge machine. The thresher was deafeningly loud, and its operation shook the entire barn, as giant arms moved up and down, pulleys spun at its side, the grain was shaken from the shafts and dropped into a hopper to be bagged in burlap, while the straw blew out the back, there to be moved aside for later baling. Fine dust from the straw clouded vision and clogged lungs. The whole operation was a safety nightmare – exposed gears, pulleys, belts, and moving arms just waiting to trap and mangle a little boy. Of course we were fascinated.

We decided to look down into the innards of the machine, my cousin Paul and I, so we climbed up on to a support beam, a vantage point which gave us a good view down into the maw of the massive machine. Seeing us, Uncle Eddie, yelled above the roar the machine that we should get out of there and do so quickly, threatening us with serious physical harm. The possibility of falling in simply had not entered our minds. But I clearly remember the event, as it was an example – no, more, it was characteristic of yet another adult giving an order to us kids without an explanation of the underlying principle behind the order. Rather than developing understanding, what Paul and I felt was embarrassment and anger.

I wonder why we had not been given even rudimentary instruction in what was safe and what was not. I still wonder. And feel some bitterness to this day.

Better than it grew wheat and oats and corn, the farm grew pests. The pests – rats, mice, caterpillars, mildews and blights were ever present, and usually seemed to be winning the slow race toward a productive harvest.

Which brings us to the bagworm story. One year bagworms came to grow in the walnut trees.

Bagworms look like small caterpillars. They knit a tight skein of white fibers about themselves which, when first seen, look kind of pretty. But underneath that protective whiteness, an effective barrier keeping the birds from eating them, they set about reproducing, enlarging their castle each day as their brood expands, while in the process, they completely eat the tree. Stand close, and you can actually hear them munching away. Their low pitch rumbling growl is a soul-disturbing sound.

Eddie, Tom, Paul and I took umbrage. Those were *our* trees, *our* walnuts. We would do something.

We asked my dad what could destroy them. He told us killing them was almost impossible. The usual sprays were not effective. (We even had DDT then.) "They knit that bag to protect themselves. Keeps the poison off the young ones," he explained.

But were we not enterprising, thoughtful, inventive boys? We figured out a way. Cutting down a few infested branches, we piled them together near the gasoline storage tank. Okay, you now know what's coming.

Paul, sitting on the tank, pumped about half a pint of gasoline on the pile, and Eddie lit it off. How disappointing. The bags slowly smoldered away, burning poorly. We looked at each other. The solution became obvious.

Who has not held their finger over the end of a running garden hose to make it spray water? Speaking for myself, I could make water spray eight or 10 feet. Naturally the same technique would work with gasoline. I indicated to Paul, still sitting on top of the tank, to pump vigorously. And being an uncommonly strong kid, he pumped with all his might. As I held my thumb over the end of the nozzle, pointing it toward the smoldering bagworms . . .

WOOOOOM. A yellow-white flash. I was instantly ablaze. I dropped the hose, fully certain the fire would travel backwards to the pump and kill my three cousins – Eddie and Tom had hidden behind the tank. I actually thought this as I ran away, down the hill, rolling through mud, tearing off my clothes the best I could.

Then, as quickly as it had started, it was over. Other than a lack of eyebrows and eyelashes, I didn't even get a first-degree burn. Well, maybe a few pink spots on cheeks and arms.

The four of us came together, shaking a bit. We were just a touch fearful about what would happen next, but as I reassembled and put my muddy clothes back on we huddled, deciding among us that it might be best not to tell our dads about the experience.

Bag worms – 1; farm kids – 0. And so the score stayed forever more. We would never spray gasoline again; turns out we were trainable after all.

On the way home, Dad inquired offhandedly about the mud

and the lack of eyebrows. I just shrugged my shoulders. He arched an eye, tilted his head a bit, turned back to watching the road, but said nothing more. Good Dad. Mom on the other hand . . .

Farms are exceptionally filthy places. Manure, a polite term, is everywhere. Thus infections are common.

One summer an abscess began to develop at the base of my thumb. I was not surprised, and interested in the process, watched it grow and mature over course of three days. The abscess itself was truly fascinating – a wild, wicked looking infection that seem to have a life its own, an abscess that drained yellow-green foul-smelling pus from a tiny hole in its center. When it began to hurt seriously enough to interfere with our play, I asked my dad about it. He looked. He touched. He mumbled his, "I'll be go to hell", then took me into the basement, filled the wash basin with almost scalding hot water, and into the water poured half a bottle of the mercuric chloride[41]. "Soak your hand in here for a while. I'll come back later." So I did, and began massaging my thumb a bit. Eventually, with enough squeezing, out through the pus came a small black piece of something that looked for all the world like a shriveled insect. *To treat any abscess, you have to get the core out*, I had been told, and that I had just done. So I knew I would get better. I dried my hand off – it was now

---

[41] We used this to treat infections in the cows. Of course Mercury is toxic. Exceedingly so. What did we know back then?

stained red from the mercury, and went back to play.

Thinking back, I knew mercury worked on cows, which were huge. So of course I knew it would work on somebody as small as me.

I expect you might not like this story or approve of Dad's treatment (especially if you are a *helicopter parent*). The story might appear to show a parental indifference to providing a son quality medical care. Perhaps even to show a careless disregard about the son's health. I disagree. Living on a farm gives you a strong immune system because of the repeated (essentially daily) infectious challenges. If you were to Google *asthma in city children*, you will find that city kids have less robust immune systems, and you would find that a recent medical therapy introduces parasites into these kids to help them increase the vigor of their immune system to help combat their asthma. Yes, worms. Anyhow, having a robust immune system certainly did benefit me years later when I found myself a patient in a military hospital. But that's an interesting tale for another time.

This next farm story is a bit dicey to relate. I've given a great deal of thought even to whether it should be put it down on paper, because it excites so many intense and complex emotions, not in farm kids, of course, but in feminists. The story has to do with sex. Not human sex, but animal sex. And I am just a little concerned that you might want to draw human parallels. Actually, you might want to skip this part.

An American Boyhood

An American Boyhood

Since you have decided to read on, may I give you a little background. My cousins and I could only rarely tell when a female animal was in heat – that is, when she was receptive to sexual intercourse. And then only when we came upon them during the actual act. Second, the entire reproductive cycle was not a mystery on any farm. Third, and this may surprise you, though we talked *ad nauseam* about human sexuality, we did not connect what we saw the animals doing with what we suspected our parents were doing. At least till later when we were much older. How dumb we were.

But now on to the cow. Uncle Eddie one morning said simply, "Take the cow to the bull". So my cousin and I did as we were told. It was not an easy task. The cow was, well, irritable. And generally out of sorts. She was uncooperative, balky, unwilling to be led. One might use the term *bitchy*, but the connotations and male usage of that word might strike too close to the human experience and cause certain readers distress.

Back to the bull. We knew the bull well. The bull was scary. Awesomely so.

How scary? I have to interrupt with a little aside: We had been repeatedly warned to keep out of the bull's pasture. "NEVER go in that pasture," Aunt Alvina had threatened. Which we did, just to aggravate him a bit, which aggravation guaranteed a charge. No sweat, we scampered back under the barbed wire, each charge producing a self-satisfied and nervous giggle; each charge ratifying our personal courage; each success making us foray a little farther into the pasture. Sorry for the digression; I couldn't help it. And remember, as excuse for this digression, there was no TV yet. We provided our own entertainment.

So we took the cow to the bull, reluctant as she was. I opened the gate, Eddie's stick prodded her in to the pasture, then we closed the gate as quickly as we could. The bull lifted his head. He walked slowly toward her. Walked around her. She peed a little. He slowly mounted. Eddie and I looked at each other. *How could he find where to put that huge thing*, we wondered. *Certainly he could not see down between his legs*. Then there was the act itself – it was violent beyond belief. I thought the bull was going to kill her. But she made no attempt to run away, and to my great surprise, she lived through the encounter. The bull finished, then completely disinterested in her, wandered away to the far end of the pasture. (Please do not attempt to draw human parallels).

Now the dangerous (to me) observation. As she ambled back to the gate, I noticed the change – the striking change in her personality, in her behavior. She walked back quietly, even serenely, to her own pasture, semen sloshing out of her vagina, running down her leg. This was a contented cow. Wow. What a change. Draw your own conclusions please.

I thought of this indelibly imprinted experience many years

later in medical school when we were studying human sexuality. After some introspection, a trait rare in me when I was a medical student, I decided not to bring up my observations of the event and the obvious changes in the cow's mental status. Good for me, because it turns out that the psychiatrists kept files on each of us med students, and I was truly afraid of what they might have thought of me and my analysis. I dread to think what would've happened had I opened my mouth. In fact, I'm a bit nervous about this story now.

Then again, I wonder if the Professors of Women's Studies might not benefit from a summer living and working on a farm. Just a thought.

And another farm story: A few years ago, I suffered through a dinner where conversation was, up to a point, manipulated by a child - woman who rhapsodized about her summers on a farm in Sweden. She told us of "waking up to the trilling of the birds, and the smells of cooking pancakes". Then she walked through wildflower covered meadows, felt the warm summer breeze in her hair, and drank fresh, chilled milk when she wished. Then finally, when day was done, was tucked in to bed, down comforter tucked up to her cute little chin. I think the soft lowing of the cows and the echoes of yodelers were interspersed throughout her story. Finally, a point came that I could stand no more BS. I observed that my primary memories of the farm were of repetitive drudgery, battling insects and weeds, the vicissitudes of what I often perceived as malevolent nature, the need to shovel tons of cow manure, and above all, the frequent killing – yes the pests, but also the butchering of animals for food. There was a dead silence. I kind of ruined the dinner, in retrospect. The host, a city boy throughout his life, was horrified. And my disruptive words almost started a fistfight, as I had interrupted what turned out to be his wife's often-played game. It seems her husband took offense. As people often do when the games they play are brought to a sudden halt.

I wish farms were sweetness and light, that there was never a worry about a sudden rainstorm beating down the wheat, nor discovering that infestations of corn worms had suddenly appeared, and I wished the so-expensive cows never developed an undiagnosable disease. In some ways, I wish I had had that woman's idealized experiences. But working farms are, in my experience, primarily about work.

Fortunately, I didn't bear the brunt of daily farm drudgery, and only worked when my dad took me there. My nine cousins who lived on the farm full-time did. When we played together, it was only after the work was done. And Uncle Eddie allowed us to play only grudgingly. We were confused at the time, my other city cousins and I, about why uncle Eddie had so many children – nine was unusual even in Catholic families during those years. Mom explained (her disgust of him obvious on her face) that he was deliberately breeding free workers for his farm. "He intends to get rich on the back of his kids", Mom said. *Would any father ever deliberately do something that awful*, I wondered? It was hard to believe, but facts were facts. My ever-recurring remembrance of him is the image of him driving down the lane to go buy feed or some other such errand (no physical labor in that) while we kids worked the fields and fed the animals.

And I should talk more about those so-called dumb cows: We didn't own those cows – they owned us. We ran to their schedule – they were fed twice a day, milked twice a day no matter the season, whatever the weather, even during illness or death in the family.

You now know some of the reasons that Americans are leaving the farms in droves, and relocating to the cities. I have read that before our Civil War, it took 22 people on the farm to produce enough food for 23. Now one person can produce food for seven, at least in America. It is critically important to know that everything beyond food production can develop in any culture only after that culture produces an agricultural excess. Without extra food, there can be no artist, no art. To divine the weather and so know when to begin to plow and plant, to nurture the seedlings, to harvest the wheat and corn, to feed the animals, then butcher them for meat, and then to sell the excess, that is the foundation of all cultures. It would be a critical lesson for any city boy or girl to learn.

I certainly have mixed feelings about that farm. The lessons learned there were priceless, but oh so hard.

One lesson taught over and over again was that the harvest bounty must be wrestled from the land with unending work – plus some significant luck. And I learned that some adults, even blood relatives, can be cruel, and maybe even enjoyed hurting others, especially us kids. I learned that danger lay in every corner of that farm, whether it was the possibility of tumbling into the pigsty, falling off a high ladder, or getting oneself caught in the exposed machinery. So about that lethality I mentioned at the beginning of this essay: both my cousin Eddie and his dad died on that farm. On the other hand, I developed lifelong friendships with my cousins, boys and girls alike, friendships bound in shared blood and shared work.

Complicated, isn't it? Especially if you work on a hardscrabble farm.

17. ST PETER'S GÖTTERDÄMERUNG[42]

Nearing the end of eighth grade, our gang, a certain four guys I palled around with, had begun to wonder, to question, and seriously to doubt, well, just about everything. We were troubled by the differences in what we experienced each day in our admittedly narrow but rapidly expanding world – and what the priests and nuns told us we must believe about that world, a world they called dangerous and evil. And dangerously, evilly sexual. That world outside St. Peter's gates.

---

[42] A powerful word from German mythology, and the title of one of Wagner's operas. Its literal meaning is *twilight of the gods* (small g), an indication of the ever lessening influence of supernatural beings in the pagan human sphere. Those people in the German myths, having been hurt and frustrated by the gods' interference in their lives just started ignoring them and discounting their influence. Which made them angry. The gods, that is. Pretty good metaphor for us boys in St Pete's, isn't it?

To begin with, we were learning to recognize the many incongruences between the words the adults said and the more truthful language their bodies spoke. Ever so slowly our analyses and insights became more accurate. (Okay, I admit a 14 year old brain has a long way to go, but . . .) The mental process progression was, first, confusion – then, following in confusion's shadow, doubt. Angst producing, worry inducing doubt. Doubt about *everything* they had taught. We concluded that the multiplication tables were probably OK, but everything else was up for grabs.

As we stumbled and mumbled toward our eighth grade, we had begun to think about the here and now, to test the reality of what we could see, hear, and touch against *the doctrine*. Though never philosophers, we had at least become better observers. And we often, in fact almost always found our reality opposed to their ideas and beliefs, especially their ideas of what happens when we die. Could eight years of dogma be, well, not real? And to compound the problem we were reminded almost every day that there was a set of rules for us, and a different set for them.

So how do 12 or 13-year-old boys' brains handle the disconnect, the dissonance, the contradiction between adult authorities' so-called truths and how they behaved and acted out?

Short answer: We did not. But we were sure trying.

By now in this narrative, it will be no surprise to you to realize that the nuns hated our nascent cognitive growth (a growth probably obvious to any perceptive adult, right?). Anything other than a rote repetition of the catechism was met with stern disapproval, but now that we were bigger, less often with the flat of a ruler across our backs. Since the sixth grade episode when Rich Rawlins[43] literally took down Sister Josephine in front of the class, the nuns had become, well, a bit wary. But the psychological abuse, the attempts to brainwash persisted. Great philosophers, far better intellects than us had figured out the answers, the nuns told us. We heard of the writings of Thomas of Aquinas, a saint no less, and Francis of Assisi, another saint, but strangely, we didn't get to read the actual discourses. Nor were we asked to show any intellectual skepticism. Just the opposite, in fact.

As an aside, I should say that I can't speak for the girls. None of us even vaguely understood those strange and wonderful creatures back then (nor do we today, come to think of it). But that small group of us boys, okay but not great students (troublemakers, actually), began actually to think. And more and more frequently, we thought about the conflicts between what *we* saw and felt, and what *they* said was real.

What an exciting time. Exciting - but alienating. Unable to trust any adult, we felt so alone.

Please let me stop for a moment.

---

[43] She had slapped him in the face in front of the class because he made mistakes reading out loud. It was a nearly fatal error for her. Richard had already been held back two grades, and was near 15 years old. He disappeared that day and was never seen again.

This is sounding like we were profound pubescent philoso-phers. May I bring in a little perspective: At age 12, almost all we dreamt about, thought about, talked about was sex. Not that we were getting any. But we sure wanted to know, well, everything. We were a mass of raging hormones, hair grow-ing in new and unusual spots, and pimples. Lots of pimples. Fields of pimples. Acres of pimples. Continents of pimples.

Enough of that. And on to something dark.

No one in my immediate group had been sexually abused by a priest, but we knew this to be one of the dark secrets of that place - *some thing* whose name could not be uttered.

So, though we could not quite say the words, we were, well, wary of spending time alone with any priest. There was this thing that they called celibacy – which, they said, was *a higher state of being*. Yet more words we simply didn't believe. More disconnects between words and actions. Keeping our distance was more prudent than we knew.

The nuns were different entirely from the priests, and were a group entirely more complex. Nor could we keep away from them.

Every one of the nuns in that convent wore what looked like a wedding ring on her left hand ring finger. I asked Sister Mary Agnes about it. "I am married to Jesus Christ." *Wow. Married to some guy dead 2000 years? Necrophilia anyone?* I won-dered. No fool by this time, I said nothing, but brought this revelation up at one of our secret lunchtime meetings in the cloakroom. We didn't have the words then, but had we been caught, the nuns would have used words like "conspiracy" and "sedition" to describe our meetings. Turns out other guys had heard the same explanation of those rings. We looked at each other. Thoughtful silence. Some toe scuffling on the floor.

And then the flood gates opened. "I been[44] in that convent," Johnny O'Halloran confided. "They live in cells, like in prison." I had an idea where this was going to go, but said nothing. Silent moments passed. Then, "Yeah, me too." Pat Flaherty and I spoke almost as one – we had taken piano lessons in that convent. "It's too quiet in there, spooky," Pat added, "and it smells really weird. Never saw one of the cells, but I heard about 'em too." I agreed with a nod. More silence. Eddie Klasnic, looking over his shoulder, then drawing closer: "I heard they aren't allowed to serve wieners at dinner. Have to cut them up in little pieces. Afraid they'll take them whole back to their rooms and then, well, use them." Well, this was certain blasphemy, and we looked toward the ceiling fully expecting a lightning strike. Our active imaginations about secret convent sex went wild.

Then Eddie Mason shut us down completely and absolutely. First, he was the oldest (and therefore most experienced and wisest) and second, we had met his dad, who was a real lawyer, a man we held in awe. And his dad, a forceful but quiet

---

[44] "Been" was pronounced as bin, like Gin. And you might notice we often did not bother to use verbs. The "have" was understood.

man who seemed to speak in capital letters and who knew without a doubt (on this we were certain) absolutely *every-thing in the world*, had given Eddie the word on the nuns. "Dad says there are some people in the world who just aren't inter-ested. In sex, I mean. And that we should not think of them as women. I mean real women." Well then, that explained some of their behavior – but only some. But never this idea of need-ing to be married to somebody dead for so long. This core nunly belief continued even in the face of Eddie's dad's words to puzzle and to confuse us, but we came to no concrete con-clusion, nor ever any understanding. Nonetheless, the cracks in their stone fortress had begun to appear.

As the days went on, once we had talked and fantasized about sex, that is our own lack thereof, we spent more time churning over and over in our minds and talking about this founda-tional idea they had crammed down our throats: that their avoidance of sex made them superior – to us, and to our par-ents. That celibacy was a higher state. This precept didn't sit well with any of us. (You, Sister Mary Francis, think you're better than my mom 'cause you don't do it? Not a chance.) Anyhow, we weren't sure that the priests and nuns really had given up sex – at least all of the time. By that age we had watched and talked to enough adults to make us, well, more than skeptical. And second, everybody else in the world seemed to think that this sex thing was not only okay but pretty spectacular. The cracks in the foundation widened.

Maybe we had not entered twilight, but our Catholicism sun was definitely moving down toward the horizon.

An American Boyhood

A tangential but important thought comes up: For eight years we had heard that we must work every moment to achieve a "State of Grace", by following the commandments, but especially by avoiding impure thoughts, thoughts which always seemed to have to do with sex. (Good luck with that with all those raging hormones.) But then this idea of *grace* took a different turn, thanks to Mom. I don't remember the exact details, but we had gone to see a ballet. She didn't have money for even good tickets, so we were off to the side of the stage, but up close. I didn't think much of the guy in tights – it was impossible not to keep staring at his crotch, but the ballerina soared in the air, dipped, and spun effortlessly, all the while up on her toes, toes covered only by the flimsiest silk and cardboard shoes. Face serene, she smiled throughout her entire dance. It was effortless. Or so it seemed. And then I noticed her flared nostrils, and the sweat. Sweat drenched her face, streaking her mascara. This woman was working to her limits, and maybe a little bit beyond, but anyone further back in the audience could see nothing other than her elegance. Since Mom had been a dancer, I asked her about this dichotomy later at home. "Woman was a professional. You want to be a professional, you make it look effortless. Absolutely effortless. And you know how she makes it look effortless? Practice practice practice. Over and over again. Until you make whatever you're doing look easy." At that moment, she had stopped drying the dishes, had put down her towel, and was looking directly into my eyes. A perfect communication

- verbal language strong and clear; body language even stronger. That Mom moment has stayed with me to this day – even more than the ballerina's image. Way to go Mom.

And so I vowed to myself to become graceful – full of grace. But that's not what the nuns meant or wanted of me.

In ninth grade, the gang was talking about our continuing existential dilemma at the water fountain (for the moment we had exhausted our puny sexual imaginations). For each of those years we had been fed daily the nuns' view of the universe: That we had been born in sin, and that unless we changed our very nature, we would burn in hell forever. We did not come to any conclusion at that moment. We were simply too young to understand – let alone answer – profound philosophical questions that have been giving thoughtful people heartburn for centuries. There was a long silence, we looked at each other, looked around to ensure there were no nuns within hearing distance, shuffling our feet nervously. Then Pat Flaherty summed up our current state of conflict in perfect adolescent fashion, "What if it's all bullshit? What we been doing here for the last nine years?" Truth is, we were not much into Pascal's dilemma[45], or any other philosopher's quandary. We were, after all, just pubescent boys.

---

[45] Pascal's dilemma, simply stated, says that if there is no God and you have believed in him, you have lost nothing when you die. On the other hand, if you don't believe in God and He is real, then when you die you are in profound kimchee. Let me apologize in advance to real philosophers for this oversimplification.

But for sure, twilight had fallen . . .

. . .yet on the other hand, and at that moment, the horizon was not completely dark. In my ninth year at that school, I saw just the smallest glimmer of light and hope.

I came to believe I had found the answer to my philosophical angst – and a positive one at that. The hope came in the form of Sister Mary Bridgitte, my homeroom teacher. She was old but not too old – maybe 22 years of age, and, when she walked by, an exciting scent of recently scrubbed, wonderfully womanly skin trailed behind her. Standing next to her desk, asking her to explain some question – an often made-up question – brought a quickening of pulse and an embarrassing warmth to my face. Even that black-and-white medieval dress could not disguise her narrow waist and full breasts. She looked like Ingrid Bergman in that 1945 Christmas movie "Bells of St. Mary's", but ever so much prettier than the actress. And she was my last hope. She didn't look like the others; she didn't act like the others. I hoped, I prayed I could I talk to her as a human being. I hoped she would help me explore important questions, to help me with my doubts. *She is not like the others*, I came to believe – my triumph of hope over history.

One morning when we were alone in homeroom, I tried to engage her in conversation. I asked simple questions at first, then more probing ones. *Sister, I need to know . . . how can it be that . . . a beautiful baby could be born in sin? My sisters certainly were not*, I added. Those words were heresy, profound heresy.

I had questioned, worse, expressed my disbelief in the fundamental foundational premise of Christianity. Too late I recognized that real human beings had been actually fried, burnt up, for questioning that belief. But I had stepped off the edge of a cliff. As I was falling, the clouds thundered; lightning struck.

Immediately her face flushed, strikingly red, powerfully contrasted against the starched white of her nun's habit. Angry eyes flashing, shaking in rage, she answered me with a cold fury, "Sit down. Don't you dare ask questions like that. Or you will get the back of my hand across your face."

I walked back to my desk. For the longest time, I sat in silence, overwhelmed by this powerful communication. This was one of the few times that the words and the body language of an adult matched. The whole transaction was, well, ugly.

The prior nine years came slowly and clearly into focus. Finally able to speak, I smiled, asked for my report card, left the room, left the school, and walked the two miles up the hill to the public high school.

The counselor's door was open, so I knocked softly on the frame. A tall slim man with graying hair, white shirt and tie motioned for me to enter. I found warmth. Better yet, I found dignity. Extending my report card to him, I said, "Mr. Erwin, I'd like to come to your school." He smiled, nodded, and took the card.

I never set foot in St. Peter's, never ever again.

18. EDDIE

One November morning during my 12th year, Eddie
killed himself.

An American Boyhood

Eddie was my cousin, my best buddy, a few months younger in age, but near same in size, in temperament, and in abilities. Here we are about three, probably closer to four. That's Eddie on the left. I'm the one wearing the tie.

We were as close as it was possible for two boys to be. Well, because of the blood, maybe closer. We played together, worked together, slept together, and, on occasion, fought together – sometimes between ourselves, and sometimes, the two of us against other kids. I don't think there was ever any clear winner during our many fights; it was the process that was more important. And then the making up, of course, which brought us even closer.

Mostly we though, we worked. Work was primary because of the farm. First work; only then, and *maybe* then, play. But when we played, we played hard.

The summer prior to his death, Eddie and I had gone together on our first ever real vacation. How Eddie had gotten away for those two weeks we will never know.

The hard part of that trip: Two young boys, vigorous boys, relegated to the back seat. All the way to Cape May, New Jersey. Driven by Maiden Aunts Mary and Minnie. In their 1939 black Chevrolet sedan. At 55 miles an hour. The whole route. At 55 miles an hour (yes, I've already said that). Just wanted you to understand.

Each stop along the way was yet another chance to teach us manners. "When you stir your iced tea, don't let the spoon clunk the glass." And that's just one small example.

Nonetheless, it was a great adventure. Save for the newly opened Pennsylvania Turnpike, the roads were generally poor, and both Mary and Minnie were scrupulous about the speed limit.

No one in the family could afford to rent a beach place, but one of Mary's cousins had married a man who had "done well" and who had a large summer home just a block from the boardwalk. And we had been invited.

It was on this trip – playing on the beach, interacting with the adults – that some fundamental differences between us began to show up. Eddie was more immediate, fun-loving, caring little for adult supervision. I was more concerned about the adults' opinion of me and was, in general, what the nuns would call *an obedient kid*. Well, usually. Differences notwithstanding – or maybe because of them – Eddie and I became closer than ever throughout those two weeks. We slept together, played in the surf together, laughed, made funny faces trying to attract the girls, and shared meals together. And of course did our best to aggravate the adults –

all within reason, of course. We knew we had to get home somehow.

When I returned to Greenock, I found myself surprised how much I missed him, and went back to the farm every chance I could. Of course this made Uncle Eddie happy as he had now another pair of hands to work.

As my birthday approached, my mother told me that this one would be a big deal – in the family turning 12 was considered significant. Only later did I learn that it had to do with the onset of puberty. Whatever. I wanted my cousin to come to *my* house for a change – it had never before been permitted. In all those years, except for our trip to the beach, he had never been away from home. No surprise, Uncle Eddie said, " No". Actually, his words were a bit more firmly said than that. He pointed out that Eddie had already had a vacation – and only a few months ago. But my dad intervened, said that he would come to pick him up at the farm then take him home after- wards, not a small commitment of time for my dad on his only day off.

Well, Eddie could come to visit, but only if he had completed his work by lunchtime, his dad said.

Eleven-year-old boys, no matter their considerable eye-hand skills, have scant judgment, and attempting to get the hay raked before my dad arrived, he drove too fast along the hill, rolled the tractor onto himself, crushing his skull underneath.

His dad blamed me. Absolutely blamed me.

Wow. Nonverbally, of course. But those looks, those vibes were unmistakable.

Though this was certainly not my first confusion about adults and their strange communications, this was certainly the most intense, the most profound, its effects the most long-lasting. And then the strangeness continued, and even got worse.

A few days later, I found myself standing in front of the casket, looking at my cousin's forever stilled body. He looked smaller than he had been, now tucked into that awful box. His smile had been erased by the embalmer, and Eddie's face had been plastered into a most uncharacteristic severe look. As I was puzzling this change out, feeling more angry with each passing moment, his dad and my dad came up behind me. His dad put his arm on my shoulder, and with tears in his eyes, said, "Well, at least we still have you." Yes, that *sounded* good. It was a strongly positive statement, on the surface. I was surprised by his charity, his kindness. Perhaps he no longer blamed me for Eddie's death. And he kept repeating this phrase over and over and over. But something was wrong. I could not move. He was holding me immobile with that hard hand around me, at the same time pinching my shoulder. That doesn't sound like much, does it, but he had really strong farmer's hands. He kept on and on, and the pain soon brought tears to my eyes, almost driving me to my knees. What could I do? I had never been in such a bizarre situation. I simply couldn't move away. My own uncle wanted to hurt me – he *was* hurting me – but secretly, not in a way that might let anyone else notice. And no one else did. Dad, standing next to me was lost inside himself, staring into the casket.

Finally Dad led me away, and Uncle Eddie was forced to release me – or otherwise be found out. (Saved! Thanks Dad.)

You may wonder about this and suspect my memory. I don't blame you. But I assure you, this episode was real. I'll go into Uncle Eddie's psychopathology in the Men chapter.

After the funeral, I bore bruises for days. What a message. It took me a long time to figure out the two different messages, and which one was truly, critically important. But I knew to keep away from him ever after. When he looked at me, he had murder in his eyes. No surprise, I spoke to no one about the incident. Especially to no adult.

But as months and then years passed, Uncle Eddie's profoundly pathologic transaction lit a fire of curiosity in me, a curiosity that would continue to the present day. What are these transactions, I wondered? Why do we humans have such difficulty saying what we mean? Or do we? Perhaps it is the listener who has the real difficulty. Many years later, in the 1950s, in a series of masterly scientific articles, a classically trained psychiatrist, Eric Berne, invented a new psychiatric field called transactional analysis. When I received this train-ing (which came actually after med school), and supplement-ing that training insight by reading his two popular books[46], I began remembering and thinking back through my innumer-able difficulties understanding adults, most of my childhood failures to understand the big people became explainable – understandable – at least in part. But I must ask you to hold on for a bit – I will save this exploration for the next to last chapter.

But during the long sad days of that wake and funeral, I had learned two critical life rules: first, and most importantly, that kids can not trust most adults to be honest in saying what they mean, and second, though death is a common part of life in the country and on the farm, the loss of a loved one was some-thing else entirely, and my irrational anger toward the loss death caused would, at least in part, drive my wish to defeat this stealer of loved ones.

How ironic. When you become a physician, you are doomed to ultimate failure: sooner or later, all of your patients die. It is not a thought docs dwell upon. At least we try not to. Not to pull too dark a curtain over the profession, it does help us understand the human condition, and at times, even post-pone the inevitable.

---

[46] Eric Berne M.D.; *Games People Play*; and *What Do You Say after You Say Hello?*

No matter my valuable insights gained about the big people and their willingness to deceive little boys – and at times even hurt them – the overarching lessons I was left with were that, at any time, a loved one could be taken away, only a black hole in my soul remaining. And that the hole is permanent, irreversible, and just awful. I still miss Eddie.

19. MY COUNTRY CLUB

What's this *My Country Club?*

OK, so no poor boy from the hills can join this – or any other country club for that matter. But he can work at one. And feel some possessiveness because of his experiences while working there. After all, the Club was only a short two mile walk up the hill from our home – and the club held opportunities even beyond any boy's dreams. The boy knew about the opportunities, because his mom and Ray Bills told him so. (Ray Bills was the caddy master, the controller of all jobs, and thus all powerful in that small world.)

From the eighth grade throughout high school, in between digging ditches, working in the scrapyard and working in the mill, on weekends, rain or shine, plus all summer long, and sometimes even in the winter when the snow was not too deep, I was on the course or in the clubhouse with *the members* (which is what we support staff called those men and women we worked for).

An American Boyhood

When in the clubhouse, I shined the members' shoes – a skill that would help me later when I was on active military duty. Pots and pans in the kitchen always needed to be washed, and working in that commercial kitchen gave me the priceless opportunity to watch Chef Allan and learn a chef's skills – and be inspired by him to create my own plated masterpieces when I had grown up.

But above all, I worked outside. I was a caddy.

Simply put, *to caddy* was to carry a member's golf clubs around the course, being instantly available to provide him with the club he wished, and above all, to keep track of his ball – no matter how or where he sliced or hooked it into the woods. The caddy's job was never simple, as you will see.

We always carried two bags – *a double* – cheaper for the two members, and ultimately more money for us. There was supposed to be a weight limit for each bag – a limit of 35 pounds. But the weight could never be questioned by someone so lowly as a caddy, and with the elegant multicolored leather bags and a full set of clubs favored by all *cognoscenti*, bags hovered around 50 pounds. Golf course fairways added up to some 6000 to 7000 total yards, tees to holes, 18 holes per course. But carrying two bags back and forth between two golfers easily doubled the distance walked. And we strove for two rounds per day to make it worthwhile to walk up the hill to the club. About 15 miles, carrying 100 pounds. Two dollars plus a twenty-five cent tip per member per 18-hole round; nine or ten bucks a day. Not bad, all in all.

It didn't take a great deal of perception to walk the course 20 or 30 times and not know every bump, every wet spot, every possible ball's lie and from that lie, the distance to the pin. Watch the movie "The Greatest Game Ever Played" (something I recommend to everyone, because the movie is more than about golf) and you will get the idea that the caddy is an indispensable member of the team, confiding to his player distances to the pin from his ball's lie, the appropriate club to choose for the next shot, and above all, providing critical psychological support. Not so in my life. "Kid, what I want from you is to keep your mouth shut, and don't lose my ball." Well okay then. But once a little experience was gained, we could watch a member during the first hole's play, then predict with remarkable accuracy a) their competence; b) their style; c) most importantly, whether they were having a good day (maybe a bigger tip), or, a bad day – doomsday for us caddies, when we would smilingly accept the blame for every bunker shot or missed putt.

Some caddies were indifferent; but a certain number of us loved the game and would always attempt to help our golfer (note the possessive *our*). We had our pride.

Always – as I stood well beyond the tee to get a better view of the ball's flight – I could get to the ball before the member, check whether it was perched upon a tuft of grass (helpful) or had rolled down into some fairway low spot (trouble), factor in how he was doing that day, and pull the appropriate club from the bag, proffering that club to him. *Let's see, this is a lofting gentle 7-iron to the green.* But almost always he would ignore me, take the eight iron, and land short, in the sand trap. Which was, *res ipsa loquitor*, my fault.

And God help the caddy when the member sliced the ball deep into dense Pennsylvania woods, woods which lined each fairway. (There were times when I actually believed the woods held some siren song for a flying ball). We quickly learned to walk the periphery of the course on some slow day, to find, clean and assemble our own collection of balls the members had previously sliced into the woods. To the non-golfers, you should know that all balls are identically made and similar in performance but individually and characteristically marked – as a *Titleist 3* for example, so that each member of the foursome can identify who owns a particular ball when they come to lie close together. This collection in your pocket, then, when your member had sliced his ball half the way to the river or hooked it into the next county, you could, after an appropriate looking-for-the-ball time, surreptitiously drop a same titled ball in some reasonable spot. Golfers are no fools, and we knew that they knew, but I never – not once – had one call me on the subterfuge. Probably a sin on my part. A venial sin, of course.

Any golf course is a great place to peek into the essence of human nature: usually good, sometimes the bad, and on occasion even the ugly. I mean you might learn something about life and come out ahead. You *might* come out ahead – unless an unruly member bent his club around your head in frustration after a bad swing, or if you didn't get hit by lightning during one of the summer thunderstorms, or if you didn't pick up leeches or get pneumonia after wading into the pond to retrieve the club thrown by a frustrated member.

Caddies are invisible (even more so than people in other service jobs). And being invisible, we could overhear the most remarkable conversations. "Ben, just call Eddie Janosczyk tomorrow morning. He's the union shop foreman in that area of the mill. Get together with him tomorrow afternoon, take a bottle of Chivas Regal, and slide a $50 bill under it. That little problem of yours will go away." *So that's the way mill problems are solved.* Or another: "No way Ed, I want that sewer job up near the high school. Don't bid low on it. You can have the one out near Renzie Park; I'll bid high on it." *So that's how city contracts are awarded, huh?* Human sexuality came in on occasion: "I got to a point where a bomb could've gone off next to me . . ." And that was uncommon. Business, yes, but sex talk was usually avoided because that intense subject had the power to ruin the golfer's concentration, and, like as not, if thinking about sex, he would hook his next shot into the pond. So most of the conversations were about making deals, about solving problems at work. Even the doctors on their

regular Wednesday afternoon on the course talked about patients – puzzling problems – or great saves, never mentioning
names though. To me, it seemed to be a time for getting free
consults. Or we marveled at their showing off, bragging about
what great doctors they were. "Most interesting case last Friday . . . 59-year-old woman, total secret alcoholic, started
bleeding . . . Family in complete denial . . . So I just . . . Piece
of cake". *Wow*. We soon developed this nagging suspicion that
if we were to get sick on a Wednesday afternoon and needed
emergency surgery, all would not end well. The docs were on
the course, or after their 18 holes, in the bar.

An afternoon came when I recognized that there wasn't a single golfer actually looking at the course itself. Think about the
ambience: rolling Pennsylvania Hills, silvery dew on morning
greens, the sweet smell of fresh cut grass, a view from the tee
on number nine down to and across the Youghiogheny river,
from that point able to see half of Westmoreland County's
farms, feel clean spring breezes, watch fluffy cumulus clouds,
notice budding trees and blooming morning glories. This golf
course was a majestically beautiful part of the world. What
golfers saw though was their ball's lie then the direction and
distance to the pin[47].

I could walk into my favorite spot on the course when a member hooked his ball to the left on number 7 fairway, and it

---

[47] Of course there had to have been a few people who recognized this beauty. I
just never noticed a single one. Nor heard a single comment about it.

came to lie deep in the rough. I never seemed to be able to find the ball immediately, even if I saw it, but always needed to walk a few steps farther. First I pushed through a few yards of low brush. Just inside the brush was a spring, and that spring fed and nourished a rampant growth of blooming honeysuckle. Honeysuckle perfume carried on cool swirls of air coming across the spring pond did something – something permanent and pleasant in a young caddy's head. Whatever it was made him recognize that this just might be the most wonderful place in the world.

Smell honeysuckle today, close my eyes, a smile forms, and I'm remembering that boy walking through yellow blooms just off number 7 fairway. Many years later when I learned the neurophysiology of that smell/remembrance phenomenon, I wondered if the scientific knowledge might away the magic a little bit.

Nah. It didn't.

On a particular day the smell was just too intense, the sky too magnificent, the sun too warm. I committed the cardinal caddy sin. I opened my mouth. I said something (and I suspect today that what I said was weak, even inane) to the member, something about beauty. I was rewarded with a frown, a grunt, and an intense keep – your – mouth - shut glare. The member was off the fairway in the rough, only concerned, intensely concerned, about the lie of his ball. So I remained quiet ever after; I did not blame him. After all, he had bet a dime on the hole.

I keep saying *he* – but there were those rare times when the ladies were *allowed* to play. And yes, I said that correctly. The men *owned* that golf course; the women were allowed to play only at certain times and on certain days. In that decision, I absolutely – and I know I was backed up 100% by every other caddy at that club – agreed with the men. Because we dreaded caddying for the women. It wasn't so much that they were bad golfers, even though they were often lousy. Being a poor golfer trying to improve was a person we looked upon with favor, and helped as much as we could. But that was rarely the case. For example, at our club, there wasn't one woman in a hundred who could shoot a round in less than an honest 90, and they cheated (on nearly every stroke) when the other women in their foursome were not looking – usually by moving their ball around to get a better lie. Plus, the greatest sin to a caddy, they were invariably cheap. And to be cheap was unforgivable after our priceless nonverbal support and help. A dime tip for 18 holes was routine, and those 18 holes seem to take forever. For Ever.

But those were not the key reasons we dreaded walking with them. We dreaded the women because they were rarely serious about the game. Most of them talked constantly about inanities, not seeing – even ignoring, when I subtly pointed out – the elegant solution to the problem their ball's lie presented to them. For many of us caddies truly loved the game, and hated when someone disrespected it. So you now know what golf is, at least what and how caddies see it. And you know what it is not. It is *not* just a game. Ever.

And another insight: Years later, remembering those conversations, and hearing that women wanted to play with the men for business reasons, I knew they had a point. Not that I would dare agree out loud back then. The course was where business problems were solved and important deals struck. And those few women who learned to play really well, right alongside the men, almost invariably did well in their deal makings.

Since many of us caddies loved the game, our love caused us moral problems when carrying for the cheaters. Real cheaters were uncommon, and being uncommon, they were oh so conspicuous, so disgusting, so loathsome. Consider this: a rich guy is playing for 10 cents a hole (okay, in today's dollars a dime would be a significant amount of money – about two bucks, in fact). He deftly dubs his ball into the sand trap on number 16. Now well out of sight – actually our heads are below the green where the other three guys are walking around, planning their putts, he says, "Now Johnny (they never learn our real names), when I say *fore*, you throw a handful of sand up onto the green." And then he picks up the ball, yells *fore*, and throws the ball up toward the pin. Of course a caddy would say (could say) nothing, but we would feel just a bit, well, unclean. I fully recognize today that the dishonesties that we took part in on the course – our helping with a lost ball for instance, were all part of a whole, but my Catholic background then excused the former as a minor (venial) sin, whereas picking the ball up and throwing it toward the pin was a disgusting mortal sin against the game we revered.

And then there was the locker room. Working in the locker room even more than on the course, we learned that there were strata within the rich people's society. How interesting it was to a naïve kid to come to recognize: old money, inherited money, plus boarding school English placed the member at the absolute apex of the pyramid. After 18 holes and a hot shower, you might hear, "Eddie, would you please mix me one of your very superb, very cold, very dry martinis?" On the next social step down, a supervisor at the mill (the value of hard work was recognized in this WASPy society) it might be, "Eddie, martini please. Cold, dry and wet." At the very bottom, the new rich – generally coarse men with Pittsburgh accents (*younse or yunz* for example, for *all of you*), men who had made money from and immediately after the war: flat of hand slap on bar, "Gimmea martini." Okay, there were exceptions. But how you talked did show a whole lot about who you were. Mister Shaw got it right in his Pygmalion.

One day on the course I heard, for the first time in my life the word *Jewess*. A ladies' foursome. "And then Madge showed up . . . You know she is a Jewess, don't you, wearing this huge rock on her hand . . ." The conversation turned powerfully negative. And then it struck me. Of course by that age I knew that people held and enjoyed their prejudices. And I knew that as I grew up in the country, we were a bit isolated living in our bend in the river, but it had not occurred to me until that moment that there were no Jews in the club. Nor were there at St. Peter's school. These differences never came up in conversation at home. It was not until high school that I actually met a Jewish boy. Was I that naïve? Was I that stupid about anti-this and anti-that? Sadly, I must answer yes. That naïveté would cost me in my future dealings with people, which is another sad story for another day.

Given that list of negative tales, you might think that golf brings out the worst in people. If so, I've given you the wrong impression, as golf often brings out their best. And though I don't play the game today, I respect the people who do, and I will always be thankful to them. After all, during my senior high school year, the Western Pennsylvania Golf Association, funded by all of the golf clubs in Allegheny County, gave me a full scholarship for eight years of school. By the time I had finished medical school, more than 20 caddies had made it successfully through their scholarship program, and many more were to follow, at least until golf carts made us obsolete. Without the game of golf, without golfers, without what I learned at that club, I would not be a surgeon today.

Not just on the course, but in each and every one of my jobs throughout my childhood and adolescence, all of them menial, I learned the difference between rich and poor people, and discovered that rich or poor was more a state of mind than the size of a bank account. But more, doing those jobs, especially at the Country Club, allowed me to learn from people who taught about human nature. Moreover, I confirmed to myself that honest work is actually ennobling, something my parents, my grandparents, and my teachers emphasized to the point of tediousness. Though I always hated and dreaded any drudgery, the work gave me a purpose, even some stability. Then later, reading in school, the ancient Greeks confirmed in more rigorous and eloquent language their concept of *right work*, a life precept I have tried to live by, to teach my own students – and above all, teach my own kids.

I loved that club. It was a privilege to work there, to walk the fairways, and above all, to get to learn from some really fine people – people both in service and in the membership.

And no, they did not talk to me before they made that movie "Caddy Shack." But they should have.

20. TIPPING POINTS

moving toward dreams and futures

Yogi Berra, in many minds the greatest American philosopher, said, "When you come to a fork in the road, take it." Ah, yes. How can you beat that wisdom?

And I had come to a fork in my own road. That junction, that branch problem caused me considerable angst as I grew toward adulthood, and only in retrospect can I say that my primary decision was correct. Which in my case, was, taking Yogi's advice, to take both paths leading from the fork. And since the paths led toward two different professions, you might appropriately wonder how this could be possible. May I explain?

Now first, to set the scene, let me tell of two experiences – intensely remembered experiences – that created my bifurcation point, my personal, anxiety producing fork.

The two paths leading onward became apparent not so much as an instant of inspiration, but appeared slowly, rather like the sun climbing above our hill, first peeking through the elms. No flashbulb exploded into my mind's eye, there was no *aha* moment. I instead the clarity came slowly, gently. But when the sun was fully up, its light was intense.

Both experiences occurred in my 11th year -- when I was growing rapidly, getting stronger, at a time when I was becoming aware of myself.

Both insights began at the farm: The Kerber Family Dairy Farm. Please let me give you a bit more background about that place, as you have barely met it in chapter 17.

As the crow flies, the farm was only about 5 miles from our house, to the east across the Youghiogheny River. But getting there was not so easy. First, we had to drive north from our home, cross the river at Versailles, go further north toward McKeesport, then turn just beyond the deep pit coal mine and slag pile toward the east, turning right again at a decaying amusement park with the incongruous name of Rainbow, then south over winding, narrow, blacktop roads into Westmoreland County, turning off into dirt roads toward Guffey Hollow, and finally onto a red dog[48] topped rutted lane that

---

[48] Red dog was a soft stony substance left over after low-grade unsellable coal was burned. The burning occurred at the mine -- where all of this half shale half coal had been dumped. Sooner or later all dumps caught on fire. Great mounds of it could be seen near all the mines in western Pennsylvania, smoldering, adding to the general filth of our air.

led to the barn and house. The better part of an hour's drive from our home finally saw us pull into the open area before the barn.

The farm lay on nearly 300 acres of depleted western Pennsylvania dirt, and its rolling hills gave up its timothy hay, alfalfa, wheat, and corn grudgingly and only after serious work. The farm began as a family project in the 30s, with all three brothers and a sister equally involved, but soon evolved into the oldest brother Edward (Eddie) taking control and living on the land, with the only girl in the family, Mary Catherine, providing the operating capital. Mary, one of the early and successful feminists had a mid-level executive position at Westinghouse, and lived at the farm in a single room under dismal circumstances with her lifelong friend, Minnie Schwartz (whom we knew as Aunt Minnie). I'll introduce them fully and in real detail in the chapter on women.

Though the farm was poor, the fields covering those gently rolling hills were incredibly beautiful. What little boy would not notice such beauty – though, in a boy way, perhaps unconsciously. What he would notice, and did exploit, was the boundless opportunities for play. There were more cousins on the farm than anyone could keep track of, and every Saturday, we worked (chores must be done first, and we were cheap labor), we played, we laughed, we fought, yet we always stood united against the adults. Ah yes, and there was danger. Variety is certainly not the spice of life, danger is, especially to little boys.

The path to this family farm started originally as a high class horse breeding and boarding facility for the country club set. Located in the 1930s near our Greenock home (more importantly, near the rich people who frequented the Youghiogheny Country Club), economics eventually dictated a move to more open land, and a turn toward dairy farming. By 1945 the farm was home to maybe 100 cows, mostly Holstein Friesiens, and a few Jerseys, the latter which we kept for our personal milk.

You've probably heard, but it bears repeating: you don't own cows. They own you. It is not possible to miss or even ignore a milking time – the cows will remind you. Worse, I had thought shoveling tons of horse manure was awful, but at least it was dry. Cow manure was not. Enough said about that – the memories are too unpleasant; the images unappealing. Especially if you are about to have dinner.

My cousins drove the tractor, a huge Farmall F 30, from the time they could reach the pedals. How I envied them their skills and their bragging rights. Driving anything at age 9? A little boy's dream. And how angry I was at my father for not teaching me this critical skill.

My dad, you will learn later, worked six days (or more correctly nights) a week (night turn, it was called), 11 PM to 7 AM, for most of his career. On his single day off, Saturday, he would come to the house, change clothes, and take me with him to the farm. Working on the farm was his only relaxation,

I think. And it was my one priceless opportunity to spend time with an otherwise tired father.

Mom simply hated it that I went to the farm. She kept telling Dad that the farm was simply too dangerous, especially the casual way Uncle Eddie ran it.

Which gets us to the point of the story.

One day we kids, cousins Eddie, Tom, Paul and I were tasked with taking a wagon load of empty gallon jars down to the farm's dump. (Today that place would be called a landfill.) We were vigorously throwing the bottles off down into the gully, having a grand time, smashing them against the rocks and against other unbroken jars. The harder we threw, the greater the shatter effect. I walked in front of one of Paul's mighty swings, and took one of the gallon jugs squarely on my forehead, which hard anatomical structure turned the jug into about a thousand pieces (maybe I exaggerate), many of which spread out over my face opening young skin more cleanly than any scalpel blade. I think I had at least 20 significant cuts, and if you have ever seen the skin of any kid's scalp and face bleed, you knew my appearance. My three cousins froze for one long moment, looking at me in horror. (Years later, Paul admitted that he believed in his heart he had killed me.)

I took me only a second to assess.

"Take me to the house. In fourth (the fastest) gear."

There was no movement. Then Eddie said, "Dad doesn't allow me to go in fourth." (Going fast was thought to be too dangerous.)

I strongly motivated him with a loud voice and a real threat on his life.

So off we set, as fast as we dared, we three standing on the tractor's rear draw bar, bouncing, hanging on literally for our lives, leaving an easily followed blood trail up the pasture.

My Dad got most of the bleeding stopped with all 10 of his fingers on the multiple cuts, and I was only a little woozy as we started the long drive to his cousin Bill's general practice medical office in McKeesport – about 40 minutes away.

Make a picture in your mind – a skinny 11 year old boy, filthy from the farm, smelling of and covered with cow sweat and cow manure, T shirt drenched with sickly sweet smelling blood, trying to cover his face to put pressure on the bleeding sites with a dirty rag, walking into a doctor's treatment room.

And then .... experience number one – An Epiphany – began.

First, into my wooziness, into my impaired consciousness flooded the doctor's office smell . . . clean, sweet ether- tinged, cool air. (Today, when I smell ether, 60 plus years on, I close my eyes and I am back in that wonderful room . . .)

Next noticed was the quiet. Any farm is a noisy place, and the noises are complex -- organic as well as machinery originated.

Everything from insects buzzing, cows lowing, pigs grunting, pumps churning, the tractor barely muffled -- all intrusively and irritatingly loud – and then to this room: nothing. No noise. Only controlled, peaceful, soft, calmness. The toxic adrenaline levels in a thirsty, blood depleted and shocky little boy began to ebb.

Though vision was a little dim, I did notice the pale green walls, a walnut examining table, and clean sheets – all senses thus softened, soothed and cooled. Soft and low indirect lighting finished the picture (then again, the darkness probably indicated I was likely going into shock). The ambience reassured *everything is in control*; my mood became tranquil; I lay down, completely comfortable and secure, and started talking to the nurse (who was also the doctor's wife). I wondered if there were some scientific reason about why they had picked the paint colors. She said, "We thought they would be soothing to the patients." She certainly hit that nail on the head. And speaking of heads, now mine really began to hurt.

Dr. Bill came into the room so quietly and smoothly that at first I did not notice him. He smiled at my dad, glanced at me, and, as he began washing his hands in the sink, said to my dad, "Your wife is certainly going to be concerned and mightily unhappy about the sartorial effect of this incident." My first thought was, *I may not know what those words mean, but I know what he's talking about. And he is right – Dad is now in real trouble.* My second thought was *My God, is this man clean.* He smelled of bleached white doctor's blouse and pants, antiseptic soap, clean skin, and minty breath. I was in heaven. Of course, maybe the low blood pressure from the blood loss addled my perceptions.

I expected to be sewn up, but after cleaning my face with warm soapy water, and with no local anesthesia, he neatly closed the cuts using stainless steel clips. *Now this is incredible*, I thought. I wanted to watch. He laughed when I tried to cross my eyes to see the cuts on my nose. When he had finished, I carried more metal on my face than I ever thought possible. Then over the metal the nurse placed fluffy white bandages. What a sight. What an impression. And – *no Novocaine*. I was proud of myself for having lain absolutely still throughout this procedure.

This guy with his starched white doctor shirt, gold rimmed glasses, meticulously clean hands and fingernails, serious knowledge, awesome skills, and above all, his confident air can actually fix humans. Wow.

Fix humans. That was for me.

Path number one became at this moment clear.

Though I savored the whole experience, there is more to the story, naturally. As we were driving home, it was impossible not to notice the pained look on Dad's face. And when I walked in the back door of our white house, my mother lost it. And yes, Dad paid, and paid, and paid. But that is another story.

Who cares about pain? Many years later, on an aircraft carrier, I talked to The Shooter, the guy who fires the airplanes off the carrier. He pointed to the motto embroidered on his white shooter's shirt: "Chicks Dig Scars, and Glory is Forever". He knew, but of course, I didn't know - at age 11.

Nonetheless, the bandages were great, and I showed them off to everyone I could.

And, two days later, the girls at school proved Shooter's motto. I was surrounded - touched even - with oohs and aahs, and questions about "How did you stand *the pain*?" An insouciant shrug of the shoulders, a crooked, knowing smile, and I walked away. Clark Gable had nothing on me. It was another important lesson for a little boy who liked girls.

The story doesn't end there. About 10 days later I went back, had the bandages and clips taken off, and was hoping for some really cool scars. What a disappointment. No Prussian-type dueling scars for me. The doctor had done such a good job that six months later it was essentially impossible to tell I had been cut. Oh well.

Could I do this? Could I be a doctor? Of course – there was no lack of self-confidence. But first there was the seemingly insurmountable problem of money for tuition.

And now on to the next part of the story. But first, even a little more background.

My dad often talked about aviation and pilots, kind of wistfully I thought, but always with admiration and great respect. As a young man he had hung around Bettis Field, a grass strip next to the old Allegheny County airport, washing planes, hoping for a ride – but never getting one. So his approving talk had set the stage for me. Then during the war, I had drawn planes, built models, and knew every fighter in our Army Air Force's inventory, plus the German, Japanese, and English planes. It's a typical story of childhood that most pilots tell.

One day we drove Aunt Mary - who was forever trying the latest technology – to our County airport. We watched her walk out onto the tarmac, then climbed the steps into a silvery DC 3 for a trip to New York. Cabin door closed, the left prop turned slowly, a mighty round engine belched smoke, then a bit of flame, as the pilot lit the engine fires. Second engine running, I waited breathlessly as the pilot taxied to the end of the runway. He stopped, the noise increased as he checked the magnetos, and when satisfied, he taxied onto the runway lining up, pausing for long seconds. That plane then roared - and I guarantee you that roar is the correct verb - down the runway, lifting off, climbing to the northeast, toward some magical path in the sky. I wanted to be on that airplane. No, more: -I suddenly realized I wanted to be that man *flying* the plane.

The hook was in the water.

A short time later my dad took us back to that same airport. In 1947 the United States Air Force had been formed as a separate service, once and forever becoming independent of the Army. And the Air Force was advertising. They had formed a jet demonstration team – flying polished-like-silver aluminum P 80s, our first operational jet. The team wasn't yet called the Thunderbirds, but would be so called eventually. The four pilots put on an unbelievable close formation routine over the field for 30 minutes, rolling, looping, all in a tight diamond pattern. They flew to the west a bit, reformed, and came back over the runway, but, coming back, I saw only three jets. "What happened to that fourth guy", I asked Dad. He shrugged, eyes on the three, who continued the show, rolling, looping in trail, as they passed from right to left. Again I wondered, *where was that fourth guy? Did he crash?* And then from behind us, a shadow, a glint of silver, and suddenly the fourth pilot flew – screamed – barely 3 feet over our heads (perhaps I exaggerated his lowness). He was not supersonic – not in that first generation jet, but was going so fast that he was a bit ahead of his sound. Milliseconds later, just beyond our heads, he pulled up to the vertical, pointing his nose to the sky, leaving in his wake a massive explosive roaring, the thunder of full throttle thrust. It was a sound and noise so intense, so unreal, it was as though giants were tearing earth and sky apart. Women screamed. Kids cried. People in the crowd peed their pants. I'm not making this up. The hair on the back of my neck became erect.

As we had concentrated on the three jets' formation work in front of us, that fourth man had maneuvered around, unnoticed and unseen, close to the ground, positioning himself to fly over our heads at full throttle. Of course his low pass was completely and absolutely illegal. I felt an ache in my chest, a yearning.

Flying jets was for me.

And the story continues.

An afternoon sometime later that summer (August I believe), back on the farm. I was standing in the manure spreader throwing cow poop onto the side pasture. In the middle of that misery – sultry humid still air, gnats buzzing into my ears and in my eyes, no water to drink, no relief in sight, the giants had come back; they were tearing apart the sky. It was characteristic, unmistakable, awesomely beautiful noise. I searched the pale blueness above and saw a single plane, a P 80, sun sparkling and glinting off his silvery fuselage. But he was flying so fast the sound was late in getting to the ground. By the time I heard his roar, he had flown almost across the sky and was nearing the far horizon. He pulled a thin disturbance, a wake behind him, a tiny white line that stayed in the sky for minutes after he had passed beyond my sight, reassuring me that what I had seen was not just imagination.

I looked down at my shoes covered with disgusting wet brown stuff, smelled the heavy organic smells of a dairy farm, painfully recognized my own sweaty smell, brushed the swarming gnats away from my face, and looked back up to the cleanliness and beauty of that silvery plane in that impossibly blue sky.

Well that did it for me. I would be a jet pilot. I did not know how I might accomplish that goal, but I had decided. Path two then became clear.

And the conflict has become clear as well, hasn't it?

An American Boyhood

Fast forward now 10 years to my junior year in college.

The Air Force was recruiting jet pilots. The Navy was recruiting jet pilots. I liked the idea of nights at sea, foreign ports, mighty ships sailing in harm's way. Join the Navy and see the world, their poster said. Above all, I liked the idea of flying an airplane onto a pitching carrier deck. You bet. I took the written test for the Navy's Wings of Gold, passed the physical, and was about to sign on the dotted line when The Letter came. From Dean Ruhe: "We are pleased to offer you a position in the University of Pittsburgh Medical School beginning September 1958 – *if you finish your fourth college year with the same grade average that you have been maintaining.* The scholarship stretched to eight years, thanks to our golfers. I could not pass up medical school. Flying would have to wait.

And it did wait. Fortunately for me, the sky did not change; better yet, as years passed the airplanes did improve, and the Marines did teach me to fly.

Who can tell when dreams get planted in kids minds? I can point to specific times when mine became fixed. But what about yours? And those of your kids and grandkids?

Though it took a long time to realize my dreams, to make them reality, having dreams and being willing to bring them to reality did give meaning and satisfaction to my life, and made the journey to their realization, well, interesting.

There were adults along the way who did their best to discourage me from the pursuit of my dreams. Too grandiose, they said. They were, by and large, good people, worried that I might reap disappointment if I failed (which they thought likely).

No, we must dream. Let me end by quoting Browning:

> *Ah, but a man's reach should exceed his grasp,*
>
> *Or what's a heaven for?*

Dreams get planted in little kids' minds early on. Dreams may take a long time – perhaps even a lifetime – to be realized. Certainly mine took many years. So before you discourage a kid (rationalizing "it's for his own good") give yourself serious pause. You have incredible power as a big person.

And kids need their dreams.

Something to think about, isn't it?

21. MOM AND DAD, DAD AND MOM

This seems like a reasonable point to talk about parents.

When grandparents have a major influence on a kid's life, as did mine, their character and personality seems unchanging, written in stone - solid and constant. But parents . . . Parents are another story.

It's not so easy to pin down your mom and dad, is it?

How's this for a theory to help explain the difficulty? We grow; we evolve – but they do too. As our adulthood dawns, we develop the insight (and maybe more importantly, the curiosity) to look back and see. And then attempt to understand their struggles, their fears, their confusions as they coped with the new, constantly demanding entities in their lives, primarily us growing kids. In their middle years, the complexity and depth of our insights (we hope) increase. And, if all goes well, during those years we learn to accept their less-than-perfect personalities and forgive their less-than-perfect attempts to raise us. And then the recognition that they are no longer strong becomes painful during their decline. Finally, sadly, roles become reversed, and they become our children.

So, with that evolution in mind, to my parents . . .

. . . and Dad comes first.

I bring him in first, because of my general observation: Dads all too often get short shrift. I know mine did. And I say that based upon what I saw during my growing up years, what the Freudians taught (or more commonly failed to teach) in med school, all this added to the many experiences and insights gathered during my subsequent adult years. I'll say it again: all too often, dads get the short end of the stick.

Ever wonder why? Another theory:

The traditional family – and the changing status of husband, wife and children in that family has been an intensely accelerating and complicated evolution.

To begin with, I refer you back to the sitcoms of the 60s and 70s depicting dads as, at best, dolts. Perhaps if we were to examine changes that occurred just over the last three generations, those generations we have directly experienced, the problems our fathers faced might begin to become understandable. But any such examination is not easy: The analysis must lead to a dispassionate examination of the profound sociological changes we have passed through during the years our parents lived in their maturity – as well as those changes we continue to experience today. Because, after and beyond genes, are we not the sum of our own environment, our own prejudices, our own conditionings? And confirmation bias being the destructive influence in life it is, so we must be especially cautious in attempting any analysis. But to examine our sociologic change, I can recommend two books to give some foundation, each on the opposite sides of the spectrum[49].

Remember, the dads of my generation, during those late 1930s, the 1940s, even into the 1950s, were children of the Great Depression – a depression that continued more than a dozen years – until we entered a major world war. Our dads had been programmed, been conditioned, had developed habits and outlooks that were rooted deeply in anxiety and in the fear that tomorrow would likely be worse than today. I often wonder how they got up each morning with that terrible responsibility of children to feed, a wife to keep happy (an unstated but understood expectation), and an attempt – their best effort – to hold onto a job that could vanish at any time.

---

[49] And those books are: "All in the Family", the title perhaps a takeoff on a 1960s sitcom (which, in general, showed dad to be a dunce), by Robert O Self. The book analyzes the present culture wars with a particularly liberal/left wing bent. Perhaps more provocative, certainly more conservative, is Kay Hymowitz (yes, a woman) "Manning up: How the Rise of Women Has Turned Men into Boys". Check out some reruns of "the Danny Thomas Show" and "All in the Family" to get a sense of the disparagement of fathers during those years.

In 1945, the war ended. We, the United States, decided to rebuild Germany and Japan. Our bombers had so effectively destroyed the German rail system (along with the rest of the country) that there was, quite simply, nothing left but twisted steel tracks and rusting rolling stock. Nor were there a lot of experienced German railroaders around. We had done a job on people too. So the call went out: Any railroader who wanted to sign a three-year contract to go to Germany to rebuild the rail system would be amply financially rewarded. Mom and Dad had fevered discussions well into the nights. Snooping at the head of the stairs, I heard it all. I was all for going. I barged into the kitchen one evening unannounced, saying "You bet. Let's go to Germany. It will be a super adventure." Hard looks, sounds from Dad much like a growl, and Mom's finger pointing back upstairs were my reply. But the ultimate question came to them – what would happen when the contract ended? Would there be a job back here? After weeks, they decided. And thus we stayed in Greenock. I have always been saddened by that decision. My sisters and I would have become fluent in two languages and learned of another culture. But as I grew older, I came to understand. Dad had to be conservative. Dad was after all, a man of responsibilities.

I remember my dad primarily as a man who seemed worried. With few exceptions, worried most of the time. And more than a little bit insecure. He would look at his growing family at the table – we were voracious eaters (well mannered, perhaps, but still, growing kids) and wonder how he could earn enough just to buy food for us. As the years passed, and his salary increased, finances became less of a worry. I never saw him so happy, so contented as when he had stopped on the way home in the morning, returning from his work, bringing large cardboard boxes filled with food, food he was finally able to afford. That simple act proved to him his ultimate and absolute success as a father.

And another aside. When my own family was growing, having a steady job, I took that power to provide for granted. But now with such pervasive unemployment, dads must again be worried.

So you might see why my Dad might have been a bit worried, a bit insecure throughout our early childhoods. What shone through his anxiety though was: Dad had talent. In fact, he had plenty of it. I don't think there was much of anything he couldn't handle. He, with my essential and unflagging help, of course, practically rebuilt the house, and certainly kept it in superb operating order throughout my childhood and beyond, till we kids were gone and then many years beyond – until Mom and Dad downsized, selling the White House to a nice lady.

There are plenty of pictures of dad throughout his life. Look at photos of him when he was a boy, and you can see, as he developed into a young man, a kindness and sensitivity that we may not have fully appreciated when we were kids. Here dad is, on the right, standing next to a friend, the year before he was married. Despite the poverty – or perhaps because of

it – the fashion was to be dressed as nattily as one could. Studying the background of these early photographs gives some insight into the general poverty of the times.

As for that lack of my sensitivity, I have not a small amount of guilt that I didn't appreciate him nearly enough, nor show him my love nearly enough. And I'm especially guilty when I remember my absolute idiocy and psychotic behavior during my adolescence. But he forgave me. He forgave me because he was a good father. In later year's photos you will see he had become a strong, mature American male, fun-loving, competent, anxious to give his city friends at bit of fun in the country during our many picnics and parties. You will also see someone habitually and neurotically concerned about his weight – his big belly – a concern generally unknown in men of that generation. His concern was a constant companion during our family dinners. I still don't know where that came from, only that it was important to him. Frankly, we kids didn't much care about his belly – only that he was there.

In an earlier chapter, I spoke of his first job when a new father, an attendant in a gas station. Fifteen bucks a week. Then he was hired as a clerk on the railroad, and in a few short years got a management job called yardmaster. I now think he was more concerned about being able to perform the job rather than being too impressed with himself, but I certainly was. As the most junior yardmaster in a small railroad, he got the least desirable job – night shift – 11 PM to 7 AM, and he worked that shift until men more senior to him died. More than 20 years working steady night turn[50] – think of that. The result of his working nights was critical to us kids and our development: Dad simply wasn't around like most fathers were during normal hours. And during the day, he tried – I emphasize tried – to sleep, not an easy task with four vigorous kids running around. So our experience of closeness to our father was not like the other kids. Nonetheless he tried his best to do as much as he could with us – to share dinner, to take us to the county fairs, and once even, when I was 15, he used his railroad passes to take all of us to Miami. And of course there were the summer picnics. But we kids always wanted more of him than we could get.

He worked six nights a week, and on Saturday, his only real day off, he would go to his brother Eddie's farm and work Taking off to the farm on his only day off naturally infuriated my mother. And she never forgave him. The message from her was, *pay attention to me. Not your damn brother.* Wanting to

---

[50] For some reason, they called the 11 to 7 shift *third trick*.

spend time with Dad, and also wanting to play with my cousins, I did my best to go with him to the farm every single
week. Naturally that was not always possible during school
year, but we had holidays and the summer. The price to me
was high. Though the drive out to the farm was pleasant – we
two alone in the car for 40 minutes each way (what were seat-
belts, by the way? And if I was lucky, a 15 cent ice cream cone
on the way home), all of the chores had to be done first before
any play could begin, and Uncle Eddie was a mean and cruel
taskmaster. Of course my mother was always concerned that
I would be seriously injured. Who doesn't know that farms
are dangerous? Of course I was, injured that is, and injured
on a regular basis. Dad paid Mom's price for every injury, I
can guarantee you. And the price? Mom was a master at creating a coldness, a distance, and being untouchable in that
husband/wife relationship. And she could keep the coldness
up for a long, long time. I had to feel sorry for my Dad on far
too many occasions.

Now I must tell you two critical stories:

A point came during a growth spurt when I thought of myself
as a man. "Dad, can I use your razor?" Dad, noticing a peach
fuzz on my upper lip, kept his smile to himself almost perfectly, looked me over for a few moments, and said, "You're
working. Buy your own. *Never use my razor*." But the question
had made him see me differently, and then with barely a
pause said, "Want to play knucks?". You're likely confused, so
a little explanation is in order. *Knucks* stands for knuckles, and
is pronounced like tux in tuxedo. Each person makes a fist,

orienting their fist horizontal to the ground; the fists are brought together touching lightly. Then taking turns, one person, the hitter, attempts to break contact, quickly raise his fist, and bring his knuckles sharply down on the top of his opponent's fist – and that top is a tender and vulnerable area. Of course the defender must sense this aggressive attempt, and quickly withdraw his fist. A clear hit on the opponent's hand gets you another turn as aggressor. If you miss – you now become the defender.

Oh this poor, pitiful old man (Dad was in his 40s). How can he stand up to somebody with my lightning reflexes?"

I'll use my left hand against your right 'till you get the hang of it," he offered. I smirked a bit. *Maybe I should hold back, not hurt the old guy too much.*

Moving to strike like a rattlesnake, I hit . . . air. Just that fast he had moved his fist away. His turn: Whack! *My goodness, did that hurt. His calloused knuckles are like limestone.*

"You okay? Want to quit?"

"I'm fine," I replied shakily.

A few more strikes (he never held back) and we both agreed (I with great relief) that we'd had enough for that day. I had never touched him, and he was using his nondominant hand. The next day the top of my hand was swollen and blue. As time passed and I grew, a day came that I got better, and started to connect, so then he switched to his right hand. Again, the process started all over again. I ended up with the top of my hand blue, swollen, aching, and next to useless. Looking for even his most minimal muscle tensing that might telegraph intent, I stared at his knuckles, so hard I thought they would melt. Still I missed, yet he hit me with great regularity. On a certain afternoon, the light dawned. I began to look onto his face, into his eyes. From that moment we struck essentially equal blows on each other. When he recognized my insight, he smiled, and walked away.

And the second lesson, which was rendered at about the apex of my adolescent arrogance: One morning he came home and said, quite innocently, "Want to make some money?" *Oh yes.*

"Put your wrist on the edge of the table, put your thumb and index finger an inch apart. I'm going to hold this dollar bill between your fingers, at the halfway point, right at Mister Washington's head. When I drop it, you catch it without moving your wrist from the table. Catch it, it's yours. Miss it, and you owe me a nickel." *Well then, 20 to 1 odds, and with my Superman-like reflexes, how can I lose?*

After 20 straight misses, I owed him a dollar. And I was only making a buck twenty-five as a stock boy at Sieberg's Men's Clothing Store. It was time for despair.

Then the kicker: "Well, that wasn't quite fair. Let me give *you* a chance to drop the dollar."

There is some justice in the world after all. I held the dollar, dropped it, and he missed. *Now I'm going to take him to the cleaners.* But he caught the next three. *I've got to work two and a*

279

half hours to make this up? This is really bad. Then, as in the last story, the light came on. I was staring at Washington when he was dropping; he was looking into my eyes when I was dropping. He let me win the money back, and when we were even, walked away. Smiling.

What incredible, powerful, straight, nonverbal communications. What wonderful lessons for a growing boy.

At this moment I believe I can see disapproval in a certain subset of readers. How cruel, some of you, ah *sensitive*, people may be thinking. There must be a kinder, gentler way to teach such life lessons. You wusses.

Dad's lessons have served me well throughout my life and career: Tolerate inflicted pain with a smile; show no other emotion. In any conflict, do not communicate – anything – to the other person, especially your next move. Thanks Dad.

From what I've said, you might think I saw my dad as being able to walk on water. No. He frustrated and angered me on so many occasions that I cannot count the ways.

Just two examples: He would not help me get a job on the railroad. Brakemen were making more than a buck eight-five an hour; as a common laborer in the steel mill I made a $1.54 (and a half cent more, the office girl emphasized), and mill labor was awful work. He said, "Brakeman? It's too dangerous. You will fall under a train and get cut in half." It turned out that getting cut in half actually happened to one man on his watch. And the unkindest cut of all: "You'll get too used to the good money and won't go to school." Had he no confidence in me? Did my own father not understand that nothing would keep me from going to school. Then second, even worse, he resisted teaching me to drive. As it is today, a driver's license was a boy's key to independence, the key to dates (yes, precious, wonderful time alone with girls), the key to status in my culture; driving was the epitome of adolescent power. "You're too young." No I wasn't. "I can't afford the insurance for you." Well, that was something to consider. Finally, he gave in. But by that time I was way behind the other kids in my class. Hard to forgive, especially knowing that my cousins had been driving tractors since they were 9 or 10.

After I had survived my adolescence, during which time, like most my peers I had become psychotically stupid, even to the occasional point of hating my parents (I know I keep saying that, but my immaturity during those high school days is such a powerful embarrassment that the remembrances keep popping into my consciousness), Dad and I became better and better friends.

Some Monday mornings, having been home for the weekend and on my way to University classes, I would stop in at his railroad switching yard just before his quitting time. Once there I could appreciate the stresses that he felt trying to figure out which railroad cars could be coupled efficiently into some passing train to move those cars to their ultimate destinations – and do so with a minimum of maneuvering in the yard. In those days before computers, each railroad car's identification number plus its disposition and ultimate destination was noted on a small card. Getting the correct cars onto the correct trains were continuing minimax problems, yet he solved them well. I was proud to see that the union men, the engineers and brakemen, whom he told how the trains would be composed and what cars would be moved at what times to which tracks and when, almost invariably despised him. Despised? If you have had any experience in a union town, you know there is always a conflict – often degenerating into hatred – between management and the union members. I explained this in the chapter on Coal and Steel. On the other hand, his clerks held him on a pedestal.

Dad's full name was Charles Stephan Kerber. They used his first two initials as an epithet, as Chicken S**t Kerber. Even then I understood (having been a reluctant member of the Steelworkers union) that if the union men had liked him, if he was one of the boys, he would not have been respected, nor been a good leader. Way to go Dad.

When I began medical school, at least a day a week he would finish his night shift, drive up to Pittsburgh, and come into the cafeteria at Schenley Hall to have breakfast with me before I left for classes. Thank God that by then he had forgiven me for all my inanities, my blunders, my adolescent years of acting out. And no, I don't want to dredge up those stupidities right now – though I will allude to them in the high school chapters. Those memories are painful enough when they come bubbling to the surface at other times. The important point is that he had the power to forgive. Another *AttaBoy*, Dad.

People who study these things tell me that we are unable to remember smells. I don't agree, for I have one memory in particular. That certain smell – actually a combination of smells – remembered even today can instantly bring me back to a time in the old car, sitting next to my Dad as he drove us home from the farm. That perfume is made by just the slightest hint of Brylcreem from his hair, the wafting and swirling of gasoline and hot lubricating oil vapors finding their way into the car's cockpit, and above all, honest and intense man sweat pouring from him on a hot summer afternoon. And that remembrance resurrects the memories. What a powerful, reassuring, safeness-for-a-little boy perfume. What a man.

I was blessed to be given a good father. I do not take that gift for granted.

And now you get to answer my question: Are the Freudians correct? Is the primary relationship son to mother? I would be interested in your answer.

*   *   *   *   *   *

Depending upon your answer to that question, maybe Mom should be first in this chapter. After all, that's what the psych professors taught, and when are the professors ever wrong?

Well, let's begin a general statement about Mom:

My sisters and I got lucky in our Mom. It's that positive – but complex. I'll do my best to explain.

An American Boyhood

We were lucky on two counts. First, Mom was, though some-what, or maybe more precisely, *generally* incompetent in mothering techniques, she was kindhearted and fair, wanting the best for us, and doing her job the best she could. Come to think of it, most of my friends' mothers were incompetent. And the second count was that we lived close to grandpar-ents. Our grandparents were able to teach us skills, demand judgments, and insist upon the character development neces-sary to turn us into adults. And help Mom when she could no longer cope. And the coping problem became manifest when Mom could no longer tolerate what the aunts and uncles de-scribed as us "difficult kids."

Mom was quite short - - she told the world she was 5 feet 1 inch tall, but I think she fudged. And she was attractive – of that there is no doubt. Early pictures (this one is from her high school graduation yearbook) show a pretty brown haired woman with an easy smile and a dancer's figure.

When I was small, she mentioned the dancing

thing to me with a faraway look – then more than a small bit of anger. Turns out she had been a really good dancer in high school, and when she graduated and was about to set to go off to New York City to dance with the Rockettes[51], my grandfather put his foot down. "No daughter of mine . . . " Every father knows the words. She obeyed, but I know that she never forgave him. Goodbye, Bright Lights and Broadway. Hello, mother of four.

She could do things – the term for this ability in our family was to say someone was *handy*, and when you think about it, that's a perfect descriptor. Whether it was sewing a dress for one of the girls, canning peaches, or baking a cake, she could do it.

She kept the house clean, organized; we always had clean clothes, and in the summer, fresh cut flowers from her garden filled vases in the kitchen and dining room. She could do most everything . . .

. . . except cook. In fact, she was a terrible cook. The English are awful cooks (but then I repeat myself). The English culture seemed, at least to us kids, to produce overcooked meat (to the point of tough, shriveled blackness), limp, colorless, over boiled vegetables, plus the inevitable mashed potatoes covered with bland flour-based gravy. Despite this apparent profound failing, she seemed to have no trouble gathering people to the house regularly – be they family, friends, or at times,

---

[51] I don't believe that the Rockettes had even been invented when she got out of high school, but that's the way the myth evolved.

passersby, and then when they had assembled, to put on a well-received picnic or Sunday dinner. Obviously, something other than the cooking was going on. I give her (and Dad) credit for this seeming magic.

She gamely yet grimly put up with the excesses of four vigorous growing kids. And we were excess personified.

When I got in trouble with the nuns, a common occurrence, and she was called to the principal's office, she smiled at their nunly scowls and frowns, listened attentively to their promises of my eternal damnation, held her tongue, took their abuse, then put her arm around my shoulder, and escorted me home. Without a negative word. I don't ever remember a personal criticism when the subject was school or the nuns. I suspect she knew what I put up with, having gone to that awful school herself.

As my father worked nights throughout our childhood, she made me the man of the house when he left each evening. Literally. Yes, yes, I know, current correctness says that this is bad psychology – too much responsibility for a little boy's narrow shoulders. I have no doubt that in today's intellectual circles she would be criticized, but the concept of responsibility was certainly impressed upon my developing mind. When night came, and Dad left, she felt secure since I kept a rifle in my bedroom, along with its live ammunition. And it was a real rifle – a 30 caliber Krag-Jorgenson military rifle – not a 22. This responsibility became a matter of pride, a pride I cherished more and more as I became older. And I had no doubt in my mind that if any bad guys came, any and all would be dead the moment they crossed the threshold. My mother and my sisters would be safe. Come to think of it though, the front door was never locked. I know no one in our neighborhood who ever locked their door. Creating a simple first barrier was something else I never thought about then[52].

Another Mom story: I was one of those painfully shy kids you likely remember from your grade school days: The little boy who fumbled, held back, appearing inadequate in most social situations. Today I can admit to myself how much embarrassment I felt by anything that brought attention to me. One day, out of the blue, Mom told me she was organizing a birthday party. "You're going to be 10. You're getting big. We're going to celebrate." I was mortified. *Who would want to come to our house, who would want to celebrate my birthday? Absolutely no one.* But she baked a cake, invited a dozen kids, half of them girls. *Oh yes, girls!* For girls, I would put up with any embarrassment. She even invited Leslie Marshall – a kid a year older – who lived all the way down in Boston (You will meet him on the school bus in chapter 23. Though not really big, he was by far the toughest kid around). And every last kid who was invited came. I was amazed. Something was going on here that I clearly did not understand. And we played wonderful, innocent games. We sat in a circle, we spun the bottle, the boys kissed the girls, the girls kissed the boys, we were foolish, we giggled, we ate too much cake and ice cream, then

---

[52] And keys were usually left in the cars. After all, the logic went, someone might need to use the car.

everybody took the bus home, slightly delirious and high with happiness and comradeship (or maybe it was all the sugar). Whatever it was, how can you beat that? Mom gets the credit – all of it. Way to go Mom.

On many evenings, now poignantly memorable evenings, she gathered us around the old oak veneer upright piano, and Mom played. We sang, all of us, whoever was in the house, whoever was a guest. Even when hi-fi became available, even when television came, we were reluctant to give up this communal closeness. But a day came when, tragedy of tragedies, my boy-tenor voice changed, and I could no longer carry a tune.

What is it about the magnificence of ordinary human voices singing together – even when those voices are not so wonderful, even when they are somewhat off key – what is it that makes the heart lighter? Hear an upright piano playing slightly out of tune, and I am back during those times. As are my sisters. Mom gave us those memories.

Other than going to visit family, Mom seemed to have no desire to travel – possibly because of her insecurity about citizenship. Actually, it was the lack thereof. Being born an illegitimate child, adopted, and being brought to America at age 7, this interesting story is better told through Grandpap Mason's eyes in chapter 11. Though it is difficult to get all of the facts, it is likely that the Purser on the steamship kept her passage money for himself, so there was simply no record of her coming into the country with my grandparents. Thus she wore the stigma of *resident alien* until in her 60s, when through the aid of a friendly local congressman, the federal government decided that she should be granted citizenship.

It is difficult for any son to know, but I had the feeling that knowing her real mother had been willing to give her up caused Mom a continuing and profound existential angst. Selfishly, I had no such illusions about what my life would have been like in Northwestern England as the son of an illegitimate girl. Most doors would have been closed. And God knows what social problems would have faced my sisters in that class conscious society. I was certainly happy that my grandfather and grandmother had brought that little girl, our Mom, to America.

Lest you think that all was sweetness and light with our mother, on too many occasions she allowed a mean streak and her jealousy to show. She let us know, to the point of tediousness, that the other women in her life – Dad's brothers' wives and, most painful of all to her, Mom's friends – had *more*. More of what, my sisters and I were never sure. But what we were sure of was that she let Dad know that he was not as good a provider as she expected. Looking back, this tension, this disapproval caused us kids a great deal of distress. In matter of fact, since age 7 she had never done without – she had never been hungry, cold, or insecure. Since she came to America, she lived life as an only child in a family of two loving parents. Had she stayed in England, her adolescence and adult life would have been truly awful. But she didn't care.

Here was where she lived. And she was not happy, and she let us know it.

On the other hand, we have no information about her first seven years in England, years that were likely to have been simply awful. Where her meanness came from, I suspect, was those early first years as a fatherless and unwanted child in an impoverished family. I paraphrase the Jesuits: *give us the boy until he is seven, and you can have the man.* Or in this case, the girl. Of course we have all seen children who have survived truly awful circumstance (an orphaned child surviving in a war zone, for example) who grow up to be happy productive adults. Nevertheless, compassion, forgiveness, and acceptance is clearly called for. Who knows what abuse she suffered during those first seven formative years?

Later in our development, the girls and I were willing, and more importantly, able to forgive her those negative character traits, especially because, as she aged, finally recognizing that her kids were doing well, she let go of her dark side. She even became a bit proud, carrying her head high throughout the neighborhood. Not a small accomplishment for somebody barely 5 feet tall.

I knew that my mother smoked, occasionally had a highball, but I still remember the day that I became aware that - scandalous thought! - Mom had sex - *even while she was pregnant.* Our milkman, in conversation, had said, "I wonder how wispy little 90 pound Ellen feels when 200 pound Charlie climbs on top of her." I was aghast, horrified. I wanted to hit him. *Not my Mom.* Oh my. I'm not sure I will ever recover, or have ever recovered. (I think I was 11 at the time.) I bet you remember that moment in your life. That moment when you learned that *those old people* (your parents) actually *did it.* Ever wonder where this surprise, this horror comes from? I certainly have no idea, but it seems to be universal.

Sometimes, in that magical drifting time between consciousness and sleep, I think back to our early years, and I think of our mother and her life during those unpleasant, poverty-stricken times as she tried to raise four kids. Then I recognize just how frightened she must have been. She was frightened every day. Though generally incompetent as a mother, she learned on the job, and ultimately learned the job, and her kids turned out well.

Being given up by her mother as a child, I recognized she was always fearful that her kids would abandon her, and that she would live out her later years alone. Yet when those difficult years came to pass, her kids gathered around her – my sisters especially, who get the absolute credit for her well-being – and cared for her. Judy especially – Judy's place in heaven is assured – took her into her home during those years when times for Mom were really bad.

Before her mind left her – Alzheimer's is the cruelest disease – I know she could look at us, her now adult kids, and finally admit to herself that she was among the most successful of all moms.

What can you do for a Mom and Dad except, with compassion and understanding, say *I love you*?

22. THE MILL ON THE HILL

To leave St. Peter's School then enter the public high school was to walk thirsty from a barren desert then drink from a firehose. Or try to.

On the first Monday in September 1949 I stepped off the public school bus, and walked with tentative and shaky steps into a clean, organized, three story buff brick building on the corner of Cornell and Bailie Avenues, high on the hill above the rivers. McKeesport Technical High School, a.k.a. the Mill on the Hill. The air was electric from the excited buzz of more than a thousand kids. I wandered in, jostled by boys – and girls – all of whom seemed to know where they were going.

A new kid, a little kid, in awe, gawking like a country hick come to Paris. Come to think of it, that's exactly what I was. I had entered into a strange and slightly frightening world, a world which would demonstrate soon to students and teachers how painfully unprepared I was.

I became a curiosity. *So this is what kids from the Catholic school are like*, they whispered to each other, well within earshot. The teachers were invariably kind and understanding (and a bit surprised, I came to recognize, at how little I knew); the kids not so. I was after all an outsider. And the only kid there who had left the Catholic school. Of nearly 2000 kids, the *only* one.

For the entire first year, my sophomore year, I was completely lost. I was so deeply in over my head it was as though I had fallen headfirst down into the depths of our garage well. And I have already told you of that nightmare.

To begin with: I found an educational system that was organized – flexibly organized – unlike anything I could have imagined. In the Catholic school there had been one and only one way. The nuns' way.

Surprise: In this building known as Tech, three major discrete pathways (there were others, but less used) had been designed to lead to a high school degree. On Mr. Erwin's advice, I had chosen the college preparatory pipeline (a.k.a. *prep*). This turned out to be an extremely exacting, demanding set of courses, all taught by the best teachers in the system. In looking at this pathway, it might interest you that it was not the teachers who decided whether one entered advanced courses, it was the student – somewhat unlike today.

Or a student could choose the so-called academic pathway. *Academic* was a euphemism. The course was not rigorously academic – it had been designed for kids who wanted to get a high school degree, but who had no intention of going on further, and who didn't want to work too terribly hard during their high school career. They would thus be destined for office, sales, and other white-collar jobs. Or they were on the football team, and needed passing grades. Come to class, behave, and you would graduate. Nothing wrong with that. And in case you are thinking of looking at anyone in this pathway with disdain, those kids knew where England was on a map, could balance a checkbook, and knew the history and politics of our state.

Students who chose could enter a third, the secretarial pathway. Thinking back, there wasn't a single male in that pool; few guys ever learned to type during those days. When the girls graduated at the end of four years, they could get an immediate job anywhere in town, and be confident that they had mastered every necessary secretarial skill. And be independent of mom and dad.

I never saw actual corporal punishment in this building in the three years I was there, but discipline was rigid, was strictly enforced, and the right of the teachers to impose that discipline was accepted without question by us kids. To be sent to the principal's office was not a trivial matter, and we dreaded having to face Dr. McElroy. Essentially all the discipline was carried out by the teachers themselves, and consisted of requiring us to stay late, usually to do extra school work. We took their discipline seriously. At least the majority of us did. Of course there were outliers, but they were few and did not last long.

And unlike the Catholic school, we had actual study periods when no classes were attended. (The nuns believed firmly that idle minds, like idle hands were the devil's workshop.) We could do pretty much as we pleased during study period. A majority of the homework got done during study hall – but not by me. I had another interest: learning to use power tools. More about Mr. Nelson's shop in a moment.

So there was another building, almost equal in size to the Technical School, which lay a few miles away: McKeesport Vocational High School. The vocational kids had elected to learn immediately salable manual skills. When a boy graduated from Voc (pronounced like Coke) he might have specialized in being an automobile mechanic, a plumber, a welder, an electrician, or he had learned to operate machine tools. And so get a job as soon as he graduated. If female, she could be certain of passing the State of Pennsylvania's Beautician examination. Discipline for the boys at Voc was usually physical, immediate, and often delivered via a closed fist. No student ever made a complaint to any authority, especially not to his mom or dad. We considered that the boys at Voc were tougher than we at Tech were. You are likely not surprised.

It was we kids who called Tech the *Mill on the Hill*, a term of affection and respect. Think of what we needed to accomplish there during a short three years – we had to pass through puberty (not a small accomplishment by itself - see the next chapter), figure out who we were as individuals, determine a social hierarchy (probably the essence of high school) and even get a little fundamental education in subjects as diverse as history (especially the history of our state), basic math, or one of three foreign languages. I wish I had done a better job at all of those tasks.

But of course first I had to get *to* Tech, which, as I lived in the country, meant getting on the school bus. How I dreaded, feared, and hated that school bus.

Sociologists accept that high school is intensely, even achingly a social development ground, probably more so even than college. In trying to achieve individuality, we dressed alike, thought alike, and behaved as though we were in a herd, all the time sure we were expressing our own wonderful individuality.

*   *   *   *   *   *

You might think that most of that socialization occurs in the actual building, and though consummately important –the building pales to unimportance – and is actually trivial compared to what happens on the school bus.

Think about a mystery author who wants to develop a complicated murder mystery plot (I do not choose the murder analogy accidentally). She puts the protagonists in an enclosed space, a space in which they absolutely must interact with each other, exposing the darkness of their hearts. *Murder on the Orient Express* comes to mind, doesn't it? And now let us enter *the school bus*. (I'm surprised that sociologists and social psychologists have not studied this arena, one rich with psychopathology. But I can find only one scientific paper on school bus behavior: *Improving Student Bus Riding Behavior through a Whole School Intervention,* by RF Putnam and co-authors. Sadly, it gets nowhere near the problems we kids faced, but at least the authors recognized there was a problem.)

Now back to the Greenock bus: getting on, you would notice that the girls sat up front, the boys in back. The ultimate and most desirable seat was the final rear bench – the locus of dominant males, six of the bigger kids across. Boys never sat with girls. If only one seat remained, and it was next to a girl, the boy would stand. Well, there were exceptions . . .

On my first day I waited by the side of the road nervously, 30 minutes early. (Didn't want to miss this ride.) As the bus was essentially empty when I got on (I lived far, far out in the country), I naturally took the middle of the rear seat. And then some of the older kids from Lower Greenock got on – the seniors. What happened next, a classic boy/boy transaction, was completely nonverbal. I was grabbed by the lapels of my jacket, jerked off the seat, and slammed to a side bench. The rest of the younger kids, those who had gone to public ninth-grade school, knew the hierarchy already. But I was a quick learner, and found my place, which unfortunately was at the very bottom of the school bus heap. Even being lower than whale feces, I got daily grief from two juniors who never called me by name, but only "the uninitiated sophomore". (I should explain that freshman had their pants removed on the first ride in the schoolbus. The pants were passed to the front of the bus through girls' hands - horrors! - at which point the humiliated boy had to shuffle, red-faced, head down, to the front of the bus to retrieve and put on his trousers. And this was called an initiation.) At first I wondered if this was Protestant prejudice against Catholic. But it was not. It was just male chemistry.

By the third week, the socializing had produced a hardened, stratified group, no different from any troop of wild African baboons. (Again, choosing that analogy is not an accident.) By that point, it would have been impossible for an outsider to enter the group, let alone be accepted. Any intrusion was simply not imaginable. Another boy getting on the bus would have been devoured - much as a young wolf trying to enter a pack other than his own would be simply torn apart.

And into this rigidly closed environment one November Monday morning, two boys from the next community, Boston, enter. They are the Marshall brothers. They signal for our bus to stop, open the rear door, and aggressively push their way in. The doors close, the bus moves out, and a menacing, deadly silence spreads through the entire bus. The girls' conversations stop in midsentence, and they turn, waiting for the bloodbath.

An American Boyhood

Ray Marshall, the younger brother was just shy of 6 feet tall, about 170 pounds, and a year younger than me. Leslie Marshall, his older brother was my height, but heavier than me, about 150 pounds, and a year older, a junior. The third (unfortunate) protagonist in this tale, Roy Gill, was older, bigger, and a well-known bully.

Apparently Roy, a Greenock boy, had slapped around a little Boston kid, Eddie Janos, at the Olympia Park skating rink Saturday night. Leslie Marshall had heard, and had taken umbrage.

Now close your eyes and picture this: The Marshall brothers stand centered in the aisle. Boys standing move a respectful (or fearful) distance from them. Ray turns, covering Leslie's back (an impeccable tactical move). Leslie takes his time, says nothing, making prolonged eye contact with everyone in the rear of the bus. For most of us, time slows, and we are more than a little reluctant to meet his gaze. After looking everyone down, he comes back to Roy, slowly walks to him, and then with both fists whirling, fists moving fast as a fan at full speed, beats him about the face. This beating lasts minutes – or so it seems. Roy, no fool, does not move; he is fearful that Leslie might actually lose his temper and consequently kill him. Leslie steps back, not even out of breath, and says quietly, "Don't touch Eddie ever again." Then Leslie, even more amazing, makes prolonged eye contact (oh, how aggressive!) with every one of the bigger kids in the back. It is a blatant invitation. (*Come on. Take me on. Watch what happens to you.*) They do not move. They look down or away, which I find an interesting phenomenon. After a few more minutes – during which time silence persists – Ray pulls the stop cord, the bus slows and stops, and the Marshall brothers simply get off to wait for their own bus, which is a few minutes behind ours.

Perry Grissinger turns to me and says, a bit breathlessly, "I was afraid he was going to hit me too," and with seriously shaking hands, lights up his unfiltered Camel. And his were the only words for the next 10 minutes in the back of our bus.

All bleeding stops eventually, and of course nothing is reported to any adult. The driver deliberately does not notice. Where are the psychologists when you want them?

By the way, Ray Marshall some years later married my sister Judy. It was a good marriage. And with Ray her husband, I never worried about her safety.

*   *   *   *   *   *

Back to the school itself, and a lost little boy, academically so far behind everyone else. The big lie we had been told during the prior nine years was that the Catholic school education was so superior to the public schools. Right. I worked day and night simply to catch up, never even dreaming of getting ahead.

I signed up for Latin because I thought it would be one course where I would have an advantage over the public school kids. After all, shouldn't the Church of Rome be the best at teaching their native language? Wrong. After embarrassing myself throughout the year, I finally did translate Caesar's *Gaul is divided into three parts*. Though I never came to appreciate the language, and in spite of my difficulties, during that course I developed an awe of the Romans, and a lifelong love of history. Thank you Miss Auld.

And speaking of awe, every single teacher I studied under had earned at least a masters, and two had PhD's. Even many of the teachers in the vocational school had earned advanced degrees. Seven of our profs were valedictorians of their college class. I doubt that the profs loved us much, but they were intensely interested in and proud of their vocation, and I suspect, at the end of the year, proud that they had given us at least some tools to face our world.

Our teachers kept a dignified reserve – an appropriate gulf – between them and us, and it served everybody well. Easy grading? Grade creep? Our Profs would rather have made a pact with the devil.

You should be skeptical of my descriptions that make my teachers sound as though they walked on water, but I didn't see *any* teacher through rose colored glasses – nine years of awful experiences at the Catholic school had destroyed my faith in anyone called *teacher*. I knew there were bad teachers in Tech just as I knew there were bad students. Some people, after all, are simply no good. And fortunately, that school was big enough that I could avoid not only the bad but the mediocre – kids and teachers. But those who taught my classes, my profs, completely changed my attitude about teaching over the course of those three years, and changed it enough that I would one day become a teacher myself. Still, being the skeptic I was (and remain today, by the way), I entered my classes at Tech with my glass of respect for any teacher barely half full – they had earned that half glass by completing their degrees – but without exception, each of their *respect glasses* was brimming over by year's end. I still remember my Profs with affection, but mostly I remember them with a profound respect.

In the college prep pipeline, I soon recognized that I was simply not like the other children. The others *knew*. They knew what they wanted, they knew where they were going, they knew the study materials cold. I was unsure. I was in love with everything. Today I would be called *unfocused*. And probably placed – actually certainly placed – on heavy medication. And sent to counseling.

Pro Dunlap (we called the teachers we liked and respected *Pro*, short for Professor) excited and nurtured my love of chemistry – which became my college major. On the first day, he showed us the breadth and power of chemical knowledge. "Want fire?" He lit a Bunsen burner. We had fire. "Want an explosion?" And he threw some powdered chemical into the gas flame. Whoom. A massive orange ball of flame traveled completely across the lab desk, almost to the empty front row. This was for me. I quietly and wordlessly got up from my seat in the very last row of desks, moved front center, and never left that position.

Math was especially, painfully difficult for me. I simply had no background in math or in critical thinking. Though I ultimately passed the courses, it was just this year I began to understand geometry. So another sidebar: Reading the *Archimedes Codex,* a book written by conservator Will Noel, and Reviel Netz, who specializes in ancient science, I finally found what geometric proofs were all about. (The original 10th-century text had been scraped from the sheepskin, and covered with a 13th century monk's prayerbook. Its resurrection revealed Archimedes' original thoughts. It's a remarkable book I recommend especially today to anyone who was baffled by geometry and the need to study those proofs during high school.)

Everyone in the prep pipeline studied long and hard. But the one difference I alluded to above was that I wanted to do more. I wanted the skills to work with my hands, not just with my head, which in my group was not quite socially acceptable. The absolute and pervasive belief in the European (especially German and Jewish) intellectual community during those years was that the more you worked with your hands, the lower you were on the social scale. The true intellectual elites – the PhD scientists, for example – only gave orders to others – and wrote, of course. But not in my family. Dad, granddads, uncles, cousins – we wanted it all. Good books plus fine handwork. That was our family's leitmotif.

Enter Mister Nelson. Pro Nelson ran The Shop, a shop small by Voc standards – mainly woodworking, but there was at least a metal lathe. He was an absolutely strict disciplinarian, and more, he was a superb teacher. Prove yourself, earn his respect, and he would let you do just about anything. Once I had learned about Mister Nelson and his shop, I spent every study period I could in his company. Woodworking soon became easy, and I brought home projects that even today I'm proud of. I progressed to metal – and he actually let me use the lathe. My final project was to build an electric motor. It worked. No one was more amazed than me when I plugged it in. Mister Nelson just laughed, "Follow the plans, boy[53], and you'll be amazed what happens." What a great lesson. Mister Nelson remains one of my heroes. I wonder what would happen if a teacher called any student "boy" today?

As observant of us as Mister Nelson was, one know-it-all outfoxed him. The kid was tired of trying to make a straight cut with a hand saw, so when Mister Nelson was wanted next door in the drafting room, Mike moved quickly to the bandsaw, powered it up, and made a perfect right angle cut through a piece of pine. The cut through his left index and long finger though, was on a diagonal, and he totally ruined the piece. Bloodstains, you might guess, never come out of

---

[53] Yes, he called me boy. No, I didn't feel disrespected.

unsealed wood. The cuts – through his fingers, that is – were apparently painless (at least for a while), because he just stood there for the longest time staring at his now separated fingers lying on the saw table. And watching tiny spurts of blood from his finger stumps. Hearing the saw running, Mister Nelson rushed back, fuming that his order had been disobeyed. When he saw the blood, his shoulders slumped. He powered the saw down, then just shook his head, walked to the phone, called the office and opened the first aid box. Of course the rest of us had immediately gathered around Mike. After all, how often does any kid get to see fingers lying on a bandsaw table? We tried to smother grins, but finally burst out laughing. In our circle, laughter was the inevitable reward for profound stupidity. Think that laughter, our laughter, is weird? McKeesport was a tough town. And no, there were no lawsuits. Just a boy's embarrassment.

The downside to our two school buildings being separate was that I could not learn advanced metal working. I wanted to weld. Even more, I wanted to learn electricity. Acquiring those skills would have to wait.

Today, that system is no more, and Tech, last time I walked by, remains just a hole on the hill. The organizational foundation of our system that became so politically unacceptable was first, that the education was carried out in two separate buildings, and second, that we were segregated academically. Yes, segregated. How politically incorrect is that?

But that public education system – that separate and unequal system – was superb. In the Vocational school, where guys and gals went to learn employable hands-on skills, they exited not only with a piece of paper, but with the ability to get – and hold – a job, and they started out making more than common laborer rates. Plus they had learned basic skills in math and English, and would know the interesting history of our state (we learned that Pennsylvania was actually a Commonwealth). Graduating from Voc, the student could even find where Europe lies on a world map. I challenge you to try that experiment with the public school graduates today. Remember, essentially all of his (okay, there were a few girls at Voc) teachers had baccalaureates, and many had masters degrees. Graduating from Tech – those of us who didn't drop out – also knew we could progress, start a family if we wished, get more schooling, plus earn a living. And pregnancy was rare.

Never once had any teacher worried about our self esteem. Sooner or later, there would be a ranking of us in the class. Nobody ever told us, *"You're all winners today."* Or any other day for that matter. We were continually ranked – on the football field, on the basketball court, and most severely of all, in class. And so we were not surprised by the real world we were to enter, the real world outside the Mill on the Hill.

Let me ask an existential question of you: can the kids who come out of our public schools today do the same? Are they ready to meet a severely competitive world?

We were. More about that in the last chapter.

As it turns out, high school, as turmoil and angst producing as it was, was not, as we thought then, the apex of our life. But my, wasn't it interesting? Especially when we look back at those years with the comfortable insights provided by our greater experience.

During those three years, my profs gave me a real leg up on life in the outside world. I hope your kids and grandkids can say the same.

23. THEN THE BELL RANG

And when it did, we left those quiet, controlled, struc-
tured classrooms, hurrying through busy hallways to our
next class, to the lunch room, or, school finally out, to get together for a Coke or (if you were *bad*) a smoke. And so we
entered, fell into, were enveloped by – what? A mass of intense, super-self-centered adolescents. Pushed, bumped,
shoved to the periphery, I came to see the Witches' boiling
cauldron in Macbeth as a pretty good metaphor for us, we
with our swirling, toiling, bubbling and boiling conflicts, our
intense needs – and our confusions. What angst, what personal crisis might bubble to the surface of this life's cauldron
next? What kid could predict?

But I wonder. Perhaps my remembrances of high school experiences and feelings may not be representative. Compare
mine to yours perhaps?

From what follows, and despite the last chapter's praise for
our Profs, you might get the impression that the academics
we encountered in the Mill on the Hill were, well, not as important as what happened beyond classroom walls. Let me

put that concern to rest. In fact a small group of us, close friends all, believed doing well in class was critical, as we had come to see that the way out of our almost inevitable steel mill laborer future was to win an academic scholarship. Certainly we did not expect to get a sports scholarship for, say, gymnastics, golf, or tennis, sports us little guys could excel in. Not back then. But we also recognized that beyond the Profs, there was this great and wonderful world out there, the adult world we were desperate to understand and enter, just waiting. But first . . .

We found ourselves usually confused, unsure of how to enter that world. It seemed that every moment outside the structure of the classroom, the problems we faced and hoped to solve revolved around Peer Pressure and Popularity. Oh yes, there was that important fourth P, Pimples.

As for peer pressure, though there was more freedom to move around and choose friends than in the schoolbus I described in the previous chapter, the pressure to conform was constant and powerful.

Of course I can only really speak for myself. But I suspect, in retrospect, the adults we have become would probably agree that we were, during those days, simple herd creatures. Oh, we told ourselves (never admitting to others our insecurities) that we were stark individuals – *our own persons* (at least we insisted to our doubting parents that was the case) – but we dressed alike, talked alike, listened to the same music, and were interested in the same things – which were, for the girls, the boys. And sad to say, for the boys, usually their cars. (After all, what did we *really* know about girls? We were just guys. Burdened by having only a single X chromosome.)

And about that power to enforce conformity: Early in my sophomore year a kid stopped me in the hall between classes. A senior, someone whom I had never seen before, grabbed my arm, looked me in the eye, and gave me a simple order: "Get yourself some black spades kid." Turns out that shoes that were okay in the Catholic school were not acceptable in the public school. And so I went to the Hanover shoe store and paid 9.95 for a pair of black shoes with soles that were shaped like a dirt shovel. Some independence on my part, huh? And the senior? Well, he felt it his right, even his duty to bring me into the herd. And I never saw him again.

Levi's with turned up cuff to ankle height, white crew socks, and black spade shoes. What a fashion statement. Only John Meszaros had different shoes. Turns out his mom made him wear them because he had ingrown toenails. (Oh, how we hated that phrase, "Mom made me . . .") John hated his shoes. Because *others noticed.*

On to popularity. The word should probably be capitalized, as Popularity indicated our place in the all-important social hierarchy of the school. Our worry over that status position – a position often evanescent and easily lost – seemed to lurk just beneath the surface of consciousness like some primitive metaphysical angst. I remember seeing one girl, a friend but not a girlfriend, rushing to the girl's room, sobbing, dissolved in tears. When I could get her alone to comfort her, I asked innocently, "You sick? Something bad at home? Somebody hurt you?" "No, they hate me." Turns out her clique had suddenly decided that her behavior had become unacceptable and they had decided to punish her by shunning her. I think the transgression was about her not wearing a certain color sweater on a certain day. Or something of that importance. It was my first experience with mean girl cliques. But not my last. What power they had. And have.

So we worried about, and finally came to accept our position in the school's social hierarchy. I never did figure out what made some kids popular (and thus socially powerful) and others not. It was more than being just a pretty girl or handsome boy. Still don't know, come to think of it.

No, not every kid cared whether he or she were Popular – or not. There were the geeks who walked among us, outliers, kids who had their acts together. We never did figure out whether to hate them or admire them. Then again, maybe they were just better actors than most of us. Underneath their placid surface, they were probably in turmoil too, right?

Want to do a good scientific study? Pick some statistically valid number of popular kids in high school, control variables as best you can, then follow them for 10 or 20 years. Now find out what happens to those kids. There are few such studies.

An American Boyhood

You might be interested in Joseph Allen's book *Escaping Endless Adolescence*. Doctor Allen is a psychologist, and has been studying and following a group of popular kids for years. It's a complex book, and I don't want to reveal all the surprises, but if you – the reader – did survive the bullies, the cruel girl cliques, your pushy parents, and were not as popular as you had hoped, you will be pleased at his findings. Isn't that interesting – and something to look forward to?

* * * * * *

On to pimples.

In my small social circle, as we struggled through our adolescence it was rare for any one of us to talk about anything beyond our status and of course the sex thing. Then again, both seemed to be bound together, part of the whole.

How this manifested in my small circle was our fear of asking a girl out who was *really popular*. (Think of the embarrassment of being turned down. Think of the lunchroom gossip on Monday. Think of the knowing looks, the condescending smiles, the whispered words among the girls as we walked past.) Many years later I learned from one of the most popular girls in the class that she often sat at home on weekends because guys were simply too afraid to ask her out. She told me this with not a small amount of bitterness and irony. And we thought ourselves brave. And consummately masculine. Pitiful is what we were.

Though slow to act, we had an uncommonly rich fantasy life. Walter Mitty had nothing on us, but unlike Walter, our fantasies had to do with females, girls, the opposite sex, women. Almost exclusively.

And the girls, about a thousand of them in that building alone[54], were marvelous. Each and every one had some goodness, some attractive trait about her. Soft, smooth, lightly rouged cheeks, come-hither red lips[55], flashing eyes outlined by the blackest mascara . . . bobby socks and saddle shoes . . . multiple petticoats, petticoats which made their skirts stand out and swish as they walked. I learned from my sisters that every girl ("Every girl? Really?", I asked them) in the 1950s wore an elastic girdle, but we boys couldn't tell, as the petticoats hid outlines of slim young hips and soft buttocks. On the other hand, skintight angora sweaters showed off their breasts – *proudly* showed off their breasts. The part of a girl's anatomy that you would see first as she rounded a corner was, you guessed it. Now the one thing I could never understand was the why and the how of that phenomenon – the bras built during the 1950s made their breasts as sharp and

---

[54] The only girls not in the Tech building were those in the Beautician Course. They went to school, no surprise, in the vocational building. Conventional knowledge held those girls to be darkly mysterious and uncommonly knowing in the ways of the world. How about that?

[55] During those days, an uncommonly vivid red lipstick was in fashion. It smeared easily and was almost impossible to get off your own face. If you were lucky enough actually to get to kiss a girl.

pointy as ice cream cones. It's a puzzle to this day (and my sisters still refuse to help).

Combine the adolescent growth spurt with the nearness of those wondrous girls. What boy wouldn't have raging hormones? So no surprise about the pimples, right?

Now on to two stories, stories that bring my near daily embarrassments into sharper focus:

It was the spring of my sophomore year, just after lunch, civics class. Steam heat still on, Prof had opened the windows. A gentle warm breeze drifted in, clearing the wintry smell, rustling papers, stirring petticoats. Civics class. It was impossible to pay attention to the importance of land-grant colleges in Pennsylvania. I began to nod off, to doze, and then was suddenly startled awake by a pulsating semi-erection moving the leg of my trousers. I looked around in terror. *Had anyone noticed?* Oh yes. MariAnne Franklin was watching me, smirking. *She knew.* Feeling my face become hot, knowing the deepness of my blush, I leaned over to tie my shoes. It took a long time to tie them.

And another day, walking along the corridor at change of class time, I saw one of the juniors turn a corner then bump into a girl. She stepped to the side to move on, but her breast brushed the bare skin of his arm. He took another step. He paused, then quickly knelt down to tie his shoes. It took a long time. I watched him, smiling. I knew. I was not alone.

Of course we fell in love. Frequently, delightfully, consummately. We simply couldn't acknowledge that during those years, as wonderful as the *falling in* is, the *falling out* would then make the world an awful, dark, and painful place. At least for a week. If both in and out had not happened with such frequency, perhaps we would bear fewer emotional scars today. Then again, probably not.

And two more stories:

Marjorie Wilson sat in front of me in Latin. I hated Latin class. Even today I can *not* tell you what or even *why* the Romans needed declensions in their language. And the syntax? *Gaul into three parts divided is* . . . So I must ask, what was there to do in that room but stare at the back of a frilly, white, low necked blouse, shining black hair, and a neck whose curves, highlighted in late morning's sunlight, put geishas to shame. Marjorie was small and slim to the point of petiteness, moved with a gracefulness most ballerinas could only dream of, and always knew the answers in class. When she turned her head she showed flashing dark eyes, a small turned up nose, and velvety smooth skin the color of lightly creamed coffee. My fantasies grew, then flourished.

So a day came when I worked up the courage to ask her out. And I wish I could say I was Joe Cool during that transaction. Hands in pockets, looking down, one shoe making slow circles on the terrazzo floor, "Uh, wanna get a coke after class?"

Now how smooth was that? Avoiding eye contact, she simply shook her head, then deftly maneuvered past me (with a smooth-as-silk swish of skirt) to her next class. But am I not a guy? *Perhaps I should be more aggressive.*

So I was. More aggressive, that is . . .

. . . and that afternoon her brother, a fullback on the football team, two years older, 180 hard pounds, and two of his friends, linemen, great dark slabs of meat, 200 pounds each, surrounded me. With the brother in the middle, each lineman grabbed an arm, slammed my 137 pounds briskly to the wall, and held me tight. My toes barely touched the ground. Her brother came close – way too close – to my face. It became difficult to breathe. "Talk to Margie again I will tear your face off." And then he just stood there. Inches away. For hours. Then again, maybe I exaggerate the time. Finally, they dropped me and the three of them went back to their space. As they say, it was a teachable moment. Would you have talked to Marjorie again? Ellen Kerber didn't raise a boy quite that stupid.

Beyond that "interesting" transaction there was this thing, this concept of *their space*? It turned out that the black kids hung out together near a certain door on the side of the school. Even having grown up in the country, I knew there were black kids; I saw them all the time in town, but at that point I had no black friends, nor did I have any opportunity to get to make one. But we recognized a reticence on both sides.

With Marjorie, I had clearly broken some powerful taboo. Of course we all understood there were white kids who hated blacks, and black kids who hated whites. But I didn't run into many of them. Most of us felt a curiosity. But no matter, what kept us apart primarily was a psychological perception of differentness, a separation – an enforced separation – taught us by somebody to be sure, but a deep and powerful separation it was. At least that part of school, that black / white divide, is better today.

24. AND ON TO WORK

Which bring us to the story of the two Johns as we
move away from the school building itself.

John L Hauser III and I literally bumped into each other coming out of school near the end of our sophomore year. Picking
up our spilled books, like dogs meeting for the first time, we
smelled each other out. Figuratively, that is. It was surprising
that we had not met before, because he lived within bicycle
distance of me, just about two miles away. As different as we
were physically, we quickly found we had similar interests
outside of school. John was tall, always grinning or outright
laughing, skinny, a bit gangly, with long arms that seemed to
flop out and around as he kind of loped along. But despite his
lankiness, he had lightning fast reflexes. It was those reflexes
that kept me from ever winning a single ping-pong game
played against him.

John had one personality trait I found rare among kids back
then. He was comfortable with being in charge, comfortable
with giving orders. And that trait, which I admired and
deeply wished I had, had been taught him by his dad. I held

his dad, John L Hauser II in a mind space that few other adults occupied, one where I placed those rare adults I respected. His dad had earned that respect first by always saying exactly what he meant, and second, by trying his best to teach me about how to get to the truth of what other adults really meant when they spoke. He understood human nature better than anyone in my immediate circle. Mister Hauser had always worked jobs of responsibility, of control, and of power. For example, he had been a riverboat pilot (and since Mark Twain, one of my heroes, was also a riverboat captain I saw Mister Hauser in the same league). When I came to know him, he was superintendent of a large scrapyard. Summer coming up, I asked him for a job. And he gave me one, as a common laborer, at $1.25 an hour, which is exactly what he paid his son. No nepotism in his world.

Mister Hauser drove John and me to work – but to avoid any appearance of favoritism, he let us out of the car a quarter-mile from the scrapyard, and made us walk through the gates. Which seemed reasonable to both of us boys.

The mission of the yard was to take every kind of iron and steel junk they could find or buy and turn it into what was termed number 1 scrap – pieces no more than two feet in any dimension. Pieces that small could be fed into an open hearth furnace, and so brought a premium price. The primary tool for that conversion was a shear – kind of a scissors on super steroids. A shed, a corrugated iron cube about seven feet on a side housed a huge electric motor. That motor drove an inexorably moving scissor arm about four feet long – up and down, up and down all day long – no matter what we put into its maw. For the first part of the summer, we disassembled old railroad cars. Men with cutting torches would burn out the rivets holding the cars together, a four by eight foot piece of the boxcar would fall off, and a crane would deliver this quarter inch thick piece of steel to our shear. It took a team of three of us to pick up the sheet, feed it just so into the jaws of the shear, then turn it 90 degrees after the jaw had done its work, cutting smaller squares, then throwing the cut squares into a pile of what was now number 1 scrap. It was exhausting – and dangerous work.

Gabe was the senior man of the team. Maybe an inch taller than me, not heavily muscled, just starting to get a bit of a pot belly, but possessed of remarkable stamina. Though in his mid-40s, Gabe would finish his grueling workday with a smile and a jaunty walk out of the yard, showing no sign of fatigue. I was in awe of his ability to work steadily eight hours with only a 10 minute morning and afternoon coffee break plus a 30 minute pause for lunch. I certainly could not; I dragged myself out of that yard each afternoon. Of course he noticed, yet every day he only smiled at my weakness, and was kind. And always helpful. But he could not seem to talk much. A head nod in agreement, a shake no, always a smile – but only a rare word. He was an interesting puzzle of a man, a puzzle I never understood. Why was he willing to work so

hard for the man for so many years, John Alder and I wondered?

Which brings us to the second man of the team (I was of
course the third), and the other John of our story: and how I
got to know John Alder.

John was just shy of six feet tall, broad of shoulder and narrow
of hip, muscled with superb definition, carrying strong
hands, blessed with fine, regular facial features, and skin the
color of Hershey's chocolate. Unlike Gabe, John was smart
and could talk – and he did: talk, and talk. He introduced me
to a foreign culture, his culture, the culture of the black laborer.

And no, I was not accepted. I was looked on more as a curiosity – but never quite trusted by the other men in his circle.

John found me amusing, and got great satisfaction out of
playing with me. Particularly playing with my head. Each
morning it took him maybe as much as 15 minutes to get inside my skull, all the while, rolling eyes, showing great wonder at my naïveté. "You are certainly the dumbest white kid I
have ever met," he would say with a grin and a shake of his
head. Gabe merely watched and smiled through our back -
and - forths, all the while feeding steel into our shear. "I asked
you the simplest question in this whole world about girls, and
you fell flat on your face . . . You want me to introduce you to
some real women? " No black patois there – his English was

better than mine by far. *You are* instead of *you be,* for instance. *Asked* instead of *axed.*

And so our understanding of each other's cultures grew as the days passed, though he would never admit that he was learning as much as I was. He had what are still called Street Smarts, and I found him wise and worldly beyond any other young man I knew. Each day I continued to prod him with questions. One Monday morning his every move brought a grimace. I asked him, "John, why the whining?" "Sunburn. Too much sun this weekend at the pool." Then he looked at my wide eyes, as understanding came. "You are even dumber than the dumbest dumb white boy I ever knew. You think we Negroes (he exaggerated the word deliberately into two syllables: knee grows) don't get sunburn? God help us all." Then we both laughed. Because it never had occurred to me.

At the end of summer, we parted company, both richer for the experience. But I never forgot him.

One thing I learned during my years at Tech was that there was a differentness – an unbridgeable gulf separating whites from blacks during those days. Why there was a difference I did not quite understand, having lived in the country all my boyhood, but it was clear that I had no power to change the situation. We simply kept apart from each other.

I found the cultural separation then as now ineffably sad. And, as is usually the case, in my early experiences, it came down to the personal: I really liked Marjorie. Plus, I wanted to be accepted by those men in the junkyard – older men, grizzled men, men with darker skin and harder hands, men who had earned my respect. But they never included me in their circle of trust, and most painfully, never respected me. Never. And that hurt.

*   *   *   *   *   *

Fortunately, there were easier jobs. In general, the jobs I worked were remarkably enjoyable though not especially remunerative (I loved actually getting money put into my hand at the end of the week, even if it wasn't as much as I had hoped). Beyond the money, each job taught me just a bit more about this world the adults inhabited, the world I wanted to enter.

Two important examples:

My junior year had just started. Pro Dunlap, my chemistry teacher, recognized that I was his most enthusiastic (and, I might modestly add, most reliable) student. Remember, this is the Pro Dunlap of the demonstration explosion, and one of my real heroes. He asked me if I would like the job of "running the curtain". Yes, yes, YES.

I should explain just what *running the curtain* meant. Some McKeesport organization sponsored occasional Friday night cultural attractions. They used our high school auditorium as the venue, and they needed someone they could depend upon primarily just to show up, to turn on the lights, to ensure that the sound system was operating, and throughout the performance, to open and close the curtain, plus other necessary details to make the stage performance successful. The job itself was trivially easy; the reliability of that person was the key, as everyone else with keys to the building had gone home by the time the performance started. I felt an awesome responsibility. But I had no doubt that I was up to it. What arrogance.

An hour before curtain, I sought out the performer, asked him what he – or she – or they needed, set up the lighting, and when the performance began, remembering their cues, did my best to give them perfect support. My reward was not just the two dollars I was paid for the evening, my reward was, above all, to see the back side of the performing arts. The unseen, sometimes dark side. Wow.

Before they went on, the performers –with only a rare exception – manifested a certain tenseness. A point came when the artist (I thought of them all as consummate artists) would become distant, eyes focused away, lost in their own minds, in an impenetrable bubble.

But one exception, one confident artist stands out, a violinist who did not enter his pre-performance space, a man who took time to open himself to a scrawny inquisitive kid, – actually allowing me to hold his 16th century violin. Then, taking it back, drawing his bow across strings – I was his only audience

– creating the sweetest, most ethereal sounds I had ever heard. Then just before the performance, he came to me (I stood just inside the curtain on stage right where all the controls lay at my fingertips), and, saying he would now "tune his fiddle," asked me to go on stage and sound an *a* on the piano. I walked on stage, pressed the *a* key an octave above middle *c* a few times, looking back to him behind the curtain until he was happy with his tuning, and then began to walk offstage. There were smiles and murmurs from the audience, even a little soft laughter – and then light and polite applause. Surprised, I stopped, turned, and took a genteel bow. He was smiling, applauding too, violin held under his arm. But at that moment I had to laugh at myself, recognizing that the stage was never to be for me.

What happened next was the experience of standing just a few feet to the side of a master violinist hearing – feeling – Tchaikovsky. After a few bars, his music seemed to enter my head, and then I was gone – no longer backstage at Tech. How do you thank an artist who has given you such a gift?

The school had a grand piano for these concerts. I rolled it onto the stage for the pianists, and once in place and before anyone had come into the hall, lightly fingered the keys. That piano – a huge Steinway – made pure and magnificent, hall filling sounds, so unlike our old upright at home. On one particular winter night, a woman whose name I do not remember played Chopin. Hear that nocturne today, and I am a 16-year-old boy backstage once more.

But beyond the privilege of hearing magnificent classical music while watching professional artists perform, I came to understand how they comported themselves, how they put on their stage face, how they commanded presence as they walked to center stage, and how they let down so completely and absolutely as they walked behind the curtain at performances' end. It was like watching a balloon deflate. They were spent, exhausted. Priceless lessons for an adolescent male.

The ballerinas – especially the corps – were most wonderful of all, as the girls in the corps were my age or just a few years older. Standing in the wings, I marveled at their smiles, smiles held at all costs, smiles held in the face of muscles strained to breaking, in pain, feeling profound air hunger, trickles, then rivers of sweat running down their faces streaking their makeup. Exiting stage right, where I stood, they would literally collapse onto the wood, gulping great volumes of air, trying to mop sweat without ruining makeup. God, how I admired them. The lesson was clear for this boy: *When you are on, whenever someone is watching, you must make whatever you do look effortless, no matter the pain. Practice enough so you may always make your task look easy, performing almost to the point of languor.* Their lessons have served me in good stead throughout my career.

Another thought came to me as I watched their aplomb, their cabrioles, their glissades . . . Talk about a lightning bolt from the blue. These girls were magnificent physical specimens –

beautiful, full of grace, accomplished. As the corps milled around beside me, stretching, waiting to go on, I found it somewhat difficult to breathe. Desirable, oh yes. And then the flash of inspiration, of insight: nine out of every 10 guys they were dancing with . . . liked the other guys. Why had I not learned to dance ballet as a kid? The odds were in my favor; I might've had a chance. Sigh.

An evening came when Grandma's words lit up in my head like red flashing neon: *Faint heart ne'er won fair maiden*. It was intermission. She had left the stage, allowing herself to collapse onto the wood floor. She had stretched out, and had closed her eyes. I waited a respectful time, took 3 courage pills and a deep breath, then approached. Sensing someone coming, she opened her eyes, watching me warily. I said, "Want to do something after the show?" Good eye contact, and offering my most engaging smile, I waited. And waited. Then, " Yeah, I want to pack my body in ice and hope the pain goes away by Monday. Get lost kid." More insight gained. Valuable, but painful.

One of my more memorable curtain jobs was on a certain Friday night when Wally Taber, a professional (a.k.a. "white") Hunter came to town.

Mr. Taber had taken a film crew with him to Africa. His professional quality filming, in 16mm Kodachrome's magnificent color, plus his smooth speaking voice to narrate his movies transported me. *I am, right now, alongside him. In Africa.*

His hunts for plains game allowed him to showcase magnificent East African savannas at sunrise, thundering herds of
wildebeest in the N'gorongora Crater, buzzards circling over
a recent lioness kill, the great East African rift, and the native
Africans – trackers, herdsmen, but especially the haughty Ma-
sai. He had us in the palm of his hand within two minutes.
And then came the hunts for dangerous game. Most men in
the audience had unconsciously moved toward the edges of
their seats. I found my eyes wide, burning for lack of blinking,
breathing rapidly, standing tense, ready to run or shoot. At
one point in his movie, a massive black-maned lion charged
his trackers and him. Taber dropped the lion in full charge (I
think lions can do a hundred yards in about 6 seconds) with
his 416 Rigby, a head shot. The lion slid to a stop, stone cold
dead, at the feet of the hunting party. He treated us then to a
dramatic pause (such perfect timing!) in his narration. The
audience was absolutely and reverently silent; no one moved.
I could not breathe.

Lights out, having locked up, walking down the hill to catch
the last bus, Mister Taber's movie played over and again in
my mind, and made me dream of walking on African plains
and in African jungles. I did wonder – since we humans
started there – what it would have been like for our ancestors
to sit in the hills as night fell, listening to and realizing that
the predators were becoming active, those predators thinking

of nothing but filling their bellies, as we (I mean our ancestors) came to recognize that we might be their dinner[56]. The
winter wind blowing up from the river felt not as cold as
usual. For I was elsewhere, lost in my reveries, amazed at my
good fortune. What a great job.

In the cold light of day, I recognized that two bucks once a
month was something other than capital-intensive. After
school one afternoon, I walked down to Fifth Avenue, and
started, store by store, asking for work. At Sieberg's Men's
Clothing Store, I struck gold. For three evenings a week and
most Saturdays, I became their stock boy. Stock boy? More
political incorrectness. Today I would be an Inventory Control Associate.

The people in that store were simply wonderful.

We rarely saw Mister Sieberg, a somewhat somber, ill tempered fellow. His bad manners were always excused because
"he had breathed the Kaiser's gas in the trenches of The Great
War." He was nonetheless still a jerk who never learned even
my first name.

Fortunately for me, the day-to-day operations were run by
Mister Bucholz, who had been an infantry captain in World

---

[56] Many years later, a night would come when I would foolishly satisfy that curiosity alone in an African valley, but that's another story.

War II. I was desperate to know what it was like to lead a company of men in battle. "The Germans had 88s," was all he would say about his experiences, shaking his head, looking off into the distance, remembering painful memories. "88" referred to the unbelievably terrifying, accurate, and destructive 88 mm artillery the Germans turned against our ground troops. He simply would not talk more. I concluded the war was awful.

A soft-spoken, silver haired, perfectly coiffed and remarkably lovely woman, Mrs. Adams, did the books, but more importantly, encouraged me as I struggled with my shyness. And it was an important struggle, as I was eventually moved to the sales floor on Saturday, and needed to learn to smile and to look people in the eye.

Finally there was Jeannie, a year older than me, a lovely young lady. Being older than me, I never thought of her as just a girl. Despite my continuing best efforts, I could never, ever entice her to come down to the stock room. My failure continued throughout the year despite gentle encouragement from Mrs. Adams. The men watched my unsuccessful attempts, smiled, but offered their quiet encouragement too.

At close of business each Saturday, Mister Bucholz had me accompany him to the bank's night depository to store the day's cash receipts. Had there been trouble, I'm not sure what help I could have been, but it was a responsibility I took seriously. How do you thank an adult who actually trusts you?

Every kid growing up should have a job in sales. You learn to meet, to greet, then shut your mouth, to make eye contact, to look into the other person's face, to search out what they actually want, then help them to find it.

So this chapter ends up being about growing beyond the worries and concerns of those adolescent high school years. The classroom work was critical for our success, of course, but beyond those walls each job taught important life lessons and helped my friends and me prepare ourselves for the world of big people.

But what of today? Are my times gone forever?

Ah no, not that I can see. If you want a job, then as now, one can be found. The *me* generation has always called such menial work *McJobs*, and looked at them with disdain, such jobs being beneath their dignity. We called our jobs, quite simply, opportunities.

So my three years at the Mill on the Hill, learning in class to think, to write, to analyze, to appreciate history – and outside of class, learning how to work for and with others, surviving that fearsome and socially intense schoolbus, all the while making friends, falling in and (sadly and repeatedly) out of love, and, in the process, simply seeing oneself expand all proved that it was in fact possible to drink from the firehose.

And that it was consummately fun and enriching to do so.

Peer Pressure, Popularity, and Pimples. Plus so much to learn. Amazing days, weren't they? Emotional scars? You bet. But we grew, we survived, and, by and large, we did well.

25. GYMM'N

Gymm'n is not a word I have ever heard outside the Three Rivers area or beyond these experiences I now describe. It's pronounced *Jim - en*, two distinct syllables. It's about gymnastics. Actually, about engaging in gymnastics.

Thus Gymm'n was almost always used as a verb, as in, "Chuck, you gymm'n Tuesday night?", and translated, asked *are you going Tuesday night to the gymnasium to work out on the horizontal and parallel bars?*

I've described to you in previous chapters how football and to a lesser extent basketball were the prime sports in our Western Pennsylvania Three Rivers culture. Both are sports of cities, places where enough kids could gather together to form teams. On the other hand, gymnastics was, and still is a solitary sport, a sport that was almost unknown in that part of the nation during the 1950s. To take the idea further, gymnastics is a sport as far away from the concept of team effort as is possible to be. Gymnastics pits the gymnast against his own self, against his own expectations of and need to achieve excellence, to be the best he can be.

An American Boyhood

Today, thanks to TV, most Americans have at least a passing acquaintance of gymnastics, often at the Olympics level. And those who have watched girls and boys at that level have come to appreciate the magnificence of a strong, lithe body in controlled and dangerous motion.

Donnie Kasner was the penultimate cause of my becoming a gymnast. The ultimate cause was, no surprise, my Dad[57].

First, about Donnie. Donnie came to sit in front of me and Civics and Pennsylvania History class that first year at Tech, as we were seated alphabetically. One day he had a gym bag with him – one of those cheap half-moon shaped flat bottom canvas bags in which we carried our tennies, shirts, shorts and towel. I was curious as to why anyone would be carrying stuff like that to class, passed him a note, and asked. He scribbled back that he was going to Turners after class. That name *Turners* rang a bell.

---

[57] I have mentioned this Freudian thing twice before – having been taught that the mother is the primary relationship in any child's life, but especially as it influences a little boy's development and ultimate life. I'm not so sure. So many things – personality traits, ways of seeing the world, habit patterns, even cursive handwriting style are those I saw in my Dad, and have appeared as I have matured. Which surprises me, because I have never consciously attempted to emulate him or those traits. The observation – more a question – certainly brings up the whole nature/nurture controversy too. Whatever you believe, dads are the primary causes of more of what we become than we give them credit for. More on this in the final chapter.

An American Boyhood

Which takes our story back to Dad. Growing up in a half German family, as a boy Dad had gone to Turners, and often spoke of the place during our family dinners in almost reverent tones. "Twice a week after school we'd walk down to the east part of town, and spend the evening tumbling, swinging on the bars." He then got even a bit misty eyed about these long ago experiences in the gymnasium. Turners had come to represent a certain important, mysterious but quite wonderful place in Dad's childhood. And here I had just learned, in Civics class of all places, that 40 years on, Turners still existed.

"Can I come with you?", I whispered. (Mister Carroza would not tolerate any talking in class.) Donnie just nodded his head. And so another adventure began.

School out, we walked down Bankers hill toward Fifth Avenue, passing through a seedy section that got even more run down as we got closer to the mill and the river. We turned right on Jerome Boulevard, and walked another half-mile, finally to come to a grimy red brick building. A small, hard to read sign over the door declared without explanation: Turners. Through the door, down the hallway, Donnie brought me in to the actual gymnasium. A side horse. Parallel bars. The mats. And – fascination of fascinations, the horizontal bar. I had never seen these things. I stood there in awe, just a little afraid to enter.

Put me in a high ceiling room today, close my eyes, fill the room with the smell of stale sweat, dust, rarely washed socks and jockstraps, and my mind's eye will take me back to that gym and cause the memories of the many hours I spent there, and of poignant and sometimes painful experiences to bubble to the surface of my consciousness. For the next three years, on Tuesday and Thursday nights, as soon as we could get there after school until the last bus to Greenock was to leave the city, I would work in that wonderful place. Actually, work is not the right word. The term was *we worked out*.

A word about this unusual idea, this idea called Turners. Why did it exist? Certainly there was no great demand for gymnasts in McKeesport. Who financed that building and its dusty gym?

The story begins in Europe. In 19th century Germany, Associations of all kinds had become the fashion. This association was called *Das Turn und Gesang Verein*. Literally translated, the Tumbling and Singing Society. Imported into America by a wave of German immigrants, the club became more important in the late 1800s when the Protestant upper class became worried that the trodden masses would drink too much on Sunday, and so be unfit for work in the mills on Monday mornings. A series of so-called blue laws were passed in Pennsylvania that prevented drinking in bars on Sundays[58].

---

[58] After all, we couldn't have workers with hangovers showing up Monday morning. This was not a problem for the Brahmins, all of them WASPs, as they had their own private clubs where liquor could be served on any day. The Duquesne Club, for example, by far the most prestigious and exclusive club in

But the wily workers figured if the bosses could do it so could they, and thus their own clubs developed bars which sold Sunday legal booze. (Smart people needing a drink have always found a way around any law any politician might write.) The *Turn und Gesang Verein* was one of those. But the elders knew that it was important that the primary purpose of the club was to appear *not just to drink booze* – and thus the gymnasium became critical for them to support. By the way, the Eastern Europeans had their own version of a gymnastics society: SOKOL, founded by a Czech and brought to America by the Slovak wave of immigrants. We went to their hall for competitions a few times a year, and I must say they were the friendliest competitions I had ever been part of. We were particularly impressed by their symbol - Sokol is a Czech word for falcon - and by their bird and motto ornately carved in oak over the door to their gym: *Sokol, the falcon, is a bird, who by his swiftness and energy, symbolizes the active, vigorous, strenuous, real, Spartan life.* Wow. That was really cool, we thought. But the part of their organization which paid for all else was, as in Turner's, the bar. I know other immigrant groups had their own clubs – the Sons of Italy, the Ancient Order of Hibernians, but I knew nothing of them. I was never invited to visit, but I doubted that they had a gymnasium.

In 1916 Mister Wilson went to war. Everything German (you will likely become saddened by reading our country's history

---

Pittsburgh, serves booze on Sunday even today. By the way, new money may now apply to the Duquesne Club, something impossible when I was a kid.

of those days) became suspect, un-American, even evil, and so the *Turn und Gesang Verein* quickly became *American Turners*. Fortunately, the people had not changed, and were marvelously supportive and even proud of us kids trying to pursue such a little-known sport. So I must emphasize that the clubs did not exist only to dispense alcohol. First, I never saw anyone drunk there, and second, there were other social activities, as Turners was a place for people of a culture to gather, to speak the mother language, to share food and drink, and to talk about someday returning to the old country. Strangely, I never heard anyone sing.

But back to the gymnastics essence: What do you do, where you start when you want to learn gymnastics in a football based steel town?

Before we answer that question may I first give you just a minimal background of terms: A specific gymnastic maneuver was called a *trick* or a *move*, or if it was basic enough, it might have its own name, like *giant swing* or a *back handspring*. And when the gymnast put a series of tricks together, he performed a *routine*. Developing a routine that combined strength and grace moves with a good dismount was the way to win competitions. Or more importantly, to impress the observing female gymnasts. Or, most importantly, to satisfy yourself.

Donnie and I dressed in the locker room – swim trunks, T-shirts, and white socks for me, plus canvas male ballet slippers for him, the slippers a piece of equipment I would have to find before our next workout. We entered the gym together, finding the coach and half a dozen other guys already loosening up. Having worked on the farm that summer, I knew I was tough as nails and strong as an ox, and would soon show everyone *how it was done*. I paid for that arrogance with pain and blisters.

No matter your background, whether weightlifting or working on a farm, when you come into the gym, you will immediately find you don't have enough upper body strength to be a gymnast. And you quickly learn that your strength must be developed slowly and painfully by doing increasingly more difficult maneuvers on the equipment. Thought, time, and sweat, plus a next day's searing ache of muscles you didn't even know you had was the price to learn gymnastics. The first casualty of the training was my inflated feeling of physical superiority.

Don and the coach, John Butella, started teaching me the basics the first night. It soon became obvious: The essence of gymnastics is to take specific body strengths, to turn that strength into motion, into momentum, then, when the timing is perfect, to use that strength and momentum to move your body in graceful and what appear to be effortless arcs. It sounds easy when it's described like that, doesn't it? Sad to say, I just didn't have the strength. Or the timing. Or even the most basic knowledge.

Did I mention risk? You will, sooner rather than later, come loose from the bars, usually at high speed and some altitude, almost always while spinning and rotating one way or the other . . . and gravity always, always wins. The sound of the gymnast hitting the mat is that of a sopping wet towel slapped onto concrete.

So along with the building-up-of-strength maneuvers, you are also taught to fall. A few minutes on the horizontal bar, a few minutes on the side horse, a few minutes on the parallel bars, and then on to the mats to learn to fall. The training begins in a crouch, a tuck of the head, chin on chest, most weight supported on hands, ending in a forward roll. As soon as you can keep your wits about you (these unphysiologic maneuvers are disorienting at first) and can do several rolls in a row, you progress to a dive into the forward roll from a standing start, and then ultimately a running start to a dive to the forward roll, catching your weight on hands, tucking head, going forward, coming back up onto your feet. Mastering the skill is a prime confidence builder and is needed during almost every workout. In my years as a gymnast, we came unglued from the bars so many times without serious injury that we rarely considered serious injury something to fear. And we had – always had – spotters. *To spot* a compatriot, one or two of us would stand next to the bars, then when someone became separated, we would try to grab him, at least breaking his fall as we came together, arms and legs flailing, onto the mat. We would then untangle ourselves, chiding each other for the mistake, laughing a bit, and get on with the workout. It was an effective system, because in all my time as a gymnast, only one kid broke his neck and became a quadriplegic.

Of the equipment, parallel bars, side horse, free exercise, I was attracted to the high bar – a.k.a. horizontal bar – immediately. The high bar combined difficulty with momentum and danger to produce elegance. Consider this: a horizontal steel bar, little more than an inch in diameter, eight feet wide, supported on posts and held in place by guy wires, the bar about nine feet above the floor. So step one, jump up to the bar. Step two, get a bit of momentum going: a partial pull-up, a quick throwback of the head while relaxing the arms, and voilà, you are swinging. And so you've learned the next rule. Move the head decisively, and your body will soon follow. Step three, as you swing forward, learn to pull yourself up over the top of the bar, feet over first, to end with you paused, head up, back arched, toes pointed (always for elegance), the bar across your hips. This will be the position to start most subsequent, more difficult moves.

And in swinging forward then pulling yourself up into that position, since you're a guy, you discover a serious problem. Actually three problems. Three small appendages get in the way.

The first time I successfully performed this maneuver, a profound, primitive, and excruciating pain shot up from my crotch into the pit of my stomach, passed up through my chest and along my back, entered my skull, and made the world go dark. I fought hard to keep the tears from rolling down my cheeks. The coach looked up at me, smiled, and said, "Pinched its ears, did you? That happens to everybody – once." So we all learned that a good jockstrap was our primary piece of equipment. In fact, protecting this anatomy seemed to be more important than protecting our hands, or even our neck, something we should have been thinking about more, because flying off the horizontal bar was inevitable.

Sometimes visitors came from SOKOL, and sometimes older guys came to work out, and we welcomed them all. But generally there was a core of only eight of us guys who came to that gym, rain, snow, sleet, or shine. Eight boys out of some 80,000 people who lived in the area. It was a lonely sport. One and only one of my high school teachers ever came to our competitions. Of course I loved her for it.

And it was so energy intensive, this gymnastics. After we had worked out, showered, and packed our gear, we headed across Jerome Boulevard to a local Eat-n-Park. We didn't then know about low blood sugar, but we felt a profound and primitive need: we recognized an awful, gut gnawing hunger. After we had spent our last penny on food, the night manager, a kind and understanding old guy, brought all of his left over day-old doughnuts to the table. We divided them carefully, then devoured them.

Ah, but there is a little-mentioned benefit of being a gymnast.

First, picture what gymnastics develops in a boy: muscular definition and growth in all the right places; lightning fast reflexes; the ability to move elegantly, almost on a level with ballet; almost no body fat; and above all, confidence in your body and so in yourself. Now think what gymnastics does for girls. Girls come to possess even more elegance, even more beauty. So perhaps you can now picture this: a magnificent young woman's body covered only by a thin skintight black leotard moving with a dancer's grace along the four inch wide balance beam, combining upper body strength and precision with a ballerina's silky smooth legwork. And so you now might be able to see in your mind's eye Jeannie and Joanne Otto. Of course all of us guys fell in love with the sisters. Fortunately for us, the girls worked out on alternate nights. Had they not been separated from us guys most of the times, I suspect that we would've come unglued from the bars far more frequently than we did.

During winter of our senior year, and my third year as a gymnast, as the annual gymnastics exhibition for the Turners adults was approaching, Don decided that we would work up a two-man strength and balance routine. I weighed 137 pounds and was almost five feet eight inches tall, so being heavier and an inch taller than Don and he being the undisputed master at handstands, he got to be on top. The goal was for the guy on top to press into, then maintain a handstand, supporting himself on the hands of the bottom guy as the bottom guy moved through various positions. The low guy always began completely supine on the floor, rolling into various positions, ultimately to stand, our four arms completely straight, palm to palm, the guy on top a mirror image of the guy on bottom. If you have ever seen the two strong men at Cirque du Soleil, you know about this routine – not that we could ever have approached their strength and professionalism.

We worked and we worked. We faltered. We sweat. Don fell, again and again. Sometimes I dropped him, sometimes he just lost his balance. But ever so slowly we came together as a team. And I came finally to realize that this effort was ultimately not for the crowd, but for us. Certainly we wanted, we desperately needed, to look good, but not so much for that audience, nor for the other gymnasts who were certain to be critically watching, nor for Jeannie and Joanne Otto (well, maybe a little for Jeannie and Joanne), but for us. This work was about achieving excellence for its own sake, for us to be as good as we could be.

Donnie decided on and planned the sequence of moves, and the way they would be executed. Never telling me why, he impressed upon me that our act would be performed in slow, deliberate, elegant motions. I thought this was weird, but he had a great sense of the dramatic, and he would turn out to be correct in that judgment.

The evening came. We dressed alike, all in white, thin strap undershirts barely covering hairy chests, long, skin-tight cotton trousers held in place by suspenders, feet covered with white leather ballet slippers, hands dusted white with chalk to prevent slippage. We looked at the crowd; we faced each other, looked at each other, nodded, then my right hand in his right hand, I leaned backwards slowly to lie on the hardwood floor, he leaning backwards to counterbalance my move. Now supine, ever so slowly, bringing both arms to the vertical, palms flat, I waited. Don walked slowly to my head. It seemed as though he took 30 seconds to place his palms just so on mine, but it worked. He secured a firm grip, and then carried out a most difficult straight arm, straight leg press to a handstand.

It came to me that the people watching had stopped talking. I noticed a respectful and absolute silence in the room. But then something else happened – the people became blurry, like in a poorly focused picture, and seemed to move into the distance. And my hearing changed. The buzz of conversation downstairs, even the sounds of traffic outside – everything seemed to move far away. And time slowed. I have no remembrance of the rest of our routine, other than that we worked together flawlessly. Yes, there was applause, yes, we did bow, yes we did walk off slowly – and with grace and control. We sat together in the locker room, looking first at each other, then looking at the tremor in our hands, and oh so exhausted. And then, uncontrollable, post stress giggles.

But I barely remember any of those feelings – especially the last part of our routine. But I do remember that for just those few minutes Don and I reached some unnameable state most people have only dreamed of. Some thing, some place we could not put into words.

Oh, by the way, and back to reality, Jeannie and Joanne never gave us the time of day. So much for gymnastics as a girl attractor.

This was the one and only time two of us worked together. The rest of the time, each of us went solo. How alone that could feel.

Gymnastics has changed since those years. Thanks to television, a significant number of Americans have become aware of the sport, and many have even come to be able to judge just how good an individual gymnast is.

Let me make an aside, an observation: During the last decade, as I have watched Olympic gymnastics, two critical changes have become apparent. First, the quality of the individual gymnast has improved dramatically. The routines are at least a quantum more difficult than we had ever dreamed of performing, and the gymnasts are better physically conditioned. And if I had to pick out a group for special notice it would be the adolescent girls. More impressive and more beautiful even to the point of magnificence are those girls, barely pubescent, who have been training since they were five or six, able for example to do back flips on a 4 inch wide balance beam, able to swing on uneven parallel bars, and fly off, with beautiful dismounts, earning scores we could never dream of during my day. I love their perfection, but I worry. As a physician I hate what the coaches have done to those little girls, abusing tender and vulnerable growing bones and joints and even more importantly, abusing their psyches. It would be an interesting scientific study to follow these kids into their 40s to see how they do. Until such a scientific study is done, I will withhold comment. But permit me to worry.

On the other hand, I cannot withhold comment on the change in the fans. It is a change not for the better. Gymnastics is not about bringing gold medals home. Especially not to America, or to any other country. Gymnastics is not about a nation's accomplishment; it is about an individual's accomplishment. You will never see a gymnast boo another competitor, and we don't like it when the fans do. Just the opposite: So many times when an opponent had finished a particularly difficult and graceful routine, we on the opposing bench found ourselves spontaneously standing to applaud him. Again: Gymnastics is about the individual. And for my friends and me, gymnastics was about our quest to be as good as we could humanly be. Gymnastics is not football, not soccer.

When I walked to the horizontal bar, all eyes were on me and me alone. How terrifying that was. When I looked up to the bar, back down to my spotters hoping to see an encouraging smile, nodded to the judges, then back up to the bar, time began to slow, to expand, and everyone and every other thing receded into the distance. Then there was only the bar, the bright lights, and me. My spotters grabbed my hips, helped me jump up to the bar (at least I think they did), and I confirmed my grip. Then a pull and a swing . . . and a rarely remembered rest of the routine. I do remember walking off when I had finished, feeling only profound air hunger, and always wishing I had done better. My errors were obvious to those in the bleachers watching, certainly obvious to my critical teammates, but they were especially obvious to me.

I never heard another gymnast complain that we lost the meet because of the other team's luck or excellence, that the judging had been bad, or to say that his teammates had let him down. Afterwards, coming out of the shower, looking into the steamy locker room mirror, each of us recognized that that person looking back from that mirror got the credit, the blame, and the ultimate responsibility for what we had done.

And then, being gymnasts, we smiled, slapped each other on the back, vowing to ourselves that we would inevitably do better next time. And we usually did.

26. MEN

A recurring theme in these essays is the relationship of boys to strong men, men closely interwoven into boys' daily lives.

Yet in an earlier chapter I had noted that during my psychiatry training (done mostly by Freudians, obviously), I was taught that the primary and critical relationship was mother and child – or perhaps more correctly said, child to mother. Everything else, every other relationship, the Professors did their best to convince us, was far down the list, was distinctly secondary.

Maybe so. But now we should explore – and more importantly – critically question that Freudian premise in depth, especially through the light of my experiences. Then ultimately, and of course, you get to decide.

Let's see, because . . .

During my childhood, I found myself surrounded by men who were giants. I still feel their closeness and their powerful

influences every day of my life. Nonetheless, it's an interesting premise – that one about the primary relationship – but
we may have to modify that premise, at least in my case. And
as you read, I would ask you to wonder about the men (or
more importantly perhaps, the lack of men) in your life.

It's possible to divide the men who influenced me into two
groups. Outside of family men, and the men in the family,
men of our blood.

As example of the former group:

Glen Rojohn owned Rojohn Plumbing and Heating, a business directly across the street from the bus stop where we
waited to go home after grade school. Each afternoon we saw
him through the large plate glass front, surrounded by his water heaters and sample furnaces. A quiet man, we watched as
he sat at his desk, fielding phone calls, handling papers, giving directions to his employees, and, on occasion, looking outside to smile at us romping and boisterous kids.

It turns out, I found many years later, that in December 1944,
returning to England having bombed in support of ground
troops fighting our Battle of the Bulge, he was pilot- in -com-
mand of a B-17 bomber, a bomber that had a midair collision
with another. After the traumatic coming together, both airplanes stuck together; his plane was on top and in control,
such as it was. Though over the ocean, and having lost significant power and with damaged controls, he was able to bring

both planes back to Europe, where he had the crews bail out. One crew member died. The other 19 men, including Mister Rojohn, became prisoners of war. I didn't learn about this unbelievably skillful but unlikely outcome to that heroic action until a few years ago, as he never talked to anyone in town about his many medals. His quietness, confidence, and self containment was typical of the veterans I knew. We kids had no idea during those years after the war that we were surrounded by heroes. They simply kept their experiences to themselves. But I was always influenced by their self effacing dignity. Mister Rojohn was the prime example – but just a single example of men I had come to respect and admire. The lessons they taught were, no surprise, nonverbal, but powerfully nonverbal: don't brag, don't boast; just get the job done – and done well. Then smile, and get on with life.

That me expand on that premise: for Mister Rojohn was *not* an isolated example. In fact, men like him were prototypical, were the norm during my boyhood. These men– both in and outside of the family – were comfortable being in charge. As a generality, men in the 1930s and 1940s, at least in our circle, tended to be willing to lead, able to give orders. The men, those men I came to know intimately, were above all, comfortable in their leadership roles and more than willing to teach young boys. They felt responsible for us; more importantly, they felt a need to be our civilizing influence. They understood and knew that boys were, while growing up, little better than primitive savages. There was no problem, for example, with any man in our circle giving a misbehaving boy the back of his hand, especially if the man knew the family well, while warning him that, when his dad got home from work, he would get even more severe discipline. On the other hand, to be physically chastised was a rare occurrence in our lives, simply because we knew better. We knew what would happen.

One day, coming home on the bus, I was being obnoxious to one of the littler kids, teasing him. Suddenly I felt a hard hand on my shoulder. Wordlessly, the man, a mill worker began to squeeze (clever, not drawing attention to the silent transaction). The pain ultimately drove me to my knees. Though other passengers nearby soon came to notice, and were watching (in approval), not a word was said. I got the message. Today any adult male giving a boy a smack – or more likely a boot on his bum, even just touching him, would be arrested. And the father would likely be arrested too. Then, almost certainly, the boy sent for psychiatric therapy. I am not exaggerating – I have seen it. You may think today's mindset is an improvement; I will never agree.

When those men of the 1930s and 40s gathered together, whether it was in the hunting camp or at a bus stop, they allowed – even encouraged – us to be nearby, but we were expected to listen and learn. And especially to shut up. How unlike the boys of today . . . who are usually treated as if they actually know something. Men in those days would look at each other – would be actually astounded if a boy offered them some advice about the world. And then they would laugh. At the boy.

Of course we ran across men who were jerks, liars, thieves – and worse. But by and large, we had the power and the freedom to avoid them.

Now on to my family.

The men in my family were all short – both grandfathers were about 5'5", my dad and uncles, about 5'6". But those men, as far as my boy cousins and I were concerned,  were huge. Here is my Dad (hands in pockets), and brothers Bill (sitting) and Eddie, in 1923.

You could characterize all of the family men as mesomorphic – generally muscular, with good vision, and in their younger days, looking kind of like Arnold before steroids. As they aged, the only changes I noted were receding hairlines and the development of paunches. All of them without exception had quick reflexes and good eye hand skills. One of my cousins characterized us thus: "Kerbers have good thumbs." Isn't that an interesting way to describe being handy?

And the entire family possessed a pervasive, even profound-to-the-point-of-neurosis work ethic. Another cousin, Annie, described it thus: "Any Kerber can work the next three people right into the ground." But before you smile, let me emphasize: those words were not a compliment. To her, that personality trait was in the nature of a terrible family curse. I didn't realize how perceptive she was until, years later, recognizing that on too many occasions, we, sisters, cousins and I, have all worked harder when we should have worked smarter.

And another pic: Uncle Bill (far left) Dad, and Uncle Eddie far right, all in their 20s.

*   *   *   *   *

My dad was the youngest of four children: Eddie, Mary, Bill, and Dad. It is often difficult to be the last born (the *baby of the family,* they called him *forever, even into his 40s*). It is especially difficult in certain families, and so it was in his, but more about that later.

Uncle Eddie believed firmly and absolutely in primogeniture. Everything the family could create was to be his – by divine right, and he expected his sister and brothers to help him. He was doing God's work, after all, and living each and every day as *a devout Catholic*.

As his first career step, Uncle Eddie tried organizing a riding stable near the country club. Then he expanded that to a horse farm across the river, and finally, recognizing economic facts of life, a dairy farm. And with the dairy farm, he achieved real financial success.

But he was cruel. He enjoyed inflicting pain, whether it was taking a whip to one of his kid' s legs, or pulling clippers through my hair during one of my rare summer haircuts. How can you make a haircut painful? But he did, and caused pain enough to cause tears to fill my eyes (but I never once gave him the satisfaction of letting him see). Aunt Mary said he was cruel because he had polio as a kid, which left him with one leg a little smaller than the other (you can see it in the photo). I never believed that explanation; it was just another example of adults saying one thing to a child while knowing another.

And Uncle Eddie quite deliberately had many kids – nine of them. It was obvious to family and friends why: Kids were cheap help. None of his kids got to leave for school, nor were allowed to play after school, until all chores were finished. Homework was last on the list, and no surprise, tired kids often just went to bed. In the summer, the farm workload was crushing: we all helped in making hay, harvesting corn, and butchering livestock.

Before we had a baler, hay would be brought from the fields to the open barn doors, then a man would push a two-pronged hook into the pile. A rope led from the hook up to a pulley attached to a roof beam, back down to a harnessed mule. When I was really small, my job was to ride the mule, directing it forward, so pulling the hay up and into the loft. No matter how I kicked its ribs to urge it on, the mule would not move. Uncle Eddie saw the problem, walked to the side of the barn, picked up a length of 2 x 4, walked up to the mule, and hit the mule with all his might on the forehead[59]. The mule worked the rest of the morning. No words were said. He treated his kids much the same way. Some lesson.

He wore his Catholic religiosity proudly for all to see, but his morality was selective. He had asked a man from a neighboring farm to bring over a piece of equipment. The farmer said, "The only day I have available to bring it over is Sunday, and I know how you feel about the Sabbath." "The better the day, the better the deed," Eddie answered quickly. *So he makes his morals fit to what he wants at the moment,* I thought. And on another occasion, replying to a visitor who observed so many kids working and running around, "the Good Lord just keeps sending them." I had seen into his dark, off-limits-to-us bedroom and knew how babies came about. God had nothing to do with the process. Another dissimulation.

---

[59] Okay, I know you have likely heard this story, and you undoubtedly think it is apocryphal, but I guarantee you, it happened for real.

Uncle Eddie was actually a powerful communicator, but the communications were often opposite to the words he spoke. How confusing, then anger producing for little boys. As I grew I came to view his intellectual dishonesty with disrespect tinged by a slight but definite disgust.

I had thought Uncle Eddie was one of the meanest, toughest men in the world when I was little. But then one day he had a heart attack, and when my dad took me to see him in the hospital (I was 15 at the time), I had never seen so much stark fear on anyone's face. He lay half upright within the oxygen tent, eyes wide, face pale, fingering his rosary beads, mumbling *Hail Marys*. I grant you that having an acute coronary event is absolutely fear producing and crushingly painful, and in my years practicing medicine, I have seen many such events. But in every one of those patients, I have never seen a single one as terrified as tough guy Uncle Eddie. In actuality, his heart attack was a relatively minor one, and he was soon back at work, cruel as ever, having gained no insight about his humanity from that coronary event.

In play, my cousins and I scrambled and ran after each other on the high exposed beams in the barn. All the time. We ran. Nobody ever fell. Yet one day Uncle Eddie "fell to his death." How interesting. I wondered if one of his kids had pushed him – a premise I tried out on some of my cousins – in later years when we were much older. Most were horrified that I would even conceptualize such an evil possibility. But two of them just smiled. Knowingly.

Uncle Bill was the polar opposite of Uncle Eddie, so different that until you looked at them and saw the physical resemblances, you wondered if they had the same parents.

Both Mom and Dad held Uncle Bill up to me as example of what a poor boy could achieve. He had worked his way through Carnegie Tech (now Carnegie Mellon University) and was an architect, with a regular, secure job at the mill (security was the ultimate success marker in our family). He had married a petite, kind, and awesomely beautiful strawberry blonde lady who presented him with three remarkably normal (but robust) kids. Uncle Bill, like his brothers, could do just about anything he chose to try. He had taught himself to play the violin, made marvelous detailed architectural drawings, and as a hobby, tinted black and white photographs with transparent oil paints, a technique he patiently taught me.

Uncle Bill and his family actually lived in the city, in McKeesport, up on the hill, well away from the mills. After school, I could drop into their home anytime I chose, totally unannounced, whereupon Aunt Agnes would give me a sandwich, a glass of milk, and make feel welcome. Uncle Bill treated me as though he actually was interested in what I had to say – a gift rare from any adult, always surprising, but wonderful affirmation for a little boy. I didn't have nearly enough time with him, but his success became the imprint for my future.

He was one of the adults who made me believe that I could, no matter the obstacles, work my way through school. "But only if you work hard enough," he would always add.

* * * * * *

My dad's father, Grandpap Kerber, doesn't get his own chapter because he died when I was a little boy, and so there are few stories and scant experience to write about. But what a profound influence he had.

Grandpap Kerber first came into my consciousness at the earliest stage at which any child can form memories. Though those memories are fuzzy, I know I was old enough to be walking and talking. I was at the Manor Avenue family home in McKeesport.

Grandpap had a dog – a large, fiercely protective German shepherd. With Fritz, I could do no wrong, and we played and wrestled together continuously. It came time to go home. Being maybe three or four, and exploring my powers, I stood behind his head – backed into a corner. My mother came to fetch me. Fritz growled, showing real teeth. Mom wisely backed off. My dad took charge, approached, and with his sternest look, gave orders both to me and the dog. Fritz growled, ears back, lowering his head, baring teeth again. Showing he was really smart, Dad backed away. He verbally threatened the dog. Fritz looked him in the eye, immobile. Threats didn't work. Then Dad described the punishment awaiting me in vigorous and vivid detail – punishment that would be inflicted on me if I did not leave Fritz's side, get in the car, so we could all go home. You may have noticed that little boys enjoy saying no. "NO," I said. Dad vowed I would not be able to sit for a week. And so this stalemate continued until my grandfather came home, immediately solving the problem (Fritz obeyed him instantly). No surprise, once in the car, I had earned and received a warm fanny. But I saw Grandpap Kerber trying to hide his smile. He winked at me, and I know was secretly pleased by my independence and grit. The stinging bottom was trivial payment for that remembered smile.

Grandpap Kerber was a Bell Telephone lineman, a lineman back in the days when that job called for the lineman's complete independence and reliability. In the morning, he was given a list of tasks by the dispatcher. In the evening, he was expected to return, having completed them, in whatever order and in whichever way that Grandpap wished. Lineman then were not specialists – they did everything from repairing a phone in your home, to climbing a pole, spikes strapped to legs, stringing line. In his dark green Telephone Company truck, he traveled the back roads of Elizabeth Township as far north as McKeesport, south to Sutersville, answering all calls for help. I have photographs of him standing proudly next to that truck. I also have photographs of him in the woods, rifle in hand, next to dead white tail deer. I have photographs of him – portraits actually – showing a serious man, a man in full, a man with broad, strong face and penetrating eyes. This photo is from 1923.

What the photographs cannot show, and what I remember was his aura of absolute self-confidence, of strength, of hardness – until he saw me, when a softening smile would spread over his face, then his calloused hand gently and tenderly stroked my cheek. Could there be a better caress for any little boy?

He had directed Mom to keep a Mason jar of cold coffee in the refrigerator. When patrolling anywhere near our place, Grandpap Kerber would stop for a few minutes, ask Mom for a glass of cold coffee, put me on his knee, then spin magical stories, stories of hunting the wily white tail deer, of battling lightning, blizzards and sleet to bring telephone service into homes of the kind and good people that he had come to know. He told of his family's hard and painful times during the depression, when they lived in the Irish ghetto of downtown McKeesport. On his knee I felt awe. And pride. And love.

To set the stage for the next episode in the Grandpap Kerber saga, I must admit to having been a willful, often obnoxious little boy, too full of himself for his own good. My Aunt Mary had told me on more occasions than I want to remember, "You would try the patience of a saint." My mom observed that

Aunt Mary was being incredibly kind. Being a little boy, I was not quite sure what either of them meant, but for sure, whatever it was was not good. Then one day (about age 5) I pushed Grandpap Kerber beyond his limits. He was distracted by something, my peskiness intruded, and I clearly had suddenly and irrevocably crossed a line. And knew it immediately. Quick as lightning, the back of his hand came across my cheek. I was stunned. How could this loving man, this giant in my life, do that? With tears of hurt and rage pouring down my cheeks, I wailed, "You. Sob. Hit. Sob. Me." Immediately the ambience changed; it was as though I had pushed a knife into his heart. Anguish spread across his face. He seemed to deflate, to get smaller. He was quiet for the longest time.

"I wouldn't hurt you for the world . . ." (Well, you just did, I thought, but I was at least smart enough to keep my mouth shut.) His was a small voice that repeated as he looked down to the floor, repeating, "...... I wouldn't hurt you for the world.......". I doubt he ever recovered; of course I certainly did, and with little boy quickness. What I have continued to remember is what a painful lesson that transaction was. Those few powerful and terrible moments in his kitchen are clearly imprinted to this day. His anguish was far worse than the pain of my tingling cheek. I had learned that even a little boy has power to cause pain to someone who loves him. It was a power that I would try my best never to wield again.

An American Boyhood

When Grandpap Kerber's four children had grown and had begun bringing money into the family, the family left Strawberry Alley to buy a home on Banker's Hill – on the appropriately named Manor Avenue. The family had realized the American dream, and had gotten out of the ghetto. The first floor of the Manor Avenue house – meticulously appointed and always organized – belonged to the women of the family, women who had known hunger and the embarrassment of poverty, women who were determined to forget forever the squalor of that Irish ghetto downtown. But the basement was his, a place where he could go to smoke his pipe "And get away from *them*", he would say to me, pointing with his pipe stem, rolling his eyes to look up, as though he could see *them* (Aunts Mary and Minnie) through the ceiling.

His overstuffed easy chair sat next to the coal furnace (how warm, how snug, how comforting, I realized). At the opposite end of the cellar lay his work bench covered with tools and guns, guns in the midst of repair and cleaning. And surprisingly, in his cellar's center, he had placed a dental chair and foot powered drill. Dental work? Why not? It seemed he could do everything else. So he carried out a completely illegal private practice of dentistry – in his basement. Of course he had no formal training – but the men and women from the old neighborhood – Germans and Irish for the most part, trusted him, and I suspect, liked his prices. He taught me to work the drill – not too fast on the foot pedal – and to listen for the correct pitch of the drill to control its speed. And he showed me how to hold the handpiece correctly, making the tiniest controlled motions with the bit, all the while keeping the driving belt from rubbing a blister on the back of my hand.

But back to that tension – that coolness I felt in the house. Little boys are easily confused, then angered by adults' ability to say one thing and communicate the opposite nonverbally. As an aside, few adults appreciate just how excellent and skillful kids are at reading even the most subtle body language[60]. This dichotomy causes real discomfort – and more often, a significant anxiety. And I felt this uncomfortable strangeness as I watched Aunts Mary and Minnie interact with Grandpap. They treated him with a peculiar correct coolness – almost as though he was not welcome in his own home. It was not until I was in medical school that I came to understand the sad origin of that tension.

So some insight into that pain: When she was in her late 50s, Aunt Mary developed signs and symptoms of a cerebral aneurysm. By that time in her life, she had come to recognize that her mom had almost certainly died from a ruptured aneurysm – not, as was the family myth, a broken heart. Recognizing the symptoms, Mary had no doubt that she was going to die – just as her mother had. I referred her to a good brain surgeon, who quickly admitted her for evaluation. In Presbyterian Hospital as she awaited her work up and likely surgery, she spilled her guts to me about the skeletons in our

---

[60] Note to adults: don't even think to try to lie to kids. Do so and they will see through you – soon labeling you as dishonest. And once the kids' trust is gone, it is gone forever.

family closet. The many skeletons. Wow. Have you not been amazed at what people will reveal when they think death is imminent?

Now to the broken heart theory. The Irish side of the family was a bit boisterous, given to take the wee drop – or often a great deal more[61], a bit randy, to hear Aunt Mary tell, adventurous (her Uncle Hutchison had gone to, survived, and returned from the California gold rush, penniless of course), but severely guilt ridden as Catholic families were wont to be. And Mary's mom, my Grandmother Ann Kerber, exercised her fanatic Catholicism to assuage her guilt – for something. "Annie is a saint", the neighbors would say, as she trudged in her housecoat and slippers to mass each morning, publicly embarrassed, ensuring the world would recognize her suffering[62]. Now back to Mary: "After her fourth child was delivered, she did the Catholic thing, and slept outside the sheets," she whispered. Now what follows is my inference: Grandpap Kerber, being a virile young man, known and welcome in most homes in the county because of his job, found the temptations too much to resist. The scandal was *he had girlfriends*. Not *a* girlfriend, mind you – girlfriends. Plural. It caused a

---

[61] The Celtic curse. As the poet said, "We are a priest and whiskey ridden race."

[62] My friends and I in medical school had long discussions about whether Jewish guilt was more destructive than Catholic guilt. Though there was no resolution, in my heart I felt I always won the arguments because I was able to point out that, whereas Jewish guilt is based in the power of the family, Catholic guilt is far more intense and expansive, being the guilt of God's Entire Universe. You have every right to disagree.

certain angst in the family – in his sons somewhat, as they were loyal to their mom, more in Mary and Minnie, but especially and absolutely in saintly wife Annie. And then one morning Annie was found dead in bed. *"Of a broken heart,"* they whispered. Of course everyone knew. Then they – Mary and Minnie especially – saw to it that Grandpap paid for his transgressions. Wow.

When I was about seven, Mom and Dad took me to visit Grandpap Kerber in McKeesport Hospital. Driving there, they were uncharacteristically tense and quiet and would answer none of my questions. As we entered the building, the smell of ether and antiseptic was, at first, overwhelming, even nausea inducing. But after some minutes I found the smell interesting, even attractive, and soon developed an awe of the place. Until we entered Grandpap's room, that is. Then I saw the concern in Dad's eyes change to something else – I didn't know what it was, but I sure knew it was bad. My mother became distinctly uncomfortable, almost sick to her stomach. Then Grandpap, without his usual smile (that was strange, I recognized), pulled the sheets aside to show us a huge white bandage over his lower belly. Now Mom became faint. I had no idea what it all meant, but knew it was more than bad, probably even awful. A cold lead ball suddenly made itself felt in my belly. I came to recognize this coldness as fear. (Prostate cancer. God's punishment, they whispered.)

Time is difficult for a seven-year-old boy to judge, but it seemed that the next thing I knew, I was being brought into the music room of the Manor Avenue house, seeing my wonderful grandfather, gray and stone cold still in his coffin. The sickly sweet combination of flower perfume and embalming fluid made me want to vomit. What happened? Then I didn't know; in medical school I learned: surgery for an advanced malignancy hastens death. It was my first experience with an unexplainable phenomenon, the cruel, absolute, and irrevocable loss of a loved adult. In an instant, walking into that candlelit room, I felt a dark hole had come in to my soul.

Since then, other similar dark holes have come into my existence. The holes don't change; they don't go away; they never get smaller. It makes me wonder what will happen when there are so many holes they all come together, to coalesce. I suspect that I don't really want to know.

27. WOMEN

So many wonderful women in this world; so many wonderful women in my life. Where to start?

You have already met Mom so we can go on to explore other interesting relationships. And, as in the chapter on MEN, allow me to divide the essay into two groups: those women in the family, and those outside.

But as the foundation, I must offer a few words of defense of women in general.

The form and content of that sentence might make you wonder: *Defense? Is someone attacking women?* And my answer is that, during the years of my growing up, women clearly were second-class citizens. Divisive politicians, feminazis and misogynists aside, let's see if we can bring some light to what is often a heated and irrational argument about a woman's place in our culture. First fact: I must point out women's subservient role and disrespected status in at least one of the major world religions, and second, women's lower status in several major world societies. Those are cold hard observations, disturbing facts. Have strides been made toward equality? Absolutely. Especially in this country and in my profession. But still . . .

Now I will admit that what follows is a highly subjective, intensely personal view, a view based upon my half-century of practicing medicine and surgery.

Psychiatrists (historically usually male) point out – firmly point out even to the point of tediousness – that the primary relationship is mother to child. Everything else, every other relationship throughout our lives is less important. I have mentioned this theory twice before in these essays. And we have been reminded by others that mothers' power has a dark side. Have you not come across books, biographies mostly, that list and describe with embarrassing and painful detail how mothers have ruined the (usually) male authors' lives, have created unresolved, mostly sexual conflict, and have even caused continuing and untreatable neurosis and psychosis? Let me stop at this moment to say to those authors: Oh how tedious. How, well, neurotic of you, you pitiful man/boy. Man up, for God's sake. Take some responsibility for yourselves. Stop blaming your moms. Women have a tough enough row to hoe.

Let me talk for just one moment as a doctor, and allow me to come to young mothers' defense. Consider: a woman, usually severely, often romantically *in love*, especially in love with life itself, is beginning to enjoy her sexuality – and then one day a profound change comes about, a change her mom or her teachers never really quite prepared her for. A fetus (a parasite, as one young mom described it to me) takes over, controlling her hormones, changing her moods, altering her body. *Her* body. No matter how much the baby is wished for, the first pregnancy is a significant life altering event.

The outward change, the body change, is the easiest to see. But it is certainly not the most important change. And I am not just talking about morning sickness, which can be truly debilitating. The real change is inside – raging hormones, confusing moods. Now a generalization: not a few men find this process as, well, natural, and fail to understand its profoundness . Thank God most women sooner or later come to terms with the change in the appearance of their bodies (a change many women feel is not for the better). And good for all of us, most moms sooner or later accept the presence of another human being in their bellies – and eventually come to find awe in their ability to create. Then, just when that young woman reaches the point of equanimity, labor, frightening and painful labor begins. An anecdote: I was helping one of my OB professors during an uncommonly difficult delivery and when the baby was out and breathing well, she turned to me and said, "If men had to have the babies, there wouldn't be many people in the world." *Good point*, I thought.

Labor done, mom exhausted, the average mom's trial is not over. Organic depression, depression that is often poorly treated, often, even rarely admitted, may ensue. And sometimes the postpartum situation even devolves into psychosis[63].

Yet our culture expects that this young woman will turn on a dime to change her life – doing so without formal training or much experience – to nurture, then mold this new baby – a most profound of all human responsibilities – for the next 20 years, turning that new person in her home into a functioning, productive, and independent adult.

As a doctor and a father myself, I continue to be amazed about how well women do it. I stand in awe.

So now that you know my mindset about women in general, let me begin with the women in my family.

Though I had four aunts, we should begin with Aunt Mary and Aunt Minnie. Mary was Dad's older sister; Minnie her life companion. Minnie had been adopted into the Kerber family as a little girl – an orphan. "Orphan", in those days, usually meant an illegitimate child who had been abandoned by the father, with the mother being unable to care for the child. But

---

[63] I remember trying to reassure a mother of three children as her labor became more intense. She looked at me with anger, saying, "What do you know? Does your body turn into a great bloody cave once a year?" How does the new intern reply to a statement like that?

the facts of Minnie's case are lost in dim time. Nonetheless, Minnie had been welcomed into the family, and was loved and treated as just one more kid in the house. By the way, I have noticed that this welcoming of lost souls into our family's bosom has continued to be a characteristic trait of my sisters even to this day.

Both Mary and Minnie were strongly independent women. Today we would recognize them as two of the first feminists in Pittsburgh. They laughed together, lived together, and worked together at the Westinghouse Electric Corporation as minor executives, which was as high as women could go in those days.

Today one would wonder, then probability conclude that they were homosexual. They were likely not, having had regular boyfriends, but were cursed with a particular Catholic mind set, almost ubiquitous in Irish Catholic families during the first half of the 20th century. You would wonder about homosexuality because they lived together and never married. But anyone who went to Catholic school during those years would understand their psyche (Irish Catholic families in particular seemed always to have at least one maiden aunt) – and their ultimate life predicaments[64].

---

[64] If, for some reason, you wanted more insight into this mindset (and I wouldn't blame you if you didn't) you might try the book "Faith: A Novel" by Jennifer Haigh.

During later years, over a glass of wine and dinner, they shared their stories, mostly stories of the general difficulties women had in the Pittsburgh working world, and more painful and specific details which they suffered through, all the while trying to get ahead in a man's world. They were treated to indignities, unfairness, abuse, even humiliation – yet they persevered. An example they related over dinner one evening: their division had done well, and a bonus was awarded to everyone in it. One of the employees, a man, came to their desks. The man did not sit down. That detail was important, they said, as his standing gave him more a position of authority. He said, "John has eight kids, and is struggling. We're all going to give our bonuses to John." Which Mary and Minnie did, without even passive resistance. But their anger and bitterness had remained alive and intense, even though so many years had passed. Today that transaction causes me to feel and remember my own anger – not only that someone would demand such a thing, but on another level, that my aunts would roll over in the face of such awful injustice. But Mary and Minnie felt they had no choice in that workplace, and continued to further their careers – and did so with a certain continuing dignity. Minnie, many years later, said with some bitterness, "We were better than any man in that office. We had to be." When I heard the retelling of the story, I was well along in medical school, and asked them why they had given in. It was a naïve question; I simply did not understand the times and what the then-held prejudices did to working women.

An American Boyhood

Of average height, with narrow waists, slim hips, flawlessly proportioned legs, and generous bosoms, they recognized and were comfortable with their attractiveness, and especially with their bodies, and carried themselves, heads erect, shoulders back, with dignity, no matter the circumstance. No wonder they were pursued by men – but though the guys got close, neither Mary nor Minnie ever consented to marriage.

Both aunts dressed themselves with style. In fact they overdressed just the slightest amount, adding their gently understated touch of elegance to the professional woman's workplace. Hats were then in vogue, and, as a hobby, they both designed and created women's hats. They gave me a standing order for pheasant feathers, and every time I shot a pheasant, I would carefully preserve the skin, feathers intact, and give it to them for their creations. Their ladies' hats were awesome. Actually, in retrospect, those hats were art – sculptures that could be worn.

It became their stated objective to civilize us savages – my boy cousins Eddie, Tommy, Paul and me. The job would have discouraged a saint.

Aunt Mary bought me – I think when I was six – a 78 RPM record "Rusty in Orchestraville". The record introduced the instruments of an orchestra through the eyes and ears of a little boy named Rusty. I literally wore out that record[65]. Aunts Mary and Minnie took my cousins and me to concerts, taught us table manners, and introduced us at age 12 to alcoholic beverages. "You will learn to drink wine at meals, especially on important occasions, and here are the rules of how and how much you will drink." She actually talked like that. Would they be put in jail today for corrupting children with alcohol? The teaching worked; none of us became alcoholics.

So at least for me, their attempts to civilize, at least in some small parts, were effective and I maintained a thankful closeness, a respect, and a deep love for them throughout my life, often sharing reminiscences over good food tempered and enhanced by good wine. It turned out that Minnie, among her other creative accomplishments, was a gourmet cook.

Their quiet competence, their dignity, their refusal to lower their standards in the face of overweening male prejudice was a powerful lesson for a growing boy, one that significantly molded my behavior toward women. Today we would recognize that what they possessed was *strength of character*.

For many years, Mary and Minnie lived at the farm, as Mary was the key financial backer of that family enterprise. So plenty of female cousins – plus my sisters – surrounded them

---

[65] Friends of mine in the San Diego Symphony found a 60-year-old copy a few years ago, and it has become one of my most precious gifts.

and were part of their lives. But we – my sisters and I – never understood why, though they were willing to try to civilize us boys, they did not spend any time or energy teaching the girls about what they were accomplishing every day. Could it have been that, because the girls were not their own children, they did not wish to interfere? Or perhaps it was that they were unsure that the career path they had chosen was worthwhile. Who knows?

I loved them both. And perhaps more importantly, I respected them for how well they had done in a man's world. And to this day I thank them for their influence.

*   *   *   *   *   *

Doris and Nancy

Why bring neighbors into this close family tale? Even more curious, why bring them in as they did not enter the scene until I was in high school? Let us see.

Both Doris and Nancy moved to the country within months of each other when I was 15. Just before the Korean War began, we Greenock natives noticed a mass migration from the city. People wanted cleaner air – plus a feeling of space. Our rolling hills were inviting, and our people welcoming.

It was only natural that I would see Doris and Nancy during my wanderings, as everyone's back yard seemed to end in woods. I'd see them in their yards sharing a coffee with husband or friends, hanging up the family wash, or tending to their flowers and gardens. A smile, a quiet and polite hello, and I was immediately invited to join them for an iced tea or a coffee. The homes they created were traditional 1950s family units – the husband worked; the wife cared for the house and garden and raised their baby boomer kids.

Doris was the essence of womanhood, a lady who smiled, and smiled all the time. She saw humor in bad weather. She saw humor in the foibles of our politicians. She even found humor in her husband's and children's behavior. Now wasn't that an accomplishment – and a personality indicator? She was small to the point of petiteness, kept her curly brown hair cut short, had a narrow-waisted, slim-hipped, girlish figure despite having delivered her three children, and projected a pleasant aura around her, a halo of beauty that came from an open and generous heart. Unlike many women I observed, she could pass a mirror without a self admiring glance, and, like most men who came to know her, I found her lack of narcissism a most powerful attractant.

She would giggle at me sometimes, but always smile when I attempted humor, then, lock her hazel eyes onto mine, look into my soul, and have me spill my deepest thoughts, hopes, and fears.

Nancy, her close and dear friend, was taller, slimmer, and carried herself with stately grace. Looking at her, one saw the classiness Aikens captured in his portraits. Soft gray eyes – smile lines at the corners – unlined brow, flawless but severely regular features, and a perfectly straight nose of exactly the right size. What a composition for a painting. And like Doris, she smiled easily, laughing gently at the poor jokes of a young boy anxious to please. Pouring me a cup of coffee, she would look directly into my eyes (I would catch my breath a bit), and quote a short verse of poetry. (During those moments I understood what poetry was for.)

Talking to these women became an important part of my post adolescent and rapidly evolving life. I wanted to share what I had accomplished, what my dreams were, and above all, I wanted their advice about the world. Because they were, above all, *women*. Real women. Of course I was in love with them. Deeply, profoundly, yet innocently in love.

These two women stand out in my memory because they were the first adult women in the world to treat me not as a child, not as a student, not as an adolescent, but as an adult – actually, as a man. How kind, how understanding of them. How charitable.

You bet I had fantasies – fantasies that had Doris and Nancy teaching me the delicious and tender secrets of adult heterosexual love. But they were fantasies unfulfilled, and through the years, though we maintained contact, I never did more than shake their hands. Well, maybe there was an occasional not-so-inadvertent touch.

On the other hand, though rare, I did find evil:

In our childhood, all was not sweetness and light. And we were vulnerable, as all kids are. Some women entering our lives were truly bad.

As an example, Aunt Eva comes immediately to mind. Aunt Eva, Grandpap Kerber's sister, was, to my sisters especially, the prototype of awfulness, the kind of woman we all read about in Grimms' Fairytales, the woman who would put lost little children in her oven. A look at Aunt Eva would freeze any kid with fear: She was a big woman with sallow complexion, long face, cold blue-gray eyes, a gold tooth in front (I'm not making this up), gray hair severely done up in a bun, coarse hands, colorless and shapeless house dress, wearing, on her feet, scuffed lace-up old lady's black shoes. That was Aunt Eva. What terrified my sisters, Janet in particular, was that she smiled with her mouth, showing those long teeth – while her eyes remained an icy coldness. Sadly, on occasion, our mother turned us over to her for babysitting. The girls still have nightmares.

One evening I heard Janet (about age 5 at that moment) screaming. I ran to the basement. Aunt Eva was holding her head down over the wash tubs, rinsing shampoo off – but not bothering to test the water temperature, which was scaldingly hot. Actual first-degree burns – and bad dreams that night were the result. We were afraid to say anything to Mom and Dad when they returned.

Of course she was not the only evil wicked witch of the North. But we kids were able, by and large, to avoid bad women. Except, of course, for the nuns, sadistic wardens in a prison called school.

Overall and in general, the women in my life during those formative years carried out traditional wifely duties while living in traditional 1950's families. They all worked hard. They did the best they could, again, by and large.

Now let me be judgmental. Let me answer that question posed in the beginning, that question about a woman's needing defense: yes, during my growing up years I believe that the women in my life did need to be defended. But perhaps not so today. A further, absolutely judgmental statement: thanks to those women – the scary ones included – life was better for us kids than it is for kids now. But those subjects, those questions are perhaps better held for the last chapter.

Nonetheless, what can I say to the women in my life but *WOW*.

28. MY WOODS

The woods were so important during my growing-up years that I'd like to explore this *idea* of a woods a bit more in depth with you – and, as important, to recommend an experiment. But for the experiment itself, your experiment, you will have to wait for us to get to the next chapter.

First, *The Woods* is a term I have come to see and use as a broad descriptor, a general, encompassing idea more than a place. *The Woods* has over the years become my generic term for what others probably think of as The Great Outdoors – those particularly American spaces where you can walk without seeing a house or a road. Though I grew up in America's Northeast, where large forests of hardwoods interspersed by occasional rye and timothy grass fields covered the hills and mountains, when I moved to the West and tramped the so-called national forests, some of them contained only low growth chaparral, some were high altitude Alpine grassy meadows, and some were even deserts covered only with cacti – with nary a tree for a hundred miles. So to me, when I say woods, the word just means wildness – places and spaces beyond parks and suburbs, environments where you can wander alone and become alone, and once again discover your oneness with nature. Each of these spaces has its own beauty, its own mystery, its own ability to bring us back to our atavistic roots.

What you need to begin your own experience in the woods, your exploration of this other reality is first, some prior preparation, second, some basic knowledge, third, an open mind, and finally, most importantly, a willingness to allow yourself to enter and become part of this place, a space which is *other than civilization*. But I'm getting ahead of myself. Hold this thought till later, so I can backtrack to an early time in my childhood, to my beginning fascination with woods.

*   *   *   *   *   *

One of my favorite books when I was seven was an old, beat up, coverless original translation from the German *Grimm Brothers Fairytales*. No, that edition had not been cleaned up for children; it was anything but politically correct[66]. In that

---

[66] How this coverless, well-worn book found its way into our home I will never know, but I doubt that my parents knew its contents. The authors put into words that vague and most profound of all kids' fears – the fear of abandonment, and for good measure, added every manner of violence, plus mutilation, even necrophilia. What seven-year-old boy could put such a book down?

old grim Grimm, little boys and girls ventured, innocently wandered, were seduced toward, seemingly were pulled into *the woods* – those dark, mysterious, ever threatening woods – and soon found themselves enticed, entranced, enthralled, hypnotized – then ultimately put in ovens . . . Or some other bad but unnamable place, but whatever that badness was, whatever evil they encountered, *they never returned*. They. Never. Returned. Wow. The authors' obvious intent (in retrospect) was to scare the devil out of us. In that they were absolutely and repeatedly successful. But I always wondered where one could find such scary places, as there were woods everywhere around the house. Our woods, though inky dark, were welcoming, safe, interesting, quiet sanctuaries.

Each step deeper into our woods revealed a new beauty, another wonder. (But where were witches when you wanted them, my sisters and I wondered?) Early morning spears of sunlight passed through the canopy and sparkled dew droplets on spiderwebs, outlining their marvelous complexity and symmetry – and their location, showing us where not to walk. (No need to disturb Charlotte, or her progeny.) Stand still for a single minute, and realize all sound – save for the beating of our hearts and the occasional plop of dew drops falling from leaves onto forest floor – had vanished. Wait one more motionless minute, insect buzz began to return. And just one minute after that, the birds started to settle down, chirping, trilling, busy at tasks only they understood. By five minutes, the squirrels – still so wary – became active. The woods were once again alive. And if we walked slowly, ever so slowly, ever so quietly, we became part of our own, our private, our magical woods. But as much fun as it was for us – my sisters and me, or Reed and me – to explore together, by far the best times were my walks in solitude.

And the older I got, the more I enjoyed those walks alone. Alone with my thoughts, I could, sooner rather than later become, not an intruder, but a part of the place. And now a question to ask for your own woodsy experiment to come: where can you find solitude for yourself today? Hold that answer.

What might you notice first on entering the woods? Is it the darkness? The quietness? The differentness from home and yard? For me it is immediately the woodsy smell. Each woods has its own distinctive and characteristic perfume, a character that changes season by season.

Best and most pungent, most exciting is the heavy rich smell of the spring forest floor – perfumed wisps, some even carried on visible misty tendrils, swirling up from sunlight warmed, moist, decomposing leaves, fungus hyphae, worms, and beetles weaving their way through, and here and there even elevating and moving those matted leaves. Breathe deeply, bringing those perfumes into your head, and you knew you were in the woods. Smell today mushrooms, cool damp earth and decomposing leaves, then close my eyes, and I am a boy again, back there drawing in sharp clean spring air, knowing winter's chill is almost gone, seeing in my mind's eye the first robins listening for worms, of finding pussy willows budding near the creek.

Thinking back, what was *not* there also comes to mind: I cannot ever remember smelling flowers. Which is surprising in retrospect, I guess. But never, even in spring, even with wild flowers everywhere around us could I find a flowery smell. Wild Columbine, Wild Ginger, Virginia Bluebell, even Skunk Cabbage pushing up through the composting leaves as the snows melted were seen – but not smelled. Except for trillium, our wildflowers were small, generally inconspicuous, making up in number for their smallness. Our poor bees certainly had their work cut out for them.

Winter's smells, on the other hand, were harsh, when there were any smells at all. The air was simply too biting, too irritating to our noses. Two deep breaths caused watery mucus to dribble, even to flow from our noses. Three quick deep breaths could actually cause sharp, burning chest pain. Only occasionally could we catch the drifting acrid scent of burning coal through the skeletally bare trees and recognize its certain promise of warmth back at home. A romp in snowy winter woods required good boots, many layers of wool, and rarely lasted more than a few hours. Winter woods brought a feeling of utter stillness; nonetheless winter woods were beautiful in their own way.

In summer woods, sultry air settled sulfury mill smoke into our gullies and valleys, but when summer's breezes blew, those breezes swirled pollens around the countryside, even into the depths of the forest. Those winds carried heavy loads of pollens from that beautiful yellow ragweed flower, a plant that grew in every open sunny field[67]. But summer air could be capricious. When we were especially lucky to be walking just before a summer thunder storm, and when we felt the pre-rain wind on sweaty necks before the storm hit, we could smell a tension in the air, a kind of electric crackle. That smell was the sharpness of ozone (though we didn't know its name then). And at that moment, we knew to head away from the tall trees, to run for cover under the patches of wild grape.

I do not remember too many of fall's smells, but those I do remember are just fine. Fall was a time of the farm, a time of people at work, only rarely of woods. Fall meant harvest – and the backbreaking toil associated with it. So the primary odor I remember is that of fresh human sweat. But fall also gave us the sweet smell of roasting corn and baking pumpkin pies. Of course fall also brought colors. The trees in our woods shed their soothing greens in fall, then adopted colors of fire. Come to think of it, fall's crisp air did bring a certain quickening of the blood – as it foretold the onset of hunting season – and a reason to return, to come back into the woods.

But now an important experience: let us go back to spring woods so I can tell you of tender and aromatic sassafras trees.

---

[67] A quick aside: Asthma was essentially unknown out in the country – asthma and allergies are generally diseases of city folk. Country folk are exposed to so many pathogens and allergens that they tend to build up a robust immune system so rarely get autoimmune diseases. In fact, there are scientific papers now published recommending that kids with asthma be infected with intestinal worms. I'm not making this up. Try googling hookworms and asthma. Or David Pritchard and hookworms.

With winter over, our quest, our hunt was first to find the trees. The full-grown summertime leaves are characteristic: each leaf has three large lobes, making identification easy. But at this time of the year, leaves had not yet formed. The bark would be the giveaway: tan gray, smooth, with green in the bark's fissures, more green the closer to the root. Then, diagnosis made, size was the next critical judgment. We looked for a sapling as big as we could pull out. A mighty two-boy heave, then sassafras's sharp sweet perfume spread, immediately overpowering the smell of moist black loam still stuck to roots. Now down to the creek to wash the dirt off. Pen knife out, a slice of root bark to chew on our way home, then skin the roots to dry, finally to make the world's best tea. Could life be any better? Winter was for certain gone when we could make sassafras tea.

You have all this to look forward to, to notice when you begin to explore your woods.

For another, it turns out that even insects are important to notice; they tell their own story and sing their own song. And bite and sting, if we are not careful.

More than the insects, the birds warn the forest about me, the intruder, at least until I can get them to settle down. Then the birds work for me to show me where to find some other animal happening to pass nearby. Predators cause the birds to fuss most, and to rise, flutter and scold, but even a passing deer upsets them. Each and all, the bugs, the birds, the animals are important – all are part of this whole. Each can be noticed, deserves to be noticed and we deserve to be part of this place.

Surprisingly, the trees – which we often think of as being immobile – are what allow the birds their movement and their safety. Example: start walking up a mountain, come to the tree line – the point of elevation beyond which no trees can grow. The birds – which we think of as having ultimate freedom – go at most, only a few meters further. An interesting way to think about freedom of movement, isn't it?

A woods' sounds change depending upon place, upon time of year, and, because of weather, even minute by minute. Walk around a hill, and the tinkle and gurgle of a creek tells you what you will soon find. The hum of insects, breezes through rustling leaves, water flowing, bubbling onto and over rocks, the deep thrum of a male ruffed grouse advertising his desirability, even the squirrel's chatter make music. The woods have always contained the best music – if you are willing to pause and listen. Who says there are no symphonies outside a hall? All you have to do is open your ears – maybe more importantly, your mind. Amadeus, eat your heart out.

May I go back to spring? Spring in my Appalachian hills is the best, for it is a time of renewal, the real beginning of the annual cycle. For most of us who live in a four-season temperate climate, our year does not begin on January 1 – our year begins when the forsythia and crocus come into bloom – when we realize that, at last, the long and discouraging winter is in full retreat.

A deep atavistic itch to escape from civilization would grow in my chest when spring sunshine began to melt the snow on the south slopes, gentle warm breezes flowed through the valleys, and the creeks ran full. Then, when the smells returned, that damp fecund smell of the composting forest floor, that feeling in my chest grew into an ache, so in Woolrich jacket and pants, Browning Upland boots, a fur cap covering my short hair, a light day pack, and my Remington 30-06 slung over my shoulder, I would begin my walk into the spring woods.

I am not now hunting – it's not hunting season. But like Hemingway, I am comfortable carrying my rifle in the woods. I have no idea why I'm uncomfortable without it – there are no bears or cougars left in Western Pennsylvania. But the rifle is part of my being. I'll go into that more a few chapters on.

*   *   *   *   *   *

A short tale: Later in the season, one early summer afternoon I heard the gurgle, and coming around a hill, found the creek. My creek was in no hurry (nor was I), as it flowed quietly away – but there – a bonus. Along the near bank, the creek nourished a mass of wild mint, mint as high as my knees. Squeeze mint's leaves with even the gentlest pinch, and the leaves release their oily and pungent aromatics. First I sat in the mint grove, facing the stream, hugging my knees, simply watching the ripples and eddies flowing past, and from time to time, glancing up, searching the far hillside for . . . something, anything. Then I lay down, rolling about, covering myself with mint's aromatics. Could anything be this pleasant? Could anything this wonderful be legal? Smell mint from my backyard today, and I am that boy on that creek bank on that sunny summer afternoon.

So . . .

From my comments, you might now think that all is sweetness and light in the woods. No, as certain wariness is essential, and that wariness is dependent upon that particular woods and what lives there.

Which brings us to another short tale: It had rained lightly and softly for four days – the kind of rain you get from the slow passage of a warm front over the land — and now the sun began to make an appearance. The air was still quite humid, the pine needles damp, making walking an absolutely silent enterprise. I came to a somewhat open spot, a small, nearly flat meadow. I had taken maybe 20 steps farther, when the hair on the back of my neck stood up. Orange yellowish mushrooms, most as big as my thumb, but some as broad as my palm had pushed up through the grasses and leaves everywhere around me. And I was stepping on them, in their center. There is only one mushroom that has remains of the volva on its cap. It is the easiest of all poisonous mushrooms to identify: Amanita muscaria, the deadliest of them all, mushrooms that synthesize a poison for which there is no antitoxin. And I was in the middle of millions of them. Okay, perhaps I exaggerate a bit. Thousands, at least. But I was wondering at that point how I was going to get their poison off my boots. When I think about that killing field today I shudder, and remember hearing a story about an Indian who died after sleeping out one night on a bed of Amanita. Then again, maybe my grandfather told me the story so I would be wary of wild mushrooms[68].

And for the next category of deep woods potential problems, I blame Disney, who introduced us to cute animals who could talk. Mister Disney showed us lions and tigers and bears (oh my) who, on the big screen, had passive, or more pernicious thought, lovable natures.

Wild animals are, well, wild.

On the one hand, you won't ordinarily get bitten by a skunk, or a squirrel, or a bat if you try to get close to them. They have enough sense to avoid us humans, as we are the ultimate predators. They avoid us – unless – unless they are rabid. And if you do get bitten by a small woods animal, and you don't get the treatment (those painful shots), a rabies death is particularly gruesome. So since small animals rarely come near us humans unless they are sick, expect the worst. Unlike those lovable critters we see in the movies, the little wild creatures are not our friends, don't talk and sing to us, and if you decide to be friendly to them, and they come toward you, you are apt

---

[68] Later, a chemist friend of mine explained that their toxins are amines: wash them off with plenty of Heinz white vinegar. PLENTY of it, multiple times: dilution is the solution to the pollution.

to get a surprise. An unpleasant surprise. Wariness is indicated. By the way, if it bites you, kill it and bring the carcass with you. Especially the head. (To know where to take it, Google "Center for Disease Control and Prevention".)

More importantly, some American woods are the homes of predators who have the ability – and the inclination – to prey on us. Prey, as in eat. A woods truism: There are many things in the forest you can eat to stay alive. There are also things in the forest that can eat you to stay alive. Uncommon, even rare, yes. But take bears seriously in places like Yellowstone.

For the past three decades in California, more mountain lions have attacked solitary runners (usually smaller female runners) than the year before. For many complicated reasons, the numbers of bear maulings and cougar attacks are not well publicized, but, as the big animals' populations are increasing, and as we encroach upon their habitat you can expect even more encounters. But the biggest hazard of all is the human attitude that you learn from Hollywood movies that humanize animals. Again, I blame Disney.

*   *   *   *   *   *

Another short tale: two friends have a mountain home in Eastern Oregon. It is their habit to spend weekends there, and take, as they say, "peaceful walks" through the woods at dusk. One evening returning – they were close enough to home to see the warm glow of light in their cabin window – they heard a strange sound, a sound they described as a snuff – like *some thing* clearing its nose. They turned, and barely made out the outline of a fully grown mountain lion not 30 meters behind. She yelled, "Go away!" (Well, that ought to scare a hungry mountain lion with cubs to feed.) He picked up a rock, and threw it. The cat deftly jumped to the side, its movements fluid, economical, silent -- then crept a step closer. They continued toward the cabin, walking backwards, saying strong words to the cat. ("SHOO" comes to mind.) The cougar took its time. They would take a few steps backwards; the cat would take one forward, then slink down into a crouch, perfectly silent, chin forward and only inches off the ground (a perfect attack posture). By the time my friends reached their porch, the cat was only steps away. They made it to the safety of their home, and locked the door. Eventually the big cat left. When my friend's wife told me this amazingly detailed and descriptive story I was amazed first by the fact that they had survived, but certainly more importantly, by her feeling of disbelief, even of insult – that an animal would dare to hunt her.

*   *   *   *   *   *

And a final tale. A few years ago I was at a medical meeting in Jackson Hole, a gentrified New West town near some magnificent wilderness areas. Yellowstone is nearby. Between Jackson and into Yellowstone you will find more walking trails through serious wilderness landscape than you can cover in 10 summers. Are there bears? Oh yes. But are any hikers allowed to carry a weapon? Not a chance. Absolutely illegal. And the Rangers, who are hours away when seconds count, carry only puny nine millimeter handguns. No surprise, some hikers get to find a body some days after a meeting between a 430 pound grizzly bear and an unfortunate fellow. Rangers recommend pepper spray and bells to keep the bears away. A local joke has it that you can always tell grizzly scat as its smells lightly of pepper and contains little bells.

One more (thankfully final) time: I blame it on Disney, having created this childlike belief that animals are humanoid, animals that won't bother us if left alone. Did you ever watch the movie *Bambi*? How about the *Seven Dwarfs*? Good. Now go to the Internet and look up pictures of bear maulings. And be reasonably cautious. The key word is reasonable.

But enough of that. Is not my intent to frighten you away, only to make you prudent. And to be prudent means to be prepared. We can expand upon your preparedness needs in the next chapter.

But to put the words in perspective, I want to share my love of and leave you with my awe of the woods.

When I walk to the edge of a cliff and suddenly recognize I can see as far away as tomorrow, when I come to the bank of a stream, and, looking hard, finally see small brown trout through the surface glare, when I slowly lift my head over an edge of rock to watch bighorn sheep on a mountainside half a mile away, when I sit at the base of a tree and watch as a woodpecker buries an acorn in her newly made storage hole, I recognize the truth in Coleridge's definition of awe: you are in awe if you find yourself in the midst of something that makes you feel you are nothing.

Which brings me back to my existential reason for this chapter, and the reasons for my recommendations to you in the next. When I have had my fill of civilization, when I have had enough (or too much) closeness, I remember that the woods showed me, when I was that wandering boy, my place in the world. And then I know I must leave the cell phone, the computer. I must go back.

For the woods keep me in awe.

29. YOUR WOODS

Perhaps you are now open to some experimentation. Yes?

I should first give you a little bit more background for the words that follow so I may lead (actually entice, even seduce) you into performing your experiments. And yes, I know we are now walking together, going beyond passively reading a simple memoir.

As I grew older, my relationship with forests expanded, and no longer was the few square miles of woods around our home enough. Pennsylvania was blessed with mature second growth forest during my early years, but if we wanted original growth forests, we could just drive south, barely across the West Virginia border to Coopers Rock State Forest, where we could find 50 square miles of pristine wilderness. Or East, a scant hour to the Appalachians.

The Appalachian Mountains are old – almost half a billion years old, and, though once as high as the Rockies, they have been worn down, eroded by eons of geologic time, and are now only a few thousand feet high. But the Appalachians are complex, and the ecology is unbelievably (and wonderfully) diverse. Best yet, you can walk for days without seeing another person or sign of human intrusion. If you keep off the path. And you will see how important it is to stay off the path, for we are not going hiking in the wilderness.

This is good place to talk about hiking. I guarantee that I'm not being critical of hiking. Hiking is a most wonderful outdoor activity that brings great satisfaction to large numbers of people, and I'm told that to hike the Appalachian Trail from New York down to its southern end in Alabama is quite an accomplishment, beauty around every turn of the path. But with hiking, there always seems to be a goal – to get to a certain place, to make good a certain pace, to stay at a certain hostel, to spot certain birds. But above all, there are those paths. The paths say "STAY ON ME." Admit it – you likely have seen those signs: Keep to the Paths. And of course the paths themselves indirectly imply, "I will lead you to . . . wherever I (the path) want you to go. Stay on me and you cannot get lost."

I never go on paths. For I am a hunter. And you can be too, but perhaps not in the way most people – maybe even you – think of hunters. For this is not about guns, not about killing.

So how does a hunter walk through woods? Well, it depends upon the mission, the day's goal, and upon your level of experience. For myself, by the time I finished high school, at age 17, I felt experienced, knowledgeable, an old hand (how wrong I was, as I learned later in the Marines).

And now my goal is to seduce you into trying a few experiments: e.g. to learn your own way to hunt through your own woods.

The first, and most common way, is simply to walk through – gently, quietly, and slowly, to discover that particular woods' nature; to smell, to hear, to feel its breezes now up, now down the gullies depending upon the sun and time of day; to experience its character; ultimately to become part of – one with – that woods. To learn that particular wood's character, its topography, its geology. To discover what has gone before you – whether it is nature (a storm or fire, for instance) or an animal, or perhaps even another human. In walking this way, you look up to the treetops, then to the distance and around, and then down to the forest floor. Looking down, you search for *sign*. Sign can be as simple as a bruised fern, bent and broken by a larger animal's passing. Sign may be an animal track. The ability to read such tracks, to make sense of their meaning comes only with significant woods experience. A good tracker can tell whether the animal is running, how large it is, and how recently it has passed that point. The most common sign though is *scat*, a polite term for animal feces. Again, scat's condition can be read to determine how recently the animal has passed, the type of animal, and importantly, its diet[69]. I still remember the awe I felt for a mountain lion that had passed through her intestine – bits of bone, fur, and amazingly, an intact razor-sharp claw. She certainly had to have been hungry to take on, kill, then eat a bobcat.

Or second, you might walk quickly (but quietly) to a previously scouted game trail in deep darkness, and set up on stand, perhaps in a tree, waiting for certain animals to go by. No surprise, that's called stand hunting. Blending in with the environment in the stand is about as far away from our civilized everyday existence as I can imagine. No iPod buds, no cell phone, no Facebook, no Twitter? What are these in the woods? When civilized people try this aloneness exercise this for the first time, what most feel is, at least during their first few times out, a certain nagging unnamable but unpleasant feeling that may progress to an actual tinge of panic. Of non-connectedness. Some tell me that, as time passes, they even experience frank fear. Ask yourself: when was the last time you were ever completely away from your computer, your phone, the comfort of the familiar, of what we know as civilization?

Of course it is impossible to be perfectly motionless for the many hours required on stand, though that is the goal. So movements must be, above all, exceedingly slow, deliberate, gentle, and quiet (wool remains the best and quietest woods

---

[69] You will likely enjoy Tristan Gooley's classic "The Natural Navigator" even more after your first walk.

clothing). In the first minutes on stand, the woods begin to become alive again. And that recognition of the wood's coming back to baseline is part of the depth and excellence of the experience. Finally, the hunter begins to become part of the woods. As time passes, a certain trance occurs. More importantly, the hunter's[70] thin veneer of civilization begins to melt away. The hunter becomes more like a primitive, devolving back toward her roots[71]. All this within the first hour of sitting silently on your stand.

As an aside at this point, ask yourself: when in your life in civilization have you ever had the opportunity to sit in one spot for thirty minutes – let alone three hours, your only task to let each of your senses become fully aware of sun, wind, temperature, the smells, the creatures around you – all the while attempting to sense change, all the while ignoring little aches, itches, hungers and thirst? You might wish to try this as a first small experiment, cell phone off, to see how you will feel. You would be bored, you say, just sitting? Try it.

$$* \quad * \quad * \quad * \quad * \quad *$$

No surprise, some equipment is required for this experience – water being the primary need, plus a securely capped bottle

---

[70] And yes, you have now become a Hunter – perhaps a hunter of experiences and feelings; certainly not necessarily a killer. And by the way, if you intend to take photographs, make sure that your electric camera is set to silent mode.

[71] Oh yes, *her* roots. I refer you to Mary Zeiss Stange's superbly written book, *Woman the Hunter*, a work that will open most women's – and men's – eyes to this sometimes controversial activity.

for urine. The hunter/observer must be clean, freshly show-ered with unperfumed soap, and deodorized with non-scented deodorant. Her clothing must blend with her envi-ronment – certain camouflage patterns work better in differ-ent locales and during different seasons, and it is critical not to have washed the clothing in perfumed detergent. Whitetail deer, for example, have become so smart about us, so attuned to our civilization, that many hunters store their washed clothes in a plastic bag filled with local tree leaves, and leave their driving shoes in the car, as those shoes might have be-come contaminated with petroleum hydrocarbons. Some go further – dousing themselves with more natural scents. I know it's hard to believe, but some hunters deliberately put skunk scent on themselves, or a bit less offensively, urine from female deer in estrus. No trouble is too great for the hunter to blend in with the environment. On the other hand, there *is* the problem of returning to home, family, and civili-zation . . .

All this to be part of the woods. You may wonder at this point; you probably will be asking the existential question *why go to all this bother?* But first, before I explain why, let us continue.

The third way, and by far my preference, is to still-hunt.

Actually the term comes from my German ancestors: *Stillehunt*; Stille meaning *quiet* or *silent* hunting. You carry pretty much the same equipment, and try to blend, but since you're on the move, there is no need for a urine bottle. Should you wish to try this technique, again as an experiment, before you even think about entering the woods, look on YouTube for a movie of an owl's seeing technique. Watch how she moves her head from side to side all the while keeping her eyes perfectly parallel to the ground. This allows a change in her three-dimensional perspective. If you try her technique next time you're out of your house – even in a park, you'll be surprised at the new things you will see.

Now back to the woods. You will not need deep forest for your first experiments, a city park will do[72]. But ignore those stay-on-the-path signs; instead keep *off* the paths: begin your first step forward, but before you place your entire weight on the forward foot, feel for the forest floor through your boot. Are there twigs underneath that might snap? If not, gently put your entire foot down and move your weight forward. Looking around, take another step, then another. Now pause maybe 20 seconds. Do the owl's seeing method – head slowly moving side to side, keeping eyes parallel to the ground. Allow yourself to see – to accept into your mind's eye – the images that come into your consciousness. Look not just ahead; look down and around, searching for the quietest possible path through the brush, and continue. Oh yes, remember to look up – something we humans rarely do. You will come to realize that seeing is neither instantaneous nor passive. You are looking *for* rather than looking *at*. Listen. Feel the breeze.

---

[72] You don't need to go to the Teton wilderness for these experiences. Thoreau wrote *On Walden Pond* not far removed from town. Though his cabin has been moved, I believe that from its original location he was able to see the church steeple, at least when winter had bared the trees of their leaves.

Imagine you are coyote and have more than our miniscule human powers of smell. And ask yourself questions, even verbalize them to yourself: what am I seeing, what am I feeling, what am I smelling? If you cover a mile in an hour, you are certainly going too fast. Then when you are comfortable in the park, try deeper woods.

But before you go too deeply into any woods, start small. With the aid of a contour map, find a section of woods bounded by roads, the roads no more than a mile in any direction. Save the Nez Perce wilderness area for later, when you have become comfortable with map, compass and counter[73].

Most everybody has heard about map and compass, but few people are aware of the counter. It's used to get to a certain place on a map from a known starting point. It's not used when still-hunting, but rather finds its use when you need to travel relatively quickly through unknown terrain. To make a counter, take a rawhide thong, tie a knot about two thirds along its length, slip nine snug fitting rubber washers on one side of the knot, and five on the other, make a little room between them, then tie knots at either end. The whole contraption is about six inches long. The next step (no pun intended) is to mark off 100 meters on some track or football field (110 yards = a hundred meters), and see how many normal steps it takes you to get to the hundred meter mark. In the woods,

---

[73] Notice I didn't say GPS. Yes, the GPS is a priceless aid – we all use it – but you can't depend upon it in deep woods. And then there's the battery problem.

pick a compass heading, and walking, count that number of steps, then move one of the nine washers toward the center knot. When each of them have been moved, you've walked a kilometer, and you can move one of the other five to the knot, keeping track of kilometers walked. You will be amazed how you can move through dense forest with confidence using your map, compass and this counter. But using this technique, your goal is to get to a certain point, not to hunt, not to enjoy the scenery along the way, but perhaps to get to a magnificent vista or some other point of interest.

*   *   *   *   *   *

This is a good place to talk about being lost. Being lost is certainly a profound fear, an atavistic Grimm-like fear. It might surprise you to learn that being lost is more a matter of time than of uncertainty of place. Let me explain with two examples.

The Lewis and Clark expedition had a goal of finding and charting their way to the Pacific Ocean. They started in Pittsburgh, headed down the Ohio to St. Louis, paddled up the Mississippi, , the Missouri, then crossed mountains – for as long as it took. Though they didn't exactly know where they were, they were not lost. On the other hand, I, hunting across Bone Mountain on the Oregon coast, having consulted my contour map, and expecting to find the car on a road two hours to the west, walked, and walked, and walked, coming instead at four hours to a cliff, and seeing no road – nothing but clouds and woods fading into distant mists. Chilled from the ever-present coastal drizzle, profoundly depressed now, I recognized that I was completely and absolutely lost. Two hours walking the wrong way. A time comes . . . and a feeling begins, that awful, uncomfortable coldness comes into your belly, then into your head – *I don't know where I am*. And then you must know what to do about being lost. But admitting it comes first. Just remember, being lost is a realization, a mind process, not necessarily an actuality.

Now, some stories to entice you to try your own experiments:

One warm autumn day I wandered through the woods, coming upon a meadow. It was early afternoon, and I had become hot and tired. A soft breeze blew into my face – you always want the wind coming toward you; no matter how we try to deodorize ourselves, all wild animals can smell humans (we humans are, after all, the ultimate predators). About a hundred meters further into the field, a dozen pines had grown – they formed a small copse, and though they were no more than 15 feet tall, provided shade and a soft bed of needles. I paused for a minute – a full 60 beats of my heart – looking around, before I stepped out of the cover of the woods. Continuing quietly toward the pines, it was my intent to lie down for a 20 minute nap. While passing through the open field I felt, well, vulnerable and exposed, but continued slow as before. I was five steps from my darkly shadowed bed-to-be when a doe suddenly stood up from it. From *my* bed-to-be. I had not seen her – nor she me. Eyes wide, head low, her mouth gaped open in surprise. She gathered herself, closed her mouth (no doubt trying to regain her dignity), continued looking at me with her liquid brown doe eyes, raised her head, stamped her fore hoof once (showing me what she thought of my intrusion), then trotted away stiff legged, head held high, indignant at my interruption of her nap, flashing her white tail at me. Surprise, surprise. To both of us. Is there any other way to attain such closeness to such a magnificent wild animal?

Later in school a biologist told us that wild animals think of only three things: food, sex, and safety. And then I thought of that beautiful doe. In just a few seconds, she had showed more emotion than some of my acquaintances. I thought that the biologist should have spent more time in the woods than in his laboratory.

It is possible to call game to you. By and large, it is the predators who will come – but occasionally young and inexperienced male deer have such curiosity. (To young deer, it is often a fatal curiosity.)

To call game, the hunter must use special care in the extreme. And that means first, to take time to let the woods settle down, second, to place the breeze in your face, and third, to break the human outline by placing a brush or tree behind you. But most importantly, it is essential to wear full camouflage – not to let a square inch of skin show. And then you call, either by voice, or with a small wooden device which, when blown correctly, can create a sound like a predator tearing apart a small live animal. The sound itself is chilling – a terrified scream of pain. Hear it in the woods, and the cry will make the hair on the back of your neck stand up.

Two observations: one day I had taken a friend out to the woods to demonstrate and to teach him the technique. We were both covered in woodland camouflage; we carefully had discussed fields of fire so that we would not shoot each other. I placed him at a sumac bush and walked away. When I reached my bush some 50 meters away, I turned back – but with a chilling realization: that I could not see him; his camouflage was too perfect. That loss of sight was terrifying to me. There was no way I could shoot without knowing exactly where he was. I walked back over toward him, and 20 meters later he became apparent. He laughed at my concern, no surprise, but I stuck a small twig in the ground to mark his location.

Another day, again camouflaged, I was sitting at the base of a stunted Pin Oak, overlooking a meadow, drifting drowsily along, snoozing in the late afternoon sun. The woods were quiet save for the humming of insects. A louder buzz brought me back from my reverie. The humming came from a bird – a male ruby throated hummingbird. He hung there, just six inches away from my left eye. I could feel the wind from his wings, see the iridescent green of his head, that gash of red on his throat, could look into his tiny, pitch black eyes. He hovered there for long seconds, trying to work out what this strange thing before him was. There was none of the coloring of his food on me – he was simply curious. He appeared satisfied, began to fly away, but then paused, hovering, then came back for a second, even longer look. I doubt that he ever figured me out. Finally, he flew away. You have to think about that biologist again and feel somewhat sad about his impoverished way to think about these wonderful wild creatures. I should have suggested at the time that he sit quietly in the woods.

We humans are not *really* civilized, I have come to realize, but we have been removed from our roots. And we become more removed with each improvement in our technology. I love my computer; I cannot live without it, nor without my cell phone. Our wonderful technology gives us instant access to friends, to information, and improves our lives dramatically. But there are times when technology is not appropriate, and is even destructive. Should we not recognize that there are times in our lives when we must be alone with ourselves, times when we must look into our souls, times when we must gain insight into our behaviors, our mistakes, and then dream for our future?

To become part of an environment that inspires awe, and to accept our place in it is therapy for the soul, pure and simple.

With this new knowledge in your head and hands (and, I hope, especially in your heart), you might wish to try these experiments in your own woods.

30. PAIN

I have been thinking about this essay a great deal. I've been worrying actually. Even wondering whether to include it at all. I had intended it to be of use primarily to give some insight from one little boy (no surprise, me) to mothers of other little boys, but come to think of it, this essay may even be helpful for mothers of little girls. That said, on we go.

A little background for this chapter: In grade school it was brought to my attention, soon and forcefully that the bullies had some fundamental need to be in control, to be dominant. And as part of their dominance display they would use the threat of beating up one of the littler kids to create the submissive behavior they needed. And if threats didn't work, inflicting actual pain was the next step. And being one of the littlest kids in class, I can now admit that fear of a bloody nose was certainly effective, at least in controlling me in the schoolyard. Next, I observed that the nuns inflicted pain as their method of control. And they had developed their techniques to a fine point such that just the threat of pain caused a terror reaction in most of us, at least most of the time. It was difficult for us kids to see much difference between the two groups.

Now another facet of this thing called pain. We all soon learned that in any vigorous boy's play, some pain was inevitable. And that on certain occasions, pain could be even pleasurable. For an example of pleasurable pain, I remember one boy rounding home plate, having hit a home run, the greatest look of pleasure on his face. I asked him why he was shaking his hands. "When I hit that ball, this electric shock ran up through my fingers, through my arms, all the way to the base of my head. And I knew that ball was going out of the park. God, did that hurt feel good."

But that was rare; pleasurable pain was exceedingly uncommon in most kids' lives. Usually, pain was pretty awful, and we hated what it did to us. Crying was of course for sissies back then (we hadn't yet heard of "the sensitive male"). And crying remains today as a marker for adult male sissies, except for two and only two acceptable situations. I can see those sensitive males out there cringing already.

The first man-okay-to-cry situation is the loss of a loved one, especially a child. And the second is the wounding or death of a comrade – a brother – in some military situation, most poignantly in or after battle.

So in growing up, a major aspect of a kid's developing self-control is to learn not to cry, and the corollary is that to not cry is to learn to handle pain. Notice I did not say to avoid pain. Of course we avoid painful unpleasantness when possible, but in a boy's world, avoidance is usually not possible..

There were two experiences that got me started down this path of study, this interest, and they began well before I entered grade school. The first was watching Dad and Grandpap working around the house or on the farm. Whereas I cried when I hit my thumb with a hammer (so I had first-hand experience of how much it hurt), Grandpap, after the same mistake, would frown, growl and mumble *bloody damn* a bit, shake his head, and after a few moments, go back to work, looking at me, and, like as not, admonish, "The good craftsman don't blame his tools." When Dad mashed a finger or cut himself, he'd throw down the tool, come out with his inevitable and good-for-all-problem statements, "I'll be go to hell . . .", dance around a bit, shake his hand and his head, and then get on with work. If the pain was really, really bad, I could notice a bit of extra water in the eyes, but never a boo-hoo, never a sign of self-pity. I never saw a man in my family cry. Other than at a funeral.

And so it was my goal to be like these men, my heroes. Of course in my earlier years, I failed regularly and dismally. But time passed, and I grew, so did my self-control, all the while aided and encouraged by strong men in my life.

Then, when in school, I began to observe how the other kids experienced and handled painful situations. But first, a disclaimer. These observations are about boys' pain. Not about girls and how they handle their pain, because I simply don't know anything about females, a point that is been repeatedly hammered into my head by any number of women – mother, aunts, sisters, girlfriends, wives, and so on[74]. So my observations are only about boys. Most of my observations came from the experiences in grade school, then later in the military (but the military experiences are beyond the scope of this essay).

So we boys had come to know pain – and to fear it, a fear reaching its apex in first grade. More than the bullies, the nuns had deliberately developed this fear of pain in us by their repeated and vigorous application of the flat of a ruler to various parts of our body, or the open palm of their hand to our faces. My response, surprising to myself, was to watch those interactions. And I watched, and watched some more.

I especially watched kids my age. Then I watched the older kids and their reactions during our group immunizations. The boys at the front of the line behaved as though the needle pain was so exquisitely awful that the experience was more than any human – at least any boy – could bear. And at this time, the bullies didn't seem nearly so tough. Strangely though, the girls didn't seem to be nearly as affected with the fear as we boys were. Boys' reactions ranged from screaming to physical withdrawal, to fighting to get away; the girls almost invariably became quietly tearful if and when they

---

[74] But someday I will. Hope springs eternal.

showed any reaction at all. Yet in the end, no matter the re-sistance or the reaction, everyone got stuck.

And then it was my turn at the needle.

For the first injection, I watched, curious. I found myself more fascinated by the needle, and by how it entered through my skin into my muscle. In subsequent years it was at times pushed in slowly, slowly enough that skin would dimple; other times it came in with a quick jab. Then a relatively slow push on the syringe plunger – that was certainly unpleasant, but when I thought about each experience later, the world had not ended, and I had remained upright. *Well, if that's the worst of a shot, it's no big deal*, I thought. *I can do this. But the others, the big kids, why? Why are they out of control? Why are they crying?*

I simply did not understand their reactions. But there they were; there it was.

Then, being a boy, as we advanced through the grades, my next evolution was to show off a bit. It became a matter of pride to smile (especially looking directly at one of the girls) as the needle went into my arm or the nun's ruler was slapped across my palm. The ultimate was to feign complete and ab-solute indifference, all the while trying to hide my eyes, eyes doing their best to make water run down my cheeks. My in-difference made the nuns furious. Which indifference they made me pay for.

Then a point came when I wondered whether there was something perhaps wrong with me, that maybe I didn't have the ability to feel what other people felt. (Now there was a thought.) But then one evening, I stepped into a groundhog burrow while running through a field, spraining my ankle, then needing to hobble a mile home, step-by-step the pain intensity increasing, until a point came when I was finally unable to bear that awfulness without whimpering. I then recognized that my perception of pain was real enough. And that I was certainly able to feel. And so there was another part to this whole pain thing which I did not understand.

But more surprise was to come: my outward manifestation of indifference to pain had side effects – two in particular. First, the pain seemed to go away faster. Of course I had no objective way to tell that for certain, but I was sure it was real. Then second, and way more important to a little boy, was the look on the faces of the others watching as I showed nonchalance when it was obvious that *that really did hurt*. Who would not appreciate both rewards?

A sidebar: When I was in the Marines, taking care of really tough guys whom I respected, I could divide them into two groups – much like my playground associates. First, those who seemed to do well in adverse circumstances by being in control of their injury, and second, a smaller group who completely abandoned themselves to the fear that the pain engendered. The second group tended to do poorly.

It's an aphorism in surgery that nobody has ever died of pain, but there are sure a lot of people in graveyards who died from pain medicine. A good point, one to remember.

*   *   *   *   *   *

If the job of little boys is to play, the goal of little boys is to gain control – of their environment, of the people around them, of course ultimately of themselves. There is nothing better a parent can teach a child than to recognize that pain is inevitable, never fatal, something not to be frightened of, but to be recognized, accepted, and used. To put a fine point on it, for a growing boy to learn to control his own personal pain is just one more step in developing his manliness.

A certain degree of parental maturity is required to develop and use these insights and techniques. A little boy, say age two, who skins his knee can do no better than to be gathered into the arms of a loving mom or dad, comforted and reassured. But a point comes – and I think it's around four or five years, when a growing boy needs some advice about how to handle the inevitable pain he will encounter in the world. And so, mom, having these insights, I hope you can use them to help your sons mature, to man up[75], to be eventually proud

---

[75] And yes, I am aware of the ongoing debate (and worries) over the feminization of American males. From my point, as a physician, those worries are real and appropriate.

of how they handle themselves in a difficult and sometimes painful world.

31. JUST ANOTHER TOOL?

It is a subject that can cause bad laws to be written through the best of intentions. It is a subject almost as emotion provoking as religion. It is a subject that can end lifelong friendships. Yes, this essay is about guns.

And no, we are not going far afield from the other chapters, as this particular tool was an ever present, even essential part of our family during my growing up years. Yes, just a tool.

But, given the powerful emotional overlay that often accompanies the subject, may I begin with the broadest and most comprehensive of permissions to you- and perhaps even a warning. If you have made your mind up about guns and are on either of the extremes – hate them or love them, you might want to skip this chapter. For that reason I have left the rest of the next page blank so you would not be tempted to read on.

Or worse, angered. Because as I said, in our family, a gun was just a tool. No emotion was involved.

I see you are continuing with your reading. So, some foundation.

In the 1940s and 1950s we redneck, live-in-the-country, Appalachian hillbillies *were* the gun culture. (In fact, some politician recently characterized us as retards "clinging to their guns and religion.") Come to think of it, almost all America during those days was pretty much part of *a* gun culture but we certainly were *the* culture. There were wars on of course, which added to the gun-friendly ambience, but if there hadn't been, there were still guns in every home, usually a 22 somewhere in a closet, plus a deer rifle standing behind a bedroom door. But there were more weapons about, more not talked about in polite company: the servicemen had brought home unbelievable numbers of weapons – handguns, rifles, even automatic weapons. And surplus weapons – serious weapons – could be bought through the mail. Twenty millimeter autoloading antitank rifles were easily ordered and delivered. For a hundred or so dollars. Not much of a surprise, many Americans did buy them, and put them by, along with crates of surplus cheap ammunition. Those weapons (now called destructive devices by our federal government) are still out there. Does anyone really think they have been registered? Does anyone really believe they have been destroyed, or have rusted away? Don't you wonder where they are? Don't you wonder why they are kept hidden? It simply is not something talked about is it?

But us kids?

Here I am at age 3. Yes, age 3. This picture says a great deal.

I've always had guns, toy and real, all given to me by parents and grandparents.

The picture shows a cork-shooting long gun, but we also had cap pistols. Pull the trigger on them, and we were rewarded with a satisfying crack-bang and the acrid smell of burnt gunpowder. The caps were actually small spots of explosive flash powder glued into a paper roll. Each pull of the trigger advanced the roll to the next flash and bang. We knew enough not to fire them in inappropriate places, a hay loft for example, having seen what a barn burning was like. But boy, did we use and enjoy our guns in every day play.

By age 4 my Red Ryder BB gun became my constant woods companion. BB guns always came with the apocryphal instructions from our moms: "Be careful you don't put your eye out." So we didn't. Put each other's eyes out, that is.

At age 6, on my birthday, Dad and Grandpap Mason gave me a 22 caliber Springfield bolt action rifle. A rifle was a significantly large purchase in our poor family, to give you an idea of its importance. And I got a box of cartridges. With this rifle,

I learned even more responsibility - plus another insight, an insight having to do with providing for the family, in those days, a male responsibility, even a duty.

By way of explanation: Though mine, the rifle was kept standing behind the door of Grandpap's bedroom and was not to be touched without some adult's permission. On regular occasions throughout the summer, Grandma, washing dishes while looking out the back window toward the garden would stop her work, would call me, then simply say, "The rabbit is eating our lettuce." (For some reason, never *a* rabbit - always *the* rabbit). So I would get the rifle, load two rounds, quietly and stealthily move into a hidden position, aim, squeeze the trigger -- hear a sharp crack as it fired (all the while being careful not to reveal myself, not moving other than to reload immediately for a second shot – which just might be needed). After a few moments (I never missed, point of pride), I could walk up the yard to retrieve my head-shot quarry. Both Grandpap Mason and Grandpap Kerber had taught me how to gut and skin small game, so the rabbit's preparation was my next job. The entire process was a certainly satisfying activity for any hunter[76], but not nearly so satisfying as to provide my family with braised rabbit - as well as the saved lettuce for that evening's dinner. Thinking back to those times, I can still feel the intense pleasure at having put meat on my family's table. That happiness-producing feeling of providing

---

[76] The liberal Spanish philosopher Jose Ortega y Gasset, in his book *Meditations on Hunting* states, "Man does not hunt to kill, but kills to have hunted."

for family and friends continues today when I bring elk or venison home – a feeling unchanged in intensity or quality.

On occasion, and generally as a reward for some job well done, Grandpap would allow me to take my rifle on my tramps through the woods – with two and only two cartridges. Further, I was always to walk alone; never with other boys. Why alone? From my grandfather: "One boy – half a man; two boys – trouble." I did not mind; of course he was right. It seems he was always right about matters so important. Priceless training and insights, those were.

And another lesson he taught through the gun: this lesson revolved about that *two cartridge* statement. I would ask, "Can I take the rifle into the woods?" "Yes, two bullets only," he would say. I would go into his top bedroom dresser drawer, extract two cartridges from the box, and when well away from the house, load my rifle. Grandpap never asked to see how many I had taken. One day, when I was much older, I asked him if he were not concerned that I might have taken more. He stopped his work, turned, put his hands on my shoulders, looked directly into my eyes, and without pausing, said, "The man is his word." Not a man *keeps* his word – Oh no – he was so much more direct; these words were absolutely clear. There was not a single iota of chance for misinterpretation when he used that verb *to be*. I felt he had looked into my soul, making me recognize that he had placed on my shoulders one of the essential foundations for becoming the man he expected me to be . . . *The man is his word* . . . Who could improve upon that?

There were many other not-subtle gun influences and lessons in our lives, of course. When the men got together at our place for summer picnics, a point would come when rifles were brought out, and each man tested his marksmanship skills on tin cans placed on the far hillside. In that culture men were comfortable with their guns, and more: to be a rifleman was to be manly, to be admired. And when I think back, most women felt the same about their men.

And for even more influence, may I again mention the movies of our childhood. B grade black-and-white movies? Yes, guys in white hats versus guys in black. Good versus evil. Gun violence was to be avoided as long as possible by the hero, but a reluctant final, conclusive, and absolute arbiter of conflict, their guns were. And again, in retrospect, I recognize their influences were profound and have remained with me today.

Of course it's different today in this current anti-gun culture, isn't it? You have doubtless seen James Bond carry a strongly worded letter from the English government when he goes toe to toe with the newest bad guy. Or not. All of which brings up a profound question: Is it not completely dishonest for an actor to kill large numbers of people with a gun in his movie, then appear about the country and in social media decrying gun violence? The awful and bloody movie "Unchained" and actor comes to mind. Just asking.

*　　*　　*　　*　　*　　*

Both Reed and I developed a peculiar fascination with two particular guns – guns that we came to recognize that had helped bring law and civilization to the American West. They had become, in our minds, the final determinant of peace and order in a number of dusty western towns, always wielded by a good sheriff or good citizens. Today both the Colt Peacemaker 45 caliber revolver and the model 94 Winchester 30-30 carbine live in my memories. From an aesthetic point of view, their lines are pleasing, difficult to improve upon, perhaps even perfect, much like a samurai sword. Not only in movies, but in histories we read, they were referred to as the "The guns that won the West." Today, an example of each hangs on my wall to remind me of my country's heritage. And mine.

Times have changed, of course. Now, today, do you not see this general acceptance of an individual's right to her weapons, that belief system I grew up with, has generally gone (or perhaps simply gone underground)? The question we should ask is whether this is a change for the better or worse. Are we safer? Let us see.

Today we live in a strange civil dichotomy, a culture that sees guns negatively, but celebrates their wanton use in movies, TV, and especially video games. Additionally, that the police forces have become militarized seems to be fine with the elites in our culture (especially those who can afford private protection services). But those same people usually are strongly vocal that it is inappropriate for an individual to protect herself. Yes, herself.

There are two parts to the Hollywood thing. The most obvious are the overwhelming number of movies that extol and glorify the most awful and egregious gun violence, close-ups of faces and heads blown away. You have to ask yourself whether movies like the Godfather and television series like the Sopranos help little boys' mental development. Not likely, do they.

Then there is another genre of movie where ordinary people become terrified by thugs, and the homeowner must resort to all manner of ingenious devices to defeat the bad guys. And you come to realize that a shotgun in the hands of the homeowner would have rendered the entire thesis of the movie irrelevant.

Finally, I am amazed at the profound hypocrisy of certain moviemakers and actors who make large amounts of money for these awful displays of violence – and then those same directors and actors campaign to prohibit weapons. Such personal dishonesty. Such disgusting duplicity.

So much worse is the videogame industry. Watch kids playing (without their noticing you) and you will see them blasting opponents to bloody bits rapidly and with great glee – all the while becoming desensitized to such absolute, gory, life-taking violence. This desensitization works well enough that it has become a training technique used by our military services to encourage soldiers actually to fire their weapons in combat. Is this desensitization to death's finality something we want our children to learn?

Which brings me to the two gorillas in the gun debate: We must first bring up the massacres, massacres of people, often just kids, by gunwielding young men: Columbine 1999 (12 kids, one adult killed); Sandyhook 2012 (20 kids, six adults plus mom killed); Aurora 2012 (12 killed, 62 injured). The list is actually longer, and if you do some research, you might be surprised to find that the problem is not confined to America, as nongovernmental and nonreligious massacres occur on a regular basis throughout the world (even in societies where guns are strictly prohibited). And the second, more pressing as far as number of deaths is concerned, is the problem of young black men killing other young black men. But problems both are, as I suggest we Americans have the power to do something about the awfulness.

Of course the first reaction to tragedy is to ask – no demand – some authority to *do something, anything*. A normal reaction, but one that often leads to unintended consequences that do even more damage. For an example in my field, consider that you have come to the emergency room with awful belly pain. The pain becomes so intense that you say to the surgeon, "Just do something." The next day, you might not be too happy if your surgeon just "did something." So before any good therapy happens, we first must make a diagnosis. And what is the diagnosis?

Before we proceed, we must recognize the two separate American tragedies. The first of these is the mass killing phenomenon, the one that gets the most press. The second, the far more important tragedy, the one rarely talked about in the legacy media, is the awful number of murders of young black males by other black males, usually via gun.

Well, guns are certainly the proximate tool, but the underlying causes come down basically to two factors: first, ignored or untreated mental illness. Look into the histories of the murderers, and you see that these disturbed young men have given off plenty of signals telegraphing their craziness and willingness to do violence. Yes, we have emptied out the mental hospitals. And yes, psychotropic medications work. But the truth is, when the person on the drug feels good (the medicine is working), he stops taking the drug. And then, with no support system to monitor him, the craziness resumes. And in America his signals are often ignored, usually under the guise of not wanting to encroach upon that person's freedom, or fear of a lawsuit.

A second factor that is operational (probably fundamental) in the epidemic black on black tragedy, again almost always ignored by the liberal press, is the lack of a loving father throughout the murderer's childhood. *We, our society,* have ignored all these signals.

Perhaps it is time to look into the mirror.

And in looking into that mirror, two questions come to mind: Why did we ignore these young men in trouble? And if we have failed, how can we change our behavior?

Wait, you ask. *I'm not a psychiatrist. How can I diagnose psychosis?* Again speaking as a physician, I answer *how easy that is (to recognize craziness, that is)*. Almost every adult has come across at least one crazy person. You know craziness by that uncomfortable and unmistakable feeling that develops in your gut as the conversation proceeds. But, for many complicated reasons, we have learned to ignore that danger signal, an important signal that our unconscious mind gives us. Without pointing fingers toward any philosophical or political group, we must observe that it has become de rigueur in our society to be accepting – of everyone – in the name of diversity, lest we be considered to be one of the unacceptable prejudiced groups those groups whose names end in …ist. And then, having recognized the signs, to notify the cops. In writing.

It was not always thus. When I was in medical school, we had the power to confine psychiatrically dangerous people to a hospital ward, to protect them – and us from their violence. But then psychotropic drugs became available, and we emptied out the mental hospitals. Combine that with a broadening concept of what acceptable individual behavior was, and we allowed really sick people to live on their own, untrammeled by societal norms. And hope that they took their medication. As corollary and almost simultaneously, no person of responsibility became willing to step forward to put the finger on, for example, a disturbed and violent young man. The legal repercussions were simply too great. They remain so today.

So the societal change needed for our psychotics is easy to see. I will not spell it out, but will rather quote my respected psychiatry Professor who said to us after a psych patient interview, "Crazy is so obvious. Now you have a diagnosis. Let's treat the patient." And so should we, as a society, do the same for those sad, disturbed patients, and not focus upon the tools they used. For the second, the lack of black fathers, I have no easy answers.

Now let me get back to guns themselves.

*　　*　　*　　*　　*　　*

Growing up the way I did, comfortable with guns as tools, I will admit a certain difficulty understanding the extreme views on both sides of the debate. Though many weapons have a certain aesthetic appeal and a remarkable utility and power, they do not seem to be objects requiring love. On the other hand, they are inanimate objects, and are not deserving of hate either. A psychiatrist coming from another planet to study us would wonder about those extremes, and, having studied us, diagnose in those extreme cases a severe neurosis, and in some, actual psychosis. I will admit that there might be those among us who can love (or hate) a hammer, a power saw, or an automobile. But I doubt it. Guns somehow occupy a special niche in our minds.

Perhaps it comes down to the negative thought that a gun may be an offensive weapon: use a gun, you have intended to kill someone. And there is a proscription in all religions and in all societies against killing. Or is there? Or is the proscription against murder?

And yet another perspective – especially appropriate for women. This is taken from *The Gun Is Civilization* by Mark

Kloos: "*Human beings only have two ways to deal with one another: reason and force. If you want me to do something for you, you have a choice of either convincing me via argument, or force me to do your bidding under threat of force. Every human interaction falls into one of those two categories, without exception. Reason or force, that's it....... In a truly moral and civilized society, people exclusively interact through persuasion. Force has no place as a valid method of social interaction, and the only thing that removes force from the menu is the personal firearm, as paradoxical as it may sound to some.*" Well, I think life in our country and our interactions with others is a bit more complex than that binary theory. On the other hand, if you are a small woman, elderly, debilitated, or in any way disadvantaged, it's something to think about, isn't it?

*   *   *   *   *   *

Let's leave those philosophical questions for the moment, and learn more about this tool that we call a gun, because without factual knowledge, how can you make good decisions about how you should perceive guns?

Feel free to skip the next few paragraphs if you are a gun afflictionado, as you likely know all about these descriptors better than I.

You can think of guns as being one of three types.

First are shotguns, long guns that began their historical life as tools to hunt birds. They project a mass of small lead pellets, the mass dispersing in air the farther the pellets move from the gun. In the last two decades though, shotguns have evolved into powerful self-defense weapons, because up close, there is scant pellet dispersion, and thus tremendous wounding. This is the reason both our city and county police carry shotguns in their patrol cars. Shotguns are incredibly lethal close-up weapons. Put yourself on the other side of the law for a moment, and think about how you would feel if you were a burglar intruding into someone's home, then hearing the unmistakable sound of a shotgun shell being chambered, that sound coming from the next room. Shotguns are rapidly becoming the commonest home defense weapon.

Handguns are just that – guns small enough to be held in one's hand. Handguns suffer from two primary problems. The first of these is their low power. An apocryphal story from the gun culture: lady to off-duty cop at a party: "Are you carrying a concealed weapon?" "Yes ma'am." "Why? Are you expecting trouble at this party?" "No ma'am. If I were expecting trouble, I would've brought a long gun." So the value of handguns is that they are small and are thus both portable and concealable on one's body or in a purse. The second characteristic of handguns is that they are extremely difficult to control. The bullet doesn't always go where you hope. A dark story from some years ago: I was called to the hospital around midnight. Gunshot wound to the neck. I was to evaluate whether the bullet had damaged any of the arteries to the brain. I found out from the cops guarding the perp that the guy on the table had attempted to rape one of our nurses in our parking lot. I spoke to her later, asking her why she had shot him in the neck. "Didn't mean to. Trying to aim at his heart. Guess I was excited." Which highlights the prime problem with handguns (beside their lack of power) – it's the difficulty in controlling them. It takes thousands of rounds of practice to make a handgun bullet go where you wish, and once you pull that trigger, you own that round as it travels away from you at the speed of sound. And you are responsible for the damage that it does to other people – intended or not – and to pets and property until it comes to a rest.

Finally, we come to rifles. Rifles cause worry in many people because they are, for all practical purposes, truly and purely *offensive* weapons. Use a rifle, and the average person believes you have killed with intent – rather than in defense of your own life. Complicating the perception is the negativity behind the idea of the black (or assault) rifle. The term *assault rifle* came from the German army in the second world war, and the concept of a handy, reliable, autoloading, medium power weapon was quickly adopted by other militaries, especially our own. Both our Colt M-16 and the Russian infamous AK-47 have become popular in civilian shooting circles, and for those same reasons.

So why should rifles, if they are essentially offensive weapons, be allowed in the hands of civilians? Good question. Why not just confiscate and destroy all of them?

To give you a perspective on the size of that destroy project: the sheer number of rifles in nonmilitary civilian hands is awesome. In World War II, more than 5 million Garand rifles were made for our military. I would estimate that half of these have come into American civilian possession today, principally through the Director of Civilian Marksmanship, a federal organization that also sold World War II M1 carbines and World War I Springfield rifles to qualified Americans. Then we have the Russian Kalashnikov AK-47. It is reliably estimated that more than 100 million Kalashnikovs have been manufactured. That's not a misprint. One hundred million – one Kalashnikov for every 300 adults on this earth. Who is going to destroy these rifles by any government edict? And who will have the power to come into *your* home to search for and take them?

A segment of the population finds assault rifles in the hands of civilians completely offensive and unnecessary. But we are reminded of civilians on the Lexington Common firing that shot heard round the world. They were using the assault rifles of their day.

And yet another perspective – that of the English. My English medical colleagues seem always to bring up the subject of guns when we meet at international medical meetings. Why they are so fascinated is not something I have been able to explain. In general, their demeanor is usually one of bemused contempt. I don't point out to them that they have required us Americans to bail them out during two world wars over the past hundred years – though I am tempted to do so. I have evolved the following response when their disdain comes up: "First, you have one thing we don't: The Queen. Therefore, you are subjects. We have two things you don't: First, a Constitution (this often surprises them, but the English have none), and second, rifles. These two things make us citizens, not subjects." Unable to argue those points, they generally drift back to the bar to order another Scotch.

I wonder what would happen if a historian or sociologist from another planet were to come to study us, and especially to study our history over the last hundred years. Free of prejudice, he might likely observe that the historical enemy of the individual has been some powerful federal government – whether it be Stalin's, Mussolini's, Hitler's, Pol Pot's, or any number of current African nation states (Biafra comes to mind). He might conclude that what we have to fear is not an armed mob which might form following the loss of our electrical grid, nor a race riot, but an all-powerful and intrusive federal government, a government with rifles and the will to use them on its citizens.

And for yet another insight: Do you know about the large and powerful gun underground? You should, if you are to understand the culture. It is difficult to find a hard copy of *Unintended Consequences* by John Ross but it would be well worth your while to read it[77].

So this question about guns is a complex calculus, all things considered. On the one hand, you must admit that the gun is

---

[77] Long out-of-print, original copies have become collector's items and are extremely expensive. But you can find a PDF file of the book on the Internet. A major portion of the book is historical. The facts are carefully researched and are accurate. The second part is a fictional account of successful individual's resistance to an out-of-control federal government.

a tool – but on the other, more, so much more. After all, the inventors of our country did not think it important to include hammers, saws, and drills as essential rights in our Constitution. But they certainly did the gun.

A final thought. We Americans recently suffered through another mass shooting, this one in Oregon. The usual extremists on both sides of the debate filled the airwaves and the Internet with solutions to the problem. I believe the anti-gunners held the day. Which caused me, someone whom I think is a rational thinker at least on most days, to wonder. Looking in the window as I walked by the El Cajon Gun Exchange I wondering when that Glock might snap, lose its ability to think rationally, and go on a rampage. Just a thought.

I try to be objective; I'd like to convince you that I'm objective, but obviously, I'm not. Then again, I'm not the one who gets to decide about our future. Ultimately and once again, it is you with your vote who gets to decide the importance of the gun in our country and in our society – and I suspect, it's place in our country's future.

But for a boy growing up as I did, a gun was an indispensable of my life. As it remains today.

32. ON DEATH and DYING

The first time I realized there was such a difference between city kids and us country kids was a certain Sunday when Buddy O'Farrell had ridden the bus out to Greenock to play with me. Probably during sixth grade or so.

At one point in the afternoon, Mom leaned out the window, yelled down into the back yard, "Get me a chicken." You know what followed. Buddy's eyes got a little wide as the chicken's head came off, and he had to work hard to keep his cool as arterial blood spurted toward his shoes. He seemed to grow a little distant during the plucking and gutting. I watched him closely, wondering, then even feeling a little worried (*is this too much?*). But he didn't get sick. And was able to eat his dinner, though he certainly looked differently at his fried chicken that afternoon. I watched him pick up and chew on a leg. The change, the recognition of where that meat had come from – that that drumstick had been running around the back yard just a few hours before – was so, so obvious, even to a 12-year-old boy.

You live in the country, you see death and dying and its inevitability all around. A farmer, a country person may even get used to death and dying somewhat, perhaps eventually. Maybe. But at least for me, I never got comfortable with its reality, with death's absolute finalness.

As a kid, I wondered about death. Or, more precisely, as my childish thinking matured, I wondered if there were levels, or more carefully said, degrees of deaths' importance? Did killing the Japanese beetle eating our tomato plants have the same import as killing the chicken for dinner? As I grew and could think better, the answer became obvious. So in general, that question was answered by my intent, and how I felt at the moment I brought the hatchet down, pulled the trigger, or squished the bug.

But back to that query about degrees of importance. First, at least for this kid, a hierarchy developed that was based upon place in the evolutionary chain. Bugs were at the bottom, warm-blooded animals at the top. Then there was size: I discovered that smaller animals required less emotion – and thus their deaths caused less sadness than killing larger ones. For example, it was relatively easy to kill a chicken for dinner, whereas killing and butchering a pig was more intense, even beyond being infinitely more physically complex an undertaking, though the killing was to provide food. Killing a cow was a tiring, major, all day event requiring big tools and lots of planning. And lots of emotion. This process, butchering, always carried with it a certain deep sadness for all of us carrying out the killing I think, but especially for some little boy who might inadvertently look into soft brown cow eyes just before the coup.

Second, intent played a role. I'm not talking about human intent – rather the animal's. I felt justified in killing rats scavenging and eating our chickens' food; no sadness there. The same with a head shot through a groundhog eating vegetables in our garden. We were competitors, and with my rifle, I won. And that felt good.

And third, I came to recognize a major emotional difference between farm animals and wild animals. The nuns at Christmas time always read us the story of Christ's birth – the manger, the stable and so on, but one term, one description stuck in my mind: the text described the *dumb animals* who were said to be standing around watching the event. And, come to think of it, farm animals are pretty stupid. *Dumb animals* is a perfect way to see a cow or a sheep. Compare domesticated to wild animals: we invest wild animals with flattering descriptors, like the *wily* coyote, *clever as a* fox, *fleet* as an antelope and so on.

Which brings me to a few stories illustrating.

Uncle Eddie to my cousin Paul and me: "Bring the steer to the yard." The steer could see all of the tools set up in the yard for the butchering process, but plodded along to the point where he would die, and stood there quietly. Passively. And he did. Die, that is. Paul and I looked at each other in wonder. *Why didn't he try to run?* It was yet another boys' observation, an observation without a unifying theory. At least at that moment.

Next story: One day my dad took me to a slaughterhouse to pick up some special sausage he had had made. Even then, people were uncomfortable with the term *slaughterhouse*, and often called the place an abattoir. Slaughterhouse is an ugly term, isn't it? But in my family there was never an attempt to soften reality with fancy words; we always called that place *the slaughterhouse*.

Inside, the men were busy at their work, efficiently going about converting living breathing animals to edible food, and doing so, as far as I could see, absolutely dispassionately. (You might wonder about their apparent lack of emotion. I certainly did.) One of the men opened the small door at the back of the building, and the Judas goat led in about a dozen sheep. They stood around, looking confused, bleating gently (what a pitiful sound bleating is). Chains were let down from the ceiling; the men attached a chain to one rear leg of each sheep, and then, pulling on the chain, raised the whole group off the floor, heads hanging down, necks about chest high to the men. With lethal efficiency and not a single wasted motion, they slit the throats of each sheep with long thin razor-sharp knives. The sheep had made not a single move to escape. Nor did they make a sound. And I thought of a Bible saying I had heard: *But I was like a gentle lamb led to the slaughter. . .* These stories brought to mind and made awfully concrete those descriptors the nuns had used, *the dumb animals*. Some emotion, some pity for them – but only some.

*   *   *   *   *   *

Ah, but then there is *the hunt*. And remember, the hunt is an essential part of my culture.

Yet my first kill was an awful moment. I remember the afternoon to this day. And I remember it clearly.

I was maybe five years old, still living with my grandparents, and was wandering through the back yard, lost in fantasyland, carrying my trusty Red Ryder BB gun, shooting at snails and grasshoppers (bad guys, bank robbers, guys in black hats) in the garden. A warble in the peach tree caught my attention, and without any thought, I brought the gun to my shoulder, sighted quickly and squeezed the trigger. It was an awful mistake, and I knew it immediately as the BB gun fired. She fell from the branch, fluttering to the ground. I picked her up, this tiny warm wren, and watched as twitching wings slowly became still. Worse was the change in her eyes – those once shiny black eyes became ever so slowly cloudy. I wished it were five minutes ago, but the change was irreversible. I couldn't believe I had done such an incredible thing. In the midst of this moral dilemma I came to recognize that I held in my hands absolute power, the power of life and death. At that moment I wanted no more of this. In fact, Grandma had told me that it was a sin to kill a songbird, and my guilt was profound. As the years passed though, I came to recognize that I would kill again – and must kill again to put meat on the table, but that I must handle this incredible power with the most careful judgment and restraint.

Though my feelings and my judgments about this darkness we call death were to mature, were to become more complex over the years, those feelings began to evolve in my mind from that critical afternoon.

And the evolution brings me to the hunt for big game, and the last story:

In high school, I had read James Fenimore Cooper's *Leatherstocking Tales*, and in one of them, I think it was *Last of the Mohicans*, Hawkeye, his Indian brother and dad had shot a deer. When they came up to their kill, they stopped, reverently knelt beside the deer, and prayed. Their prayer was both an apology to the animal (whom they felt was their brother) for taking its life, and a thanks for the blessing of giving its meat for their sustenance. *Of course*, I thought. *What else would one do?* I too, through the years and up to this day, when I have hunted successfully, give thanks to the animal, placing a tuft of leaves or acorns in its mouth (his last meal, a German tradition taught me by my Grandfather Kerber) and spending moments of quiet sitting with my quarry in the woods. And when I think back of those times, that prayer of thanks is as close to religion as I have ever come.

As an aside, I have tried to explain this complex sequence of events and this intense feeling to my more civilized citified friends. Always unsuccessfully.

Heavy stuff for a little boy to comprehend, to make sense of. Heavy stuff for anybody to think about, isn't it?

*   *   *   *   *   *

Animal death was one thing; human death another.

Simply put, I found human death completely overwhelming. I have told you that by age 8, I had lost my wonderful Grandfather Kerber, and by age 12, my closest friend, my cousin Eddie. My feelings around those two deaths are contained in a single word: hatred. I hated the priests who tried to console us with platitudes, empty words that did nothing to take away the profound emptiness, those black holes in my heart. I hated any God that would allow this awfulness to happen. I hated others around me who were still laughing and living. Those feelings, I admit became gentled by time, but the scars never quite healed.

I never gotten comfortable with human death, and I know few physicians who ever have. I cannot shake the conviction that every human death is a failure. And yes, I know that feeling is irrational, but there you have it. I suspect that this feeling, this need to keep death at bay is one of the motivators that cause people to go into the healthcare professions. And of course we are always ultimately unsuccessful – all of our patients die, sooner or later. Sooner or later.

But nobody I know likes to pull the plug (To make that absolute decision – to turn off the respirator).

When I was an intern and our team was trying to determine whether someone was brain-dead, I was anguishing about the ethics of the whole process. An old (as in experienced) doctor pulled me aside, said to me, "Death is so obvious," then walked away, leaving me to my moral dilemma. And when I thought about it, of course he was correct. We pulled the plug.

But I also came to recognize that there are degrees and gradations about how we feel when we are faced with this absolute and irreversible process, this darkness, especially when we assume the power to kill, and on the other hand, to try to wield the power to heal.

At this moment I wonder: does this chapter make you a little uncomfortable? It does me.

These words may be discomfort causing because we as a culture appear to have developed some societal need to put death in the background, even to deny its presence, its inevitability, and its finality.

Just two examples: Meat comes not from the slaughterhouse, but nicely packaged in plastic wrap. A city friend, believe it or not, when I was exploring the topic actually said these words to me: "Where does meat come from? From the supermarket, stupid." (I'm not making that up. I couldn't make that up.) And our funerals have become, well, neat and tidy, the bodies perfected ("She looks so natural."). We have even softened our terms: "she passed" rather than "she's dead". In fact, because we use so much denial, and because death is our ultimate state, perhaps we should shine some light in to this dark corner of existence. Denial may be good in the short term, but as a way of living each day, it is really, really bad.

A coincidence. On the other hand, perhaps not a coincidence. While working on this chapter this morning, my sister called. Mary, my lovable and beloved cousin had just died. There is no good death when one has metastatic cancer, but this one was the least bad as it could be. She was not in pain (finally we have learned control pain in the terminally ill), she was surrounded by her family, and far more importantly, she was composed and accepting of her own death. She said to my sister yesterday afternoon, "I am no longer afraid. I am ready to die." And she looked into Mary Ellen's eyes and smiled.

Mary, like most of our family, never used softening words. She didn't say *I'm ready to pass on*. In the face of this awfulness, this black loss in the family, I found my observation about her words at first trivial, maybe even demeaning. But on further reflection, her clear words, plus her smile represented and brought to mind her whole life, a life lived with clarity and honesty, a life at the end represented by her simple direct words and perfect nonverbal communication. So even during her last hours, it was her personality to reassure, to help her cousin with the impending grief.

Mary's death brings a judgment, plus a complex question to mind. And the judgment is a bad one: once again, my patient has died. Another failure. And the question? Does anything come after this cold change? I wish I knew.

As a little boy growing up in the country, my environment made me face death of all kinds with great regularity. And facing it I grew. And facing it, I went into medicine. But I have never become comfortable with death's awfulness or its absoluteness.

And I hope I never do – become comfortable with death, that is. For to do so would remove a piece of my remaining humanity.

33. ON COMMUNICATING CONFUSION

Having read the essays to this point, it's probably obvious that the two foundational principles underlying my childhood growth and development were 1), the remarkable freedoms I enjoyed, and 2), the absolute responsibility for my actions as I exercised those freedoms. But another major theme that runs through my sisters' and my childhoods is the continuing need – at times a desperate, frustrating quest – to find big people to communicate honestly, and so to teach us the ways of the world.

Of course any kid can learn about heat by putting his finger into the flame on the gas stove, but soon we all come to understand that there is a better way. And kids search for that way every single day of their childhood. They search for teachers, for you cannot learn by making every single mistake. You simply won't live long enough. So kids search for big people they can trust.

To set the stage: Take yourself back in time; try to remember that kid – the one who had just asked you *the question* – you fill in the blank – and analyze what you saw in her eyes. If she was like most little kids, you would almost certainly see trust (otherwise she would have not have come to you for an answer), probably hope (hope that you might help her with her important dilemma), and almost certainly some anxiety (having prior experience, and thus worried that yet another adult might give her mixed signals, that your words would be discordant from your body language, body language that would show your real feelings).

For myself, as a little boy trying to gain knowledge, trying simply to grow up, over and over again, the big people confounded me. And watching my friends' confusion, I came to recognize that I was not alone. What the adults too often communicated – both verbally and more importantly, nonverbally – during so many transactions simply made no sense when I tried to test the new knowledge in any world I could see and touch. The result in us was error, embarrassment, sometimes even pain, but always confusion. I thought we kids deserved better. Still do.

To put a finer point on the problem, inadequate or misleading communications from adult to child often enhances neuroses and other life problems in the developing child, but in its essence, bad communication interferes with the ultimate humanistic goal, the development of loving intimacy.

So why is clear communication so often so difficult for us? After all, didn't we invent language to satisfy this very need?

To answer, let's consider the origins of communication. And to do that, I'll ask you to do an experiment – an experiment of observation – to watch the development of a newborn baby. (And no, not a baby in your own family. We need some objectivity, after all. We can take lessons from the clinical psychologists on how it's done. They spend long hours, simply watching, simply observing, and then, only after many hours of looking, develop their insights.)

You will notice that immediately after birth, there is simply not enough functioning brain for baby to perceive the outside world, so she is able to do little more than suckle, move arms and legs randomly, cry when discomforted, respond to some startling event by a grasp reflex, and eliminate waste. All are primitive reflexes. At that stage, she and an earthworm have a lot in common.

How quickly her brain grows though. Soon her eyes can focus and converge, and she learns to recognize Mom, and that Mom's warm soft breast and secure arms are the source of her satisfaction and her safety. Her survival, her comfort, she quickly learns, depends upon her rapidly developing ability to recognize what Mom is all about. And this mental growth, this cognitive development is the critical foundation of the child's remarkably accurate and reliable ability to read Mom's (and others') body language. She learns to sense her mother's needs. She becomes possibly a better observer of her mom and mom's moods and needs than the psychologists I just spoke of. She is powerfully motivated; she must learn – her survival depends on it.

The first problems start to become obvious when our child develops language skills. Because, for our own complicated reasons, we adults don't always say what we mean. Worse, we often don't recognize the conflicts within ourselves that give rise to the dichotomy, words that might say heads, while our body language shows tails. To emphasize, when adults say one thing and mean another, it confuses a kid. Bad communications hurt.

Keeping these two means of communication – verbal language and body language – in mind, let's now dig deeper into this communication thing. And our problems with it.

Probably the best way to understand these more complicated transactions between adults and kids is to consider that even as a child we have within ourselves (our psyches) three different persona: one we have incorporated from our parents, a second our current adult selves[78], and third, residuals of our earlier childness. Certainly by eight or ten years, these three states are fairly well-developed. In terms of transactional analysis (a study of how we communicate with each other)[79]

---

[78] It may come as a surprise to you to believe that a 10-year-old can think of herself as an adult. But kids are practicing to be grown-ups all the time, so this analysis becomes a useful construct to understand behavior.

[79] I have found *Transactional Analysis*, invented by psychiatrist Eric Berne to be much more valuable in understanding human behavior (and treating abnormal

we may call these states *Parent, Adult, and Child*, in capital letters. When describing an actual other person, say Uncle Pete, we will use small case letter, as Pete is an *adult*. To summarize, it's possible when communicating with another person to interact from your Parent to their Parent, your Adult to their Adult or your Child to their Child. These straight communications can be considered the goal of honest communication. Let me emphasize: one can have straight Adult to Adult communications even when there is a significant age disparity, as when Grandma gives advice to my nine-year-old sister Judy about sewing buttons on shirts.

Let me give you an example of an Adult to Adult communication from my Dad one afternoon.

We are about nine, Reed and I, and are wrestling around in Grandma's backyard. Playing Cowboys and Indians, we take turns winning and losing. We think it natural that the loser be trussed up with a length of old clothes line. We have learned to make a hangman's noose. My Dad walks out to the backyard, puts his face about five inches from mine, and says in his few-words manner, "Don't ever let anyone put a rope around your neck." Then he looks at Reed, holds Reed's gaze a few seconds, turns back to me, makes another eye contact, turns around and walks away. Reed and I look at each other. *Wow, that was important.* I remember that transaction to this moment. His was a perfect and perfectly clear communication

---

behavior) than Freudian analysis. You would enjoy two books by Berne, *Games People Play*, and *What Do You Say after You Say Hello*.

– no preamble, no softening, no explanations, no reasoning are needed. There was no sarcasm. His combination of body language – the closeness, the intense unblinking look, plus the congruent words make us recognize that ropes around necks, even in play, can be fatal. No further words are needed. This is exactly what kids need from the big people. Dad makes the good communicator list, and he is near the top. What he was *not* doing was talking down to either of us, his Parent to our Child.

Most of the time, as we were after all kids, Parent to Child communication was totally appropriate. "Dad, I don't feel good, and I have these bumps all over my face and they really, really itch. I'm scared. Am I going to die?" A communication from my Child to his Parent. "Don't worry son. It's just the measles. You'll be better in about two weeks." And then he gathered me into his arms, carrying me into the bedroom. That sick feeling suddenly wasn't too bad. Dad's words and maybe more importantly, his actions were congruent: loving, in charge, reassuring, and confident. My fear was immediately gone. His reply was from his Parent to my Child.

Problems for kids come when the communications become crossed.

For example: We have our driving licenses; we are seniors; it is Friday night. There is beer. One of us, Mikey Kolendro becomes staggeringly, vomiting-in-the-bushes drunk. Stush (the third man in our trio) and I drive him home, guide him up the steps, into his house, and Surprise! run into his violently furious mom. She screams at him (and us) for long minutes. One phrase, and only one phrase that she keeps repeating sticks in our minds. "Don't you ever let me see you drunk again." Before reading on, let me ask how would you analyze this exchange? If this had been an Adult to Adult communication – which we, being only 17-year-old boys, thought it was, the chastising was well deserved. But in fact she was talking as her disapproving Parent to his misbehaving Child. Her anger is real - and, OK, I will admit, appropriate, but the critical (and pathological) part of the verbal message is *don't ever let me see . . .* Which said to Mikey (words we all heard clearly) that he must do his drinking in secret, hiding it from her. Turns out, that exchange happened many other times, and he ultimately accepted and incorporated her directive into his life. It was a loser's life script she wrote for him. In later years, Mikey did poorly. You are likely not surprised.

I have an even more painful, more complicated example of crossed communications.

We are in third or fourth grade, Jimmy Chisholm and I. Since Jimmy lives literally across the tracks behind the school, I often go over to his back yard during lunchtime, where we can share our lunch sandwiches and get away from the nuns. On this particular day, his mom is outside doing the wash, scrubbing clothes on a washboard[80]. His dad is sitting in a lawn chair. From his dad comes the overpowering smells of whiskey and tobacco.

"Hi Dad. What are you doing home?" An innocent question, an Adult to Adult question, reasonable because usually his dad would have been at work. What we didn't know at the time was that his dad had just lost his job. His dad's response was an immediate and powerful backhand to Jimmy's face, knocking him to the ground. Wailing, Jimmy picked himself up, ran into the house. His dad looked at me unsteadily for a few seconds, then stumbled into the house as well, slamming the door. I stood there, unable to move, completely confounded, not knowing what to do.

His mom continued the washing, seemingly unperturbed. She said to me, "Jimmy's dad loves him; he just doesn't know how to express love." Wow. I got out of there as quickly as I could make my legs move. With her words bouncing around in my head, I was totally confused.

It took many years and a lot of training to figure out those transactions. A father striking his son to vent his own frustration and powerlessness is just awful. Eventually, the kid will

---

[80] It is unlikely you have ever used — or even seen a washboard. Stuck in a tub of hot water, the woman (always the woman) pulled dirty clothes out of the sudsy hot tub water and rubbed them on the corrugated metal washboard to clean them. It was dreary, hand ruining labor.

understand though – and probably even forgive, once he develops understanding of the circumstance. But what he will never forgive or forget is the pathologic communication from mom. She did nothing to explain dad's behavior, but instead said words that were completely incongruent and inappropriate for the situation. It is that kind of dishonest communication that so terribly screws up kids. *Mom says dad loves me and yet he hits me? What kind of the world is this?* If this kind of communication is repeated, perhaps Jimmy incorporates into his own life script that it's okay to hit those who love you. Which is what happened, and sad to say but no surprise, in later years Jimmy did poorly, especially with his own kids.

Sometimes adults directly lied to us. We could rarely figure out their agenda, but knew there was something bad going on.

Other times the big people just said untrue words to cover their ignorance.

For example, a story which brings us back to the nuns: "Sister, I heard the saying the *die is cast*. What does that mean?" "When you are making steel, they pour the liquid steel into dies." It took me many years to learn that die was a singular of dice, and the saying referred to gambling, and that once you threw the die down, you could not change your bet.

And another: "Sister, I hear that people play the numbers (a common form of petty gambling in the valleys). What is that; why do they do it?" "It is an evil thing, carried on by evil people. God will punish them." What an answer. Took a long time to figure out the numbers racket, and its connection to the local Mafia.

Kids don't mind an "I don't know the answer to that" reply. Both direct lying and the cover-up were relatively easy to spot; kids are more attuned to truth than any adult can know (which makes you wonder, don't adults remember their own childhood and how good their own BS detector was?).

Two more points, and then we will sum this up.

The first gets back to the power and remarkable accuracy of kids' ability to read body language. Mom and Dad are going away for a few days. They have asked Aunt Eva to come stay with us. Aunt Eva has a problem with Janet. For some reason, she doesn't like Janet. She looks at Janet, smiles with her mouth, and says sweetly, "I'm looking forward to spending more time with you." Her eyes convey hate. Janet, who reads body language quite well being only four, is appropriately terrified. Mom heard only Eva's words. Those days that followed were long, painful days for Janet.

Sadly, over the years, as we become more language oriented, we seem to train ourselves to ignore the critical communications that come to us during every transaction. Mom certainly did with Aunt Eva – perhaps because she wanted to get away.

An opinion: Just about every adult I know would improve their lives by relearning the skill of reading body language. Something to think about, isn't it?

Perhaps now is a good time to look in the mirror and ask yourself how well you do communicating with kids. All too often, the answer is *not too well*.

But . . . We should not get too deeply into self blame, because in our favor, as adults we are often distracted, lacking in time, concerned with so many important survival problems – the education and safety of those kids, for example – and we have our own needs, fears, inappropriate behavior patterns, even at times neuroses that come into play during any transaction. And face it, kids can be really manipulative. Nonetheless, they depend upon us to learn to be productive, loving adults. Perhaps some communication guidelines are in order.

You might think about four Es before you reply to that expectant kid: engagement, empathy, enlistment, and education[81].

The engagement part is pretty easily accomplished, because the kid has come to you. Eye contact is the critical beginning, then consider getting down to their level. Sit down, lie down, whatever. Look hard for the nonverbal clues.

Empathy is more difficult. Here's where your body language comes into play. If you stop what you're doing, make eye contact, and listen attentively, the empathy bond will happen, and happen quickly.

---

[81] Doctors have an especially severe problem trying to communicate with kids. First, they are usually sick, and second, they are almost always afraid. I'm indebted to a colleague, John M Purvis MD, who proposed the 4 E memory aid.

Enlistment? Simply include them into your problem solving reply. A few questions are appropriate. And the questions lead directly to the next E . . .

Education. And this is the payoff. With a little thought, it's possible to include the kid's problem-solving abilities into your reply. "Interesting statement, Patty, but is it accurate? Is *everyone* going to New York City to spend the night after the prom?" The judgment part of what to say is often difficult, because kids need different things depending upon their level of development. When a four-year-old asks where she came from, she might not be asking for a talk about human sexuality but wondering instead about the city where she was born.

In summary: To work every day to communicate well to the children around us is a worthy life goal. We can all agree that the many thousands of transactions that occur during a kid's growth and maturation will each have an effect, but that the important and critical people, parents especially, will have a disproportionate effect. And remembering that kids are truly expert at reading body language, it simply doesn't pay to be anything other than completely honest with them.

The stakes for the kids are high, because it is so easy while raising a child to implant neurotic behaviors, behaviors that will follow them into adulthood, behaviors that will interfere with their ability to develop loving relationships. And the ability to communicate, the essential skill needed to develop trusting love is a lifelong and ultimate goal, isn't it?

An American Boyhood

My sisters and I were generally fortunate, because almost all of the time our grandparents, and mom and dad could look us in the eye and give us straight communications. Outside the family though, adults confused us so, so often.

Which leads us into the next chapter, which is about that ultimate communication, the one we all strive for . . .

34. BEYOND MEASURING

At first glance you might think that this story should be near the front of the book, given the age at which it takes place, but bear with me a few moments. And please allow me to add a few words to create a foundation: scientists go about the world measuring things: with rulers, stopwatches, and thermometers their primary tools. And appropriately so. Good for them. Now with all that in mind, let us proceed.

The story begins simply, but is, well, complicated (and wonderfully, gloriously complicated, at least for me).

Mom had a friend up the road – almost as far up as Sutersville. And one day, while they were talking, as moms were wont to do, Mrs. Anderson suggested that, since her little girl and I were the same age, we should play together.

An American Boyhood

I think I was somewhere around 10 at the time, and when Mom told me of the plan, I put my foot down. Literally put it down, stomping on the kitchen linoleum. My response was, quite immediately and simply "No." Being 10 and shy, I was certain I wanted no stranger to come to my house nor I to go to hers, unless it was my idea. As quick, as firm as my *no* was, Mom corrected me as to form: "No, thank you, I mean," which was my only acceptable come back. But you might notice that I was not corrected as to content, as *moms had decided*. Jenny and I were to play together. And there you have it. Stage set.

Arrangements made by the two moms (all-powerful moms, especially in the case of the two kids in this episode), it came to happen that one blustery November Saturday afternoon I waited impatiently but dutifully at the side of the road for the bus from Sutersville, all the while feeling a certain dread. What got off the bus was a girl pretty much my height, pretty much my age, a girl pretty much as shy as I was. Following Mom's politeness instructions to the letter ("When the bus stops, you will....."), I led the way into our warm kitchen. Mom had put out homemade brownies and glasses of milk. (As an aside, even today I'm fairly sure there is no better ice-breaker than brownies and milk. And if the day is cold, and the milk a little warm, no adult beverage could possibly in any way compete. You might want to keep this pearl of wisdom in mind.)

Bellies pleasantly and pleasingly full, now a bit less uncomfortable with each other, then dressed for the weather, we began to explore the back yard. And to play. (Of course. We were little kids, were we not?) Tossing fallen leaves at each other. Running through the woods. Skipping flat rocks across the creek, playing hide and seek around the big elms, tumbling and rolling together down the hillside. Yes, rolling together. We finally came to rest side-by-side, laughing, a little flushed from our exertions – and then she took my hand in hers.

We came slowly closer, and gently, ever so gently, surprising ourselves, our lips touched. And at that moment, the world – my world – changed. Changed forever. I am not exaggerating.

Perhaps one moment of comic relief: our noses were runny – dribbling thin watery snot at that – it was a bitingly chilly North wind, November afternoon after all. Okay, I know this sounds awful, but that gentle kiss smeared and commingled snot dribbles over both our upper lips. It was kind of sweet, the snot was, which we discovered when we separated and needed to run our tongues over chapped upper lips. Sharing snot was embarrassing at first, but we came to realize that what we had done was so exquisitely unusual and surprisingly good that it caused a mutual giggle – and another roll around, arms about each other. So, self-consciousness now completely gone, we kissed again. And again. And again.

I can explain what happened next if I use objective and rigid rules of scientific observation, rules I learned years later in school. The facts: Her tossel cap had come off, and strawberry blonde curls fell about her face as she looked down at me. Just then the dark low clouds scudding over the hillside must have parted, allowing a small shaft of afternoon sunshine to fall just right upon her hair, illuminating it. Lying on my back, looking up at her face, looking toward the sky, that fortuitous single shaft of sunlight lightened the periphery of her hair. A magical golden halo surrounded her head. Just at that place; just at that moment in time. Yes, science; scientific observation.

My science professors, each and every one coldly rational, taught that physical rules explained every physical phenomenon. They had taught me, depending upon their own discipline of course, that we were just a collection of vibrating atoms . . . Or hormonally controlled physiologic organisms. . . Or well designed entities whose sole meaning was to replicate DNA . . . Or behaviorally, Jenny and I had just engaged in pre-mating activity. I think you get their point.

Ah, No. Ten year-old kids? Pre-mating activity? Come on . . .

For there are worlds beyond science, worlds beyond our ability to measure.

Here is the realness: Looking up into her eyes, having just kissed, a glowing radiant aura had come to surround her, had come to be. A light I had never before noticed, never before seen . . . a light suffusing through her hair, a light reflecting back on her face. . . that wonderful, that soft, that beautiful face – a light that grew in warmth and intensity had entered, had expanded my very soul. And the dark sky – the entire rest of the world in fact – blurred to insignificance. *What ..... Is ..... This ......? What ..... Is ...... Happening?*

And then a thought came suddenly, pushing itself into my joyful confusion. Now I understood. I understood what those halos around the paintings of the saints were all about. And looking into Jenny's eyes again, this soft warm aura, this glow grew, spreading out from her curls, blotting out the darkness of the sky. Cornflower blue eyes looking into mine, flushed cheeks the color of July cherries, smiling plump pink lips, but above all the glowing ethereal aura of strawberry blonde hair surrounding that beautiful face.

And this, I came to realize, was reality.

You have every right to be skeptical. You should be skeptical, to wonder how I could remember that moment so clearly. But I do, because of the moment's unusualness, its intensity, its profoundness. From time to time, when I think about Jenny, about that moment's image, that feeling, that experience, and then try to commingle those memories into the starkness of my professors' sureness, cold scientists who could not believe in any phenomenon they were unable to measure, who in fact felt disdain for any thing they could not explain with a formula, I recognize there are some wonderfully important things beyond science. In fact, I have come to believe that many things beyond the measurable are more essential than those we can quantify.

This lovely little girl and I created our first experience – at least *my* first real experience – with what I can only call *the sacred*. Before or since, I have never been able to find *the sacred* in any book said to be written by the Creator of the universe, in the soaring Gothic arches of any church, during any incense scented Catholic mass, or in the depths of some sonorous Gregorian chant. Nor have I found *the sacred* in the eloquent rationality of any priest, nor in the intense and fear producing threats of black clad nuns. Try as they all might, they have not been able to show or create that existential feeling of insight and wonder about the essence of being. Especially about the essence of two human's ability to share.

I think Jenny felt this sharing of souls too. In fact, I know she did. No, of course we didn't understand what we had created at that fragile and evanescent point in time – we were after all only kids. But years later, in recollecting and reliving those tendernesses, I came to recognize that that essence of the moment, that experiential happening, came about because of a tender mutual gift. Let me repeat the key words: Tender. Mutual. Gift.

Indeed, it did take two for the creation. The creation needed we two, kids who had developed a closeness, a freely offered, completely trusting closeness. Not an insignificant learning experience for a simple little country girl and boy, was it?

But back to you: in a quiet moment, we must wonder whether this essential communication, the Tender Mutual Gift is not the ultimate quest for each and every one of us. And if so, to wonder how well each of us has done until now to create this ultimate closeness. And then perhaps wonder what we will do to find it tomorrow. And the next day.

465

On the other hand, perhaps you can think of some other experience, some other moment, another something that better defines our sacred humanness in your own life. For me, it is and always will be the willing opening of one person's soul to another, then joining, the interface, the junction of two conscious minds each able, each willing to let the other in[82].

This concept, this idea does explain many metaphysical things we come across: common human decency, for example. Altruism. Loyalty, honor. Perhaps even poetry.

Now back to that afternoon. Finally, the blue hour approached, and it was time for Jenny to go home. I stood with her along the road, waiting for the bus to come. And when it stopped, I touched her lips with another sweet and gentle kiss. She climbed the steps, but just before the door closed, she turned, tossing her red-blonde curls, looked directly into my soul, and smiled. Time stood still. I can close my eyes today and see her sparkling blue eyes and that happy smile.

Oh, and that soft, suffused light around her lovely face – her own personal halo, her sacred halo – had not faded.

It never will.

---

[82] Recently I came across a book that expanded this idea of the sacred. You might consider finding it. Roger Scruten's *The Soul of the World*, Princeton Press. It is the perfect nonreligious reply to those who want to reduce us to a replicating bunch of non-spiritual stuff. Read it, and you will find yourself smiling, happy with yourself as a person and with this unusual condition we call humanness.

35. SO WHAT?

At this point, after so many words, so many pages, my high school friend Donnie Kasner would likely look at me and, in his McKeesport accent, so simply, so succinctly say, "Yeah yeah, so what?" Which gets right to the point: Where do these essays, certainly only my remembrances, simple musings, leave us? So, so what?

The *yeah yeah so what* question brings us back to the striking comparison that began the second chapter, those two polar opposites: that pretty, overly padded, painfully constricted little blonde girl on her tricycle, and my (and my sisters') re-markable freedoms and responsibilities.

We started this project together, my writing, you reading a simple memoir, but, as we went on, I asked you, bit by bit, chapter by chapter, to question the way you see the world, to make comparisons with my time so long ago and how you see our culture today. And especially to ask you to wonder, to describe to yourself, to analyze how you interact with and teach kids today. Then, and importantly, with your insights, to wonder about their future, and ultimately to wonder about the future of our culture.

So you may be curious, perhaps even puzzled, I would suspect. You're likely wondering where this final chapter is going. Which is no surprise, as I came to wonder too. Because when I started writing it, I was somewhat less than sure myself.

Your primary, in fact your ultimate question is likely to be whether my experiences, experiences of a little boy growing up in a different time in America have anything to do with raising your kids and grandkids today, and especially whether my experiences can tell us anything about their future – and thus our future. When I sat down to write this last essay, that question bubbled up from the depths of my mind's deepest recesses. As I promised in that first chapter, this was not to be a poor-boy-does-well bio. What started out as simple growing up series of stories now finishes up as something else entirely, something that brings the problems and questions of child-rearing and what our future might contain into stark relief. Is that too arrogant a statement?

Well, the question worked for me. But you get to judge.

So let us go back to that somewhat worried and insecure little boy at his high school graduation in 1954, and the pretty and overly protected little girl on her tricycle in Balboa Park, two images that focus us on the question: could there be any two kids more different? Could my story possibly be relevant in this current complicated world the kids face today?

To answer, I hope you'll allow me to iterate and string together four simple but fundamental concepts, letting the words create a simple logic path, attempting to highlight differences but connect essentials in those two such disparate lives.

The first idea, the first concept, has to do with history – beginning with history painted with a rather broad brush, especially and particularly history of us as humans. And as we examine our history we must question whether it's even possible to learn from our past – of course the triumphs – but especially from our mistakes. For there is no shortage of lessons, as we Homo Sapiens have certainly made plenty of mistakes.

The second concept emphasizes that there are cycles great and small – cycles in the world, cycles in our own lives. This second concept hopes that we can anticipate the future knowing about those cycles that bear so importantly and repetitively in our lives.

The third questions whether we can generalize about the characteristics of different generations, and whether insights gleaned from those generalizations might allow us to understand better the current kids.

And fourth to consider then critically evaluate the current conventional knowledge about today's kids and to wonder whether if those memes are realistic and science-based.

Then finally to bring the analyses and criticisms together into a conclusion, allowing us perhaps even to predict our next years. And if you permit some hubris, I will append my personal prediction for today's generation and their ultimate fates – and the fate of our American culture. No surprise, this last part really worries me, as my personal history has been one of a generally well-meaning but naïve guy who is able to predict everything – except the future. So be warned.

*   *   *   *   *   *

Now let's expand and question that first idea, which is about human history in general. And I bring this up now because it has been my experience that there is no shortage of people who believe that the past is no guide to the future.

Early on, Mister Prince, my high school geometry teacher once told me, "You can't walk through the same stream twice." Which got me (and might get you) thinking. Well, I knew that he was literally correct, with constantly flowing water molecules having replaced the ones I last walked through, and all that. This outlook was perhaps not a surprising way for any quite-literal math teacher to think. But we are not wading through streams here, and the analogy is a hard sell because when I walk into the adjacent class room, a room where Miss Malseed forces me to confront the history of Western civilization. That metaphorically short walk becomes especially poignant when, again and again, she forces me to recognize how we humans have rarely learned from our mistakes, and so down through the ages, seem to keep repeating them[83]. Of course mathematics is absolute, and Mister Prince's observation was literally correct, but Miss Malseed's ability to weave history into a remarkable and insight producing narrative, plus the perspective of my own gray-haired experience, makes me accept as an absolute Shakespeare's take on history: *What's pass'd is prologue.*

Thus I believe that the answer to the first query is *yes*, we can learn from history, and having learned, have the power to analyze our mistakes, and with new knowledge, to alter our own future, and we hope, our children's and grandchildren's future for the better.

* * * * * *

If you accept that that hypothesis is possible, let's progress to

---

[83] I immediately wondered if we, our culture, are forever doomed to repeat history's mistakes. That started me worrying on a personal level – wondering if I were doomed to repeat my own mistakes. (Which would be really, really bad.) I'm wondering even today. Though the jury is still out, I am optimistic.

the next idea, that of cycles in our lives. It's easy to recognize the short term cycles – especially the daily recurrences – the sun comes up; the sun goes down. We wake up hungry; we go to bed tired. Perhaps a little more difficult is to recognize the cycles in our moods. Admittedly, it's more simple for a woman as she has her menses to remind her, but we men seem to wallow about without ever developing great insight into our ups and downs. Those few Americans who still farm recognize the change of seasons and their importance, but as most of us live in the city, we tend to keep nature somewhat beyond arm's length, as we have the power of turning on heat in the winter and air-conditioning in the summer. Even more difficult to analyze is our own birth, life, and (scary thought) death cycle. No surprise – lots of denial about that cycle. So the more removed we are from any daily experience of nature, the less attention we tend to pay to the great cycles, especially the one which has the potential to affect our children and grandchildren most, the evolution to maturity, then potential decline of our American culture.

And what is the American consensus about our future? How are we doing? How do we see the president? And his approval ratings? How about Congress? The kids today? Google any poll about us and you will not be encouraged. But hold that thought for a moment.

*　　*　　*　　*　　*　　*

All of which might lead us to the next cycle to consider, to ask us to analyze this whole idea of *generations*, especially to emphasize their repetitive nature, that generational characteristics repeat themselves.

What? Generations are cyclic? They keep recurring? Hold that thought for a moment. Let's consider the *idea* of generations first.

It's curious, isn't it, this concept of *generations*. It is a concept that is almost universally accepted – at least vaguely, and at least by us Americans. Even TIME magazine has devoted major portions of issues to the idea[84]. But wait, isn't that practice called profiling, assigning a certain set of characteristics to an entire group just because they were born between certain years? And we all know that profiling is simply not okay, profiling is consummately politically incorrect, and that profiling leads to all manner of evilness – racism, being the prime example. But actually, from a scientific point of view, profiling works, and it works if the sample size is large enough, and homogeneous, and the group that you studied to characterize the whole is representative of the whole. So the idea has some scientific merit, and besides, we all use the term. Or maybe it's more precise to say *many of us* use the term[85].

---

[84] May 13, 2013, May 20, 2013

[85] One scientific use of profiling: eight-year-old black girl comes to the ER, suddenly unable to speak and now weak on her right side. The physician must get the process going quickly, tentatively making the diagnosis of sickle cell disease (she is black remember, and thus profiled), and begin quickly to treat her evolving stroke. Of course other diagnostic studies are carried out simultaneously in

So, for the moment, allow me to say that at least in America, we profile groups. (You have to admit that the progressives profile the conservatives, and the conservatives profile the progressives. Each negatively, of course.) So, back to generations, which, by and large, is an idea we accept that people born during certain times have discernible characteristics. You might be surprised to learn that sociologists have been able to identify four specific generations, and that the generations follow one another with remarkable regularity, and have done so since the 1600s.[86]

Those sociologists and psychologists who study the generations generally think of each generation lasting some 22 to 24 years.

Now let's begin with a generation most Americans have agreed about: *The Greatest Generation.* Most of us have heard about that Greatest Generation, men (and women too) who were children of the depression, who then left homes to go off and fight a world war. They won that war, quite literally saving the world for democracy, then came home, and having been so destructive for four years, wanted nothing more than to build themselves a home, to build a career, to have and love their kids. The character and characteristics of this generation

---

case he is incorrect, but here time is of the essence.

[86] Strauss, William and Howe, Neil, GENERATIONS: The history of America's future 1584 to 2069, William Morrow and Company, New York, 1991

has been well documented in a book by Brokaw[87].

Next we come to mine, the *Unnamed Generation* (which is, in my opinion, the generally underappreciated generation, but that's another story[88]). We can profitably save time, paper and ink by skipping over us.

Ah, but then the *Baby Boomers* (1945 to about 1970) came into the world. Theirs came to be called the *Me Generation*. And as time passed, that became such an appropriate name. The me generation began when kids in their teens and 20s gave us Woodstock, hippies, flower power, widespread substance abuse and perhaps ultimately and most importantly, when they achieved their political maturity, they gave the country an overwhelming public debt, which hangs over everyone's head today[89].

Then we come to the next generation, often called *Generation X*, and now the most recent generation, the so-called *Millennials,* which I think our little girl belongs to. Close enough for discussion purposes.

Now let me tell two stories, stories that might clarify for you

---

[87] The Greatest Generation, Brokaw, T , Random House Publishing, 1998

[88] Say what you will, our generation fought and died in Vietnam, even knowing we were being betrayed by our political leaders.

[89] Keep that debt in mind, but let me get back to you about it later in this essay.

my own nonscientific, almost certainly prejudiced characterizations of two of the generations, the *me generation* (I have already given you a hint of my, well, somewhat negative feelings toward them, so you probably know what to expect), and another story from this latest generation, which is what gives me hope.

It is the first day of July, 1982. On July 1 of every year, a new crop of young doctors begins the first year of their advanced training. It being 1982, these new docs are, you guessed it, of the *Me Generation*. Young guy comes my office, casually dressed, short white Doctor coat, coat wrinkled and not particularly clean, a little late but not fatally late, sits down, puts his hands behind his head, leans back, feet up on my desk and casually says, "Teach me." You might wonder if he actually lived after that transaction. Yes, he did, but no, he did not, ah, do well. Sadly, that attitude, that arrogance, that feeling of entitlement was repeated, painfully repeated, by many of his contemporaries throughout those years. It was not a fun time to be a professor at a medical school. Still, eventually that generation of doctors learned, and I have to give them that. Turns out that the profession itself is a cruel and unforgiving teacher.

Now the second story, which brings us to Jessica, a *Millennial*, a fairly typical member of the current crop of young doctors. When the powers in the med school assigned me to be her faculty advisor, I wondered if she would even care about having a gray-haired godfather. That wonder did not last long.

"Hi, I'm Jessica." Comfortable and direct eye contact, a smile, clean fingernails, computer ready to take notes – but most importantly – the look. She had the look of one hungry to learn. Wow. What a change. And she did well from that first day, and is now a superb physician. You might keep this difference in mind as we continue down our meandering path.

And another data point (actually another story): Erika, age 22, a product of an upper-class Boston suburban family (probably flaming liberals, right? Oops. I think I'm guilty of profiling) has recently graduated from an upper tier college (again, probably a bastion of liberal thought, right?[90]). Having graduated, she is going to *do good*. She takes a job in the deep South. The organization she works for is supported by government money. The culture, the work ethic of the other employees is . . . well, not productive. They are Liberals with a capital L. In six months Erika becomes a "raging capitalist", her Dad's words (and in my words, a conservative. Importantly, a small *c* conservative).

But wait you say, these stories are not typical – these kids are outliers. This new generation is obviously *going to the dogs*. No it isn't, but I will freely admit to you that my high opinion of the current generation is not universal among us who have achieved a certain maturity. The word curmudgeonly comes to mind when trying to describe these older people.

---

[90] My prejudice is showing again, isn't it? Please forgive me.

So this brings us to a few more stories:

"Awful, just awful, these kids. Head down, not paying attention, she walked straight into me, just staring at *that thing* in her hands. Yep, she walked right into me, nearly bowled me over." And from another elder: "I don't what I'm going to do with Jonathan. All through the meal, sneaking looks down into his lap, trying to hide *that thing* under the table, couldn't get him to talk, and with all that's going on in the world today . . . You'd think he'd at least want to learn how to carry on a conversation." And another mother talking: "Unconscious, that's what she is. There's a whole world out there waiting to be appreciated, but as soon as she's able, she hides away in her room with *that thing*, looking down, always looking down at it." An iPhone, correct? Is it the continual texting on *that thing* we're discussing? Wait a minute, the year is 1620, and *that thing* is a bound book. By that time, it has been 60 or 70 years since Gutenberg invented movable print, and books are *the rage*. Or maybe the year is a few thousand earlier than 1620, just after the invention of cursive writing. Come on, admit it. When have you ever *not* heard old people complaining about the younger generation?

Having pored through too many op-eds (some pro, mostly con), I have come up with these characteristics of today's kids – at least according to the op-ed writers: today's kids have an abnormally high self regard coupled with a basic disregard of facts; that ignorance is the only true bliss; that commencement speakers must be disinvited if their philosophy does not hew to the current politically correct agenda. But there are more than negatives, especially in our upper tier colleges –powerful positives as well: demands for "transformative justice" (whatever that is), to mandate sensitivity training; to organize continuous external reviews of the college's structural racism, classism, able-ism, sexism, and heterosexism (these from, of all places, Dartmouth College, a school once held in high regard. And there were more demands. Seventy-two in all, as a matter of fact. You can look them up on the Internet.)

Okay, so the kids today have been, well, a bit spoiled by parents and the poor primary educational system in our country. Okay, cosseted is not a bad word either. But it's not all their fault. Nothing can top the egregious indulgences and self-importance of the non-science departments of today's colleges. I can do no better than to refer you to the Wikipedia entry outlining the Duke University lacrosse team's vilification following the stripper's charge of rape. If you choose to look up this entry, spend bit of time looking at the 88 faculty (photographs too, please) all of whom were so quick to render judgment[91]. Now that there's a bit of perspective brought by time, the review will discourage you. Notice that there is no science faculty on that list. And then the Humanities faculty wonders why they have rendered themselves irrelevant[92]. Sadly, the Humanities have committed suicide. And so our culture loses an important positive influence.

---

[91] http://en.wikipedia.org/wiki/Group_of_88

[92] And you might admit that this perceived irrelevance is a great sadness, and significantly diminishes American culture.

An American Boyhood

*   *   *   *   *   *

Now we come to a follow-on question: do the generations change (we hope, *to improve*) as they grow, learn, age, and, scary thought, achieve political power? I mean, isn't this the critical query to answer?

Which brings us back full circle, back to that overly padded little girl in Balboa Park, and the little boy you've come to know in the prior chapters – and his freedom – and her lack of same. Could there possibly be any relevance in comparing the two childhoods? Could we learn anything from the comparison?

Of course any attempted scientific analysis has to admit qualitative differences in today's culture, and the problems the current kids face.

Again, Google any poll you want, and you'll discover soon an angst in the country, an underlying worry and discomfort about the national debt – a debt hanging over each of our heads (more than $70,000 a person, and probably more, depending upon who calculates it), the unsustainable social welfare so-called entitlement programs, the lousy public educational system, the unwinnable war on drugs (at least 50 billion a year. Did we learn nothing from Prohibition?). And to all that add the dangerous and unstable world beyond our shores, and to cap it all, a growing and ominous recognition of the intrusiveness of big government burrowing its way into every aspect of our private lives every minute of every day.

Ah, but the variable in the equation is that little, over padded, overprotected girl. Dictators, whether they be politicians, slaveholders, teachers or parents (well, *some* parents. Helicopter parents), have always undervalued and underestimated the individual human drive for freedom. How will she feel when she (and her friends) come to realize what they have missed – given the bad educational system they were subjected to, the debt hanging over their heads, the overregulated life they have been forced to lead? Remember, we are now dealing with the new Greatest Generation. As did the last greatest generation, she will get mad, buckle down, fight, and win. And in so doing, rescue our culture.

Think not? Are you surprised at my conclusion?

She and her colleagues have at their disposal powerful tools. My granddaughters, for example, had computers and were computer literate at age 5. Here at UCSD kids aged 10 are taking – and completing – programming courses. Knowledge has always been power, but never more so than today. And all the while today's kids are developing a healthy skepticism. There is so much garbage on the Internet that they have become discerning, and have become able to cut through the bloviating words and images continually vying for their conscious attention. They have become able to find reasonableness and rationality within muck and mire.

When they achieve their political maturity, they will have another powerful tool at their disposal: America is on the verge of an energy revolution. Gas and oil have been found in abundance in this country, and we now have the ability to extract it from the ground. Given the recent overreach of the religious environmentalists, these kids, in their backlash, will achieve rational compromise, and will find a way to extract the energy while preserving our air and water quality.

Why am I so optimistic? Well, though my statistical sampling is small, and my population group somewhat not representative of our population as a whole, the young trainees today are so different from the arrogant and entitled young physicians who came into my office in the 1980s. They now come in prepared, bright eyed, computer savvy – and they are problem solvers. Maybe there aren't as many as you'd like. But I would argue that it doesn't take many good people in a culture to keep the culture going[93], and my positive personal experience with this new Greatest Generation extends into other professions – and specifically includes lawyers, electricians,

---

[93] Some authors have explained many group activities by the 5/40 rule. Discovered first (of all places) in an analysis of the Battle of Britain, it states that five percent of pilots accounted for more than 40 percent of aircraft shot down. *The Most Dangerous Enemy : A History of the Battle of Britain* by Stephen Bungay brings the finding to light. The 5/40 rule has been applied by sociologists and system analysts to other diverse group activities from surgical procedures to taxpaying. Extending the rule to our civilization's needs, five percent of good people may be enough to carry the day. I don't know of any way to prove this premise. I do believe that five percent is enough.

and plumbers.

On the other hand, maybe my observation, actually my pre-diction – that the new Greatest Generation will, with their skills and psyche ready to ride the energy boom to renewed American greatness – is too ambitious. After all, there is no proof to my premise, is there?

I can almost see you there shaking your head. You trust your own observations – and from what I observe, those observa-tions are mostly negative about the kids today and the future of our culture. But my name is not Pollyanna, and I am not faith-based. If I cannot test a hypothesis, I don't hold it useful.

No, my conclusions rest upon three fundamental observa-tions: first, that history repeats itself, second, that a small number of key movers and shakers in a society determines the future of that society, and third, that, as a physician-observer, I have seen enough of and made accurate observations about that group of key movers.

*　　*　　*　　*　　*　　*

Maybe it is better just to think of these essays as just a story, or more accurately, just a history. A history of one fortunate little boy's attempts to understand the big people around him, and to understand his world. And to explain his positive out-look for our future.

On the other hand, perhaps it is that I am blessed with a lousy memory. Of course there were tears, anger, frustration, fist-fights, disappointments and heartbreak during my child-hood, and that of my sisters. I don't seem to be able to remem-ber any of the downers with any intensity. On the other hand, my memories for the good times remain strong. Thinking about this disparity, it is truly a blessing to have selective memory. When I look at the old grainy pictures, which bring back memories of the adults – especially my grandparents – I see their support, hear their words of insight, remember their love, and remember their guidance, I know my sisters (the girls!) and I were truly blessed. And in the remembering, I recognize that my experience was not unique: most of my friends who grew up in those times can say similar things.

My (quiet) generation, especially those of us who lived in our part of the country, the Appalachian chain, grew up inde-pendent, responsible for our own actions, and respectful. And to emphasize, if we had one overarching and generic charac-ter trait, is was to be respectful of others' beliefs and privacy. We simply didn't try to change our neighbors' opinions, reli-gions, or philosophy. So we stepped back, watching – impo-tently, as it turned out – as the *me generation* – larger and more strident than us, became powerful and politically active. Though I cannot speak for each and every one in my genera-tion (after all, we were cursed with our own politicians), we have become appalled at the changes in our country.

I cannot even attempt to sell my boyhood as some magic time

of idyllic life in America. Women were, for the most part repressed. Black Americans were certainly and cruelly repressed. The memory of the Great Depression had burned itself deeply into and was still fresh in adult minds, especially into the minds of every one of my teachers – all of whom had suffered through it. Medical care was primitive, poverty was widespread, and there was that awfulness we called World War II.

Then maybe it's just best to recognize that where the stories all lead is to the three ideas in these essays: That freedom blended with responsibility leavened by honest communication bring resilience and love into the world.

What I've learned – trying to live a life in medicine and surgery, and do so by my grandparents' rules for the last 50 years, are three simple words: humans are wonderful. And wonderfully able. And have incredible potential. Yes, we do stupid things, yes, we are often times jerks, yes, we hurt those we love, yes, we get hurt (most often from our own bad programming, bad decisions, bad actions), but we are resilient. Plus, we have one overarching capacity – that ability to love. When I follow my grandmother's rules to show forbearance, kindness, respect, and especially love, I find, at the end of some transaction with another person – be it a short minute or one lasting a whole year, that a little bit of light and fresh air have come into what were dark spaces. And we all recognize that fresh air and light scare away the demons.

Now knowing what my generation was -- and knowing what we Americans can do, and happy with my observations about this new Greatest Generation, I walk toward our future with a light step and a confident smile. Why not come along?

An American Boyhood

An American Boyhood

Sincerest thanks to all those who proofed the book, giving up their time, energy, and mental tranquility. Thanks especially to my sisters, who provided me with particularly insightful and often severe (and severely needed) editing criticism: Judy, Mary Ellen, and Janet, each of whom reminded me frequently where the truths of the stories lay, all the while gleefully correcting my profound male biases (their words). And loving thanks to my daughters Laura and Carolyn and my son Charles who provided critical emotional support, ideas, and editing.

And to Joe Horton, a valued and trusted critic and friend.

And to Joshua Levin and Kelly Notaras of KN Literary Arts for their professional editing and encouragement.

Most photos are from family archives, though several are open source. Many of the McKeesport pictures come from a resource called "Old McKeesport", author or editor unknown. If any reader can shed light on this problem, please contact me, as I would like to credit someone for these marvelous records of a bygone time.

Any mistakes in the book are mine and mine alone. I have only sometimes changed the names of individuals in the stories, and then done so only to protect those individuals from hurt or embarrassment.

Charles W Kerber MD

San Diego 2016

The text is set in Book Antigua type.

An American Boyhood

78707735R00274

Made in the USA
Lexington, KY
12 January 2018